A People's History of Riots, Protest and the Law

Matt Clement

A People's History of Riots, Protest and the Law

The Sound of the Crowd

Matt Clement
Faculty of Humanities and
Social Sciences
University of Winchester
United Kingdom

ISBN 978-1-137-52750-9   ISBN 978-1-137-52751-6   (eBook)
DOI 10.1057/978-1-137-52751-6

Library of Congress Control Number: 2016943982

Cover illustration: © yu liang wong / Alamy Stock Photo

Printed on acid-free paper

This Palgrave Macmillan imprint is published by Springer Nature
The registered company is Macmillan Publishers Ltd. London

To Ali and Bob, my nearest and dearest

Foreword

In advanced capitalist regions of the globe, acts of collective resistance remain unusual events even if they do occur with some frequency, as Matt Clement in *A People's History of Riots, Protest and the Law: The Sound of the Crowd* demonstrates. Such acts appear unusual in part because they arise within countries whose economic 'success' has been built on the forging of an individualist mindset under which the majority of us, the majority of the time, are compelled to play the dull and isolating game of getting by to the best of our, individual, abilities. Those of us whose 'daily grind' has been interspersed with moments of collective action, protest and resistance have experienced the breaking of this stultifying, life-limiting framework if only for brief moments which are all too often dissipated as quickly as they first arose. These moments are not forgotten, however, and live in our, individual, consciousness as examples of possibility, of how things could be different, and of how, to use the slogan of the anti-capitalist movement of the early 2000s, 'another way is possible'.

The Sound of the Crowd reminds us that society has been changed in numerous ways through collective struggle—examples presented within this text span more than 2000 years of history and reveal the part which the 'crowd', 'the mob', 'the rabble', has played in bringing power to account and in helping to build progressive movements within society. The outlawing of slavery, the overthrow of absolute monarchies, the formation of trade unions, votes for women, the ending of legalised segregation in the USA, of apartheid in South Africa, and the legalising of same-sex unions, are just some of the many such progressive moments to be celebrated and in which the crowd has played a significant part. Each might have happened without the bravery of those who were willing to engage in the collective breaking of the law and standing together against the prevailing current, but I doubt it. The crowd throughout history has played a significant part in signalling to authority, and that there has been a change in the collective imagination as well as a growing unwillingness of the people to tolerate further indignities and discrimination either on their own or on others' behalf.

The crowd is a universal phenomenon. It continues to reconstitute itself throughout history and across the globe. We have witnessed a global resurgence of the crowd since the 1960s as waves of economic crises have hit various regions of the world. The growing internationalisation of capital and the interdependence of the different national economies, accelerated by the fall of the Soviet Union and China's entry into the global economy, have thus led to 'a greater degree of simultaneity and similarity in what might broadly be referred to as "class struggles" around the process of capital accumulation and…government measures to resolve crises' (Walton 1994:21). In this process, Walton argues, the relationship between the state and civil society, between government and the people, is being fundamentally redefined and old certainties cast out into the wind. Under these circumstances we will experience more protest, it will take different forms and draw in a wider layer of people.

It is clear that mainstream criminology cannot begin to comprehend the crowd and the part which collective rule-breaking has played in the removal of injustices in society; neither does it contain the tools which would allow it to empathise with those who take part in such disruptive behaviour. The discipline, after all, emerged out of the state's need to control its citizens and to mould their behaviour to its own needs and political ends. The classical 'founding fathers' of criminology were liberal philosophers who considered the modern legal system a moral good and were concerned with maintaining the individual's responsibility in upholding the rule of law. While disciplines such as philosophy, history and literature have been more open to an understanding and acceptance of the role of dissent in shaping contemporary society and social history, the role of criminology has been to condemn and to suppress dissident and law-breaking behaviours. What is more disturbing is that many of the critical voices which have been raised within criminology have also started from the assumption that the riot is a problematic and damaging event that must be understood and responded to in some way so that it is less likely to occur in the future. The perspective which they take is inherently reformist, suggesting that the inequalities of capitalism can be somehow ironed out and that western democracies can offer a space in which the crowd can be heard and their demands incorporated into policy changes, that, if we were only to listen to the voices of the oppressed and to act on their demands that social stability and justice might be restored.

The voices of the crowd, however, are all too often shouting out that there is no justice, that they have never known justice and that liberal democracy is a sham which affords them no political or social representation. Of course this cry is often poorly articulated, but whether ransacking shops, setting fires in anger or marching on Parliament with specified demands, the crowd, in its collective refusal to comply with expected codes of conduct, is presenting a challenge to the existing order of things. It is a visceral expression of a complex, deep-seated sense that the world is not as it should be. This is as true of the crowds with which we can empathise as it is with those whose motivations we find difficult to comprehend or which are distasteful to us. In an address to the American Society of Criminology in 1988, Maureen Cain reminded us that in order to transgress the very real limitations of our discipline it is necessary to engage in more than merely 'photographing the garbage can' (Cain 1990:7). It is not enough to document and comment on the reaction and response to any given situation but it is imperative that we understand what it is a reaction to. Furthermore, we must incorporate the knowledge that pain, anger and emotion do not always have a language through which they can be expressed. As a consequence, the actions of the crowd can be complex, contradictory and mystifying but we are compelled to look through these, to demystify and to find a language which can reflect and more clearly represent the realities of life and longing in the crowd's participants. It is necessary to interrogate the nature of social ordering in society and its harmful consequences, to look at the whole picture and to understand the law and law-breaking from this, clearer, vantage point. This is a political more than a criminological project.

The work of Clement is overtly political. He utilises a Marxist framework and analysis to interpret the sound of the crowd and to remind critical criminologists of the importance of taking such a standpoint. The Marxist method demands a historical and a comparative overview of the subject and this is his starting point and his concluding stance. Marxist analysis also requires active commitment to the struggle itself, to fully empathise with the subject of study and to gain knowledge and understanding through praxis—the fusion of theory and practice—and to resist the temptation to comment from the side-lines. Clement is a committed socialist and activist; consequently his analysis is imbued with the values that inform his activism and are informed by them in turn. *The Sound of the Crowd* looks far beyond the trigger events, through the particular motivations and private troubles of the actors involved on the streets, to look upwards at the systemic harms produced by the economic and political systems which allow expressions of anger, social frustration and disconnection to build so acutely and to be felt so deeply within particular neighbourhoods and social groups. Rather than looking downwards to attempt to unravel the peculiarities of circumstance that lead to unrest, to focus on the actions of the crowd in reaction to specific marginalising events, he argues that we should look upwards to the social ordering processes which lead to the creation of unwanted, surplus populations, and which then subsequently cast these configurations as disloyal, different and disorderly.

The Sound of the Crowd challenges us to think differently about the process of what is commonly referred to as 'riot'. The language which criminology generally uses to denote collective breaking of the law needs to break free itself from the limitations set by legal frameworks and the discourse of (neo-)liberalism. To see these moments from the eyes of the participants these are uprisings, rebellions, liberations, protest, a fightback. Opposing authority on the streets can also be exciting, fun, frightening, thrilling, a festival of the oppressed, a carnival (Presdee 2000). As one sixteen year old interviewed for the Guardian/LSE report 'Reading the Riots' explained of his involvement on the streets in August 2011 'What I really noticed that day was that we had control…Normally the police control us. But the law was obeying us, know what I mean?' (Lewis et al. 2011:23). And it is important for us to know precisely what such moments mean in the life of a young person who has experienced only a lack of autonomy and control in their life previously and to understand what compels people to speak out and act out in situations where to do so threatens life and liberty. As Gilmore's observations on the policing of protest (Gilmore 2010, 2012; Gilmore et al. 2016) demonstrate the failure of the state to facilitate peaceful protest, its criminalising of dissent and the violence it metes out in the course of its policing operations are the issues of concern.

So following Clement, I invite critical criminology to rethink its response to the sound of the crowd. It is not to be condemned or to be considered fearful or dangerous and never as mindless or even apolitical. As we well know it is our reaction to the crowd which defines and then amplifies its nature as deviance. It is the repression of the sound which constitutes the danger and which forces it to re-emerge in louder and more vociferous ways. When we listen to it, the sound of the crowd reveals the crimes of the powerful and of state-sanctioned violence, it speaks of the misappropriation and privatisation of what should be held for the common good. This sound is not one to be considered as outside of the law but as necessary to the functioning of society, as a counterbalance to power and authority which is held in the hands of the few. Any society which feels it necessary to silence the crowd needs to be treated to the best of our critical attention.

Karen Evans
University of Liverpool

References

Cain, M. (1990). Towards transgression: New directions in feminist criminology. *International Journal of the Sociology of Law, 18*, 1–18.

Gilmore, J. (2010). Policing protest: An authoritarian consensus. *Criminal Justice Matters, 82*(1), 21–23

Gilmore, J. (2012). Criminalizing dissent in the 'war on terror': The British state's reaction to the Gaza war protests of 2008–2009. In S. Poynting & G. Morgan (Eds.), *Global Islamophobia: Muslims and Moral Panic in the* West. London: Ashgate.

Gilmore, J., Jackson, W., & Monk, H. (2016). *'Keep Moving!'*. The Centre for the Study of Crime, Criminalisation and Social Exclusion, Liverpool John Moores University and Centre for Urban Research (CURB), University of York.

Lewis, P., Newburn, T., Mcgillivary, C., Greenhill, A, Frayman, H., & Procter, R. (2011). *Reading the riots: investigating England's summer of disorder*. London: The London School of Economics and Political Science and The Guardian.

Presdee, M. (2000). *Cultural criminology and the carnival of crime*. London: Routledge.

Walton, J. (1994). *Free markets and food riots: The politics of global adjustment*. Oxford, UK/Cambridge, MA: Blackwell.

Acknowledgements

This book has been the fruit of many years helping to organise and attend protests and demonstrations, some of which—such as Trafalgar Square in 1990 and Welling in 1993—ended up being labelled as 'riots'.

My academic career started out when living in Bristol, a city whose history is littered with riots. My thanks go to radical historians and sociologists whose work and advice have benefited me there: John Lever, Andy Mathers, Steve Poole, Steve Mills, Will Atkinson, Kevin Doogan and Roger Ball. Thanks also to those who helped me gain the work experience to progress: Sean Creaven, Christina Pantazis and Carolyn Brina.

I am grateful to Julia Willan at Palgrave Macmillan for commissioning this book and Dominic Walker for helping with its completion as well as the secretarial support and sound advice of my wife, Ali Swindells. Others to be thanked include Simon Sandall, Simon Hallsworth, Steve Hall, John Lea, Brian Richardson, Stephen Mennell and Ryan Powell— and comrades and friends in Southampton including Kate Swindells, Vincenzo Scalia, Bobby Noyes and Glyn Oliver.

Contents

List of Tables

1

Introduction

Urban rioters of all historical eras tend to engage in a fairly standard set of behaviours: they stage marches (often from one space of symbolic significance to another); they chant slogans (both advocating their cause and denigrating their opponents); they perform petty acts of vandalism (for example, smashing windows, doors, street signs, etc.); they loot stores and houses of valuable objects (or, in food riots, of basic staples); they make threats through symbolic actions ...; they skirmish with rival gangs or mobs (or sometimes are content with mutual displays of intimidation); they threaten hated individuals with violence (and, occasionally, actually lynch them); they set fires (a more serious action that often provokes a response from the authorities); and finally, they attack or are attacked by representatives of the government (such as police, soldiers or militia). These behaviours are all familiar enough to require little further elaboration. (Aldrete 2013, 425)

Interestingly, these examples are not from the twenty-first century, but describe the pattern of protest in ancient Rome. Clearly there are parallels between past and present which may help us to gain a more appreciative understanding of how and why riots and other acts of protest such as demonstrations and strikes come about. Criminology mushroomed

© The Editor(s) (if applicable) and The Author(s) 2016   **1**
M. Clement, *A People's History of Riots, Protest and the Law*,
DOI 10.1057/978-1-137-52751-6_1

in the 1960s through its ability to explain how and why millions were 'becoming deviant' (Becker 1963; Matza 1969). Before this time, social science categorised actions (and people) as either normal or deviant. This functional approach tended to see 'normal' as something desirable— 'deviance' was its anti-social opposite. If any group were opposed to the norm—which by definition would include protestors—they were deviating and needed correction. Mainstream criminologists would tend to blame the deviant themselves, whereas more liberal views acknowledged the role of structures in shaping attitudes and therefore sought to change the structures. The sociologists of deviance in the 1960s and 1970s started to develop a more critical perspective, which viewed those trying to change the way in which mainstream society denied their civil rights not as victims of structures but active agents for change whose situation—with the movements that developed around these issues such as racial and gender oppression—needed to be appreciated. For David Matza,

> Appreciating a phenomenon is a fateful decision, for it eventually entails a commitment—to the phenomenon and to those exemplifying it—to render it with fidelity and without violating its integrity. (Matza 1969, 24)

As the movement of resistance to capitalism expresses itself in various different actions, those who fail to commit themselves to an active appreciation of the struggles going on around them will end up joining policy makers in stigmatising the poor and criminalising protest. This book explores how adopting an appreciative viewpoint towards the actions of the crowd becomes increasingly important in an era of riot and protest on the global stage: 'the moral bind of law is lessened wherever a sense of injustice prevails. It is tantamount to asserting that chaos and tyranny reign instead of order and society' (Matza 1990, 102).

The sound of the crowd, or more accurately the actions and intentions of a large group of people who find themselves resisting the normal atmosphere of compliance with the rules and methods set by society's ruling institutions, is important because it is a collective statement. It comes out of peoples' interdependence—their reliance on each others support in stressful situations of extreme injustice and blatant disrespect. As Joop Goudsblum summarises it:

1. Sociology is about people in the plural—human beings who are inter-dependent with each other in a variety of ways, and whose lives evolve in and are significantly shaped by the social figurations they form together.
2. These figurations are continually in flux, undergoing changes of many kinds—some rapid and ephemeral, others slower but perhaps more lasting.
3. The development of human knowledge takes place within human figurations, and is one important aspect of their overall development. (Goudsblom 1977, 6, 105)

Social scientists must therefore take an interest and develop an appreciation of crowds protesting, whether we call them groups, figurations, classes or mobs, in whatever form the action takes. As Egypt showed in 2011, crowd action can lead to revolution and there is discussion and examples below of how revolutions in the ancient world, in Rome, in medieval Italy, early modern England and later France place mass popular action at their centre. These actions can be called direct democracy—where groups of people are assembling, arguing and acting decisively in situations that often begin as a form of self-defence, a desperate attempt to counter what has been called the barbarism of the existing order, or a civilising offensive by the ruling powers (Powell 2013). Processes of decivilisation, where society is thrust backwards by its rulers towards violence and anti-social barbarism (Mennell 1990), can provoke resistance from groups of people (figurations) against—for example—measures that are unjust and austere.

When France's Louis XVI left the poor to starve, the French revolutionaries in 1789 called the Queen, Marie Antoinette, 'Madame Deficit'. The Paris crowd stormed the Bastille, the giant fortress and prison at the heart of the city, freed the prisoners and burnt it down: they started the 1789 French Revolution. When Louis's troops in turn massacred hundreds at the Field of Mars 'it was easy to see that the violent compression of so powerful and elastic a spring would be followed by as violent a recoil' (Macaulay 1889, 350). Macaulay's phrase was actually describing the events of another revolution, in England 101 years earlier, and are reproduced here to illustrate how these themes of acts of violent repression provoke popular resistance. In the process, the people within the crowd—the body, or constitution of this group, or figuration—themselves change their consciousness, the blinkers narrowing their vision of a possible future come off, and they can start to believe that collective action can change their world for the better (Rudé 1964). This book contains only a small sample of such struggles. Many other events could, and maybe should, have been included, such as the 1917 Russian Revolution (Lenin 1917). But because the focus here is on appreciating events labelled as criminal or the product of a deviant subculture, I concentrate more on 'second-order' struggles that do not overthrow the existing order, but are so often present and which emerge out of the contradictions between different sections of society. I focus on crowds of people assembling, marching, demonstrating, rioting and occupying spaces, such as public squares, main streets and workplaces. Much of the evidence is a product of reviewing the histories of crowds acting together to change their circumstances. Once again, Aldrete's Roman examples illustrate that these kinds of actions have been with us for at least the last 2000 years:

> Statues often became the focal point for urban unrest, and a number of riots culminated in the pulling down of or attack upon the statue of a hated public figure. Thus, in 55 BC, statues of Pompey were stoned by an angry crowd, in 40 BC, statues of Mark Antony and Octavian were smashed during food riots … Crowds might also express their hatred for an individual by attacking his house, a symbol closely associated with his identity. This was a popular type of behaviour during the late Republic, when Cicero, his brother Quintus, Milo, Lepidus and the assassins of Julius Caesar all had their houses burnt or damaged by vengeful mobs. (Aldrete 2013, 430)

The events that sparked the idea of writing this book were the global renaissance of crowd actions that occurred in 2011 (Žižek 2012; Badiou 2012). Most prominently, the uprisings against tyranny in the Middle East, known as the Arab Spring, but also the European and American social movements centred around city squares protesting against austerity and inequality, and the British equivalent which consisted of several mass demonstrations throughout the year and a series of riots concentrated into five days in August. We were told by many commentators from the academic world and the media that the 2011 English riots were not political or social in the way riots had been in the past. Politicians also weighed in with their self-interested condemnations which seek to distance the act of riot from any kind of legitimacy. And yet, in past riots we tend to find the kind of political, social, economic and moral rationales employed by those taking part which have clear parallels with twenty-first-century injustices in the minds of protestors today.

As we have just seen, throughout history crowds have expressed their hatred for an individual by attacking his house. In Britain you could add the Chief Justice Lord Mansfield in the 1780 Gordon Riots, or the Conservative ex-prime minister and general, the Duke of Wellington, in 1831, who was so worried about such attacks he installed metal window shutters that earned him the nickname the 'Iron Duke'. Aldrete adds that 'a similar displacement of hostility felt for a group being directed against its "home" can be seen in the burning or threatened burning of the senate-house, as happened in 44 BC and 56 BC' (2013, 430).

This is an important area for criminology for several reasons. Firstly, it was the spike in mass protest in the Western world around May 1968 which provided the ammunition for the growth of a radical sociology of deviance whose key ideas have become central to the understanding of criminology today. Labelling theory, moral panics, media critique and appreciation of so-called deviant subcultures all emerged out of this atmosphere of protest, as I will explore with particular reference to the UK and the USA. Secondly, the way in which the major concerns for criminology have shifted over subsequent decades tells us a lot about the forms of repression practised by states anxious to maintain social control, and the manner in which many of these pioneering sociologists of deviance adapted their interpretations of social reality as the possibility of fundamental social change appeared to recede, accelerating the emphasis on realism and reform rather than idealism and revolution. I maintain that the return of the crowd to the centre of world events over the last five years or so highlights the shortcomings of some of the grander claims of realists and post-modernists about the supposed irrelevance of class inequality and the dissension it produces.

This account will take a long-term view of this phenomenon and illustrate how people have been protesting for thousands of years. Summarising Engels and Marx I will describe how the process of the formation of those key institutions, the state and private property, emerged out of these protests as social forces undermining the mass of peoples' control over their lives. Those classes became established in authority over the great majority, their aim was to make all others outsiders—that is to undermine and remove the grip they once had over aspects of their existence. Criminologists need to appreciate how the concept of the law has evolved over the centuries. The law is never simply a monolithic tool of oppression, not even today. Lawyers, after all, earn their living by interpreting it in the interests of their clients. Of course, for much of history, the law has been a tool in the hands of the state to protect its interests and those of its powerful friends, but that is not where law began. Originally, law was made by people collectively and justice was the result, that is they enacted judgement, allegedly to protect the weak from the strong, but certainly to ensure the business of everyday life was governed in the interests of the community. People were not rebels, seeking to overthrow authority, but constituted authority themselves—in common.

Of course, as societies developed, hierarchies and inequalities emerged. The powerful forged institutions advancing their specific, or class, interests. Often, these would clash with the ways of life and the desires of the mass of the community concerned.

In fourteenth-century Europe people often asserted political rights by taking control of city squares. In Florence, companies of citizens assembled in the piazza and voted on the recommendations of their leaders. The nobles had historically believed they were the only class fit to rule and this was the way the new rising classes, the merchants and artisans, could contest their monopoly. Sometimes, lower ranks of workers, such as the Ciompi or wool-workers guild in 1378, rioted in order to win voting rights and a say in government. In the nearby highlands of Tuscany 'the men of the mountains still elected their own priests in convocations [assemblies or figurations] that enlisted the presence of all the adult men of the parish … at the sound of their church bells' (Cohn 1999, 50–52).

Cohn shows how these communities were able to rise up and resist unfair taxation by Florence's rulers. Even though the official chronicles describe these revolts as defeated, in fact they won significant concessions which ushered in the introduction of a fairer and more universal system of taxation, thus probably ensuring the future economic success of this city state in its later 'Renaissance'.

Three years after the Florentine textile workers' revolt, masses of English peasants, artisans and merchants rose up against corrupt government, winning the support of much of southern and eastern England, including London, for their cause and marching in so great a number that they prevented an army being able to repress them. The high drama of their protest was played out in public. The young Richard II persuaded the rebels to trust his promise to reform, rather than resume their revolt after the nobles had killed their leader, Wat Tyler (Hilton 1973; Barker 2014). Once again it was unfair taxation, in this case a poll tax, that had sparked the rising.

Throughout history, whenever the common people assembled, their motivation was often fuelled by a sense of injustice—creating a need to muster strength in numbers in order to respond to the tyranny of a ruler whose acts of violence constituted a threat to their wellbeing. It's a social (pro-social) movement of the majority that is needed to counter the anti-social or unjust actions of the powerful few. In England, the 1285 statute of Winchester institutionalised the idea of the community policing itself against internal and external threats, electing accountable constables and creating the hue and cry (call and response) that would galvanise all members into active defence of their interests.

Because the common people governed many aspects of everyday life within their own communities it was logical to see law and order as a part of this, so for them any threat to common customs and local democracy was itself a criminal act which should be countered by community action. This was the logic of the musters on village greens where church bells summoned the people to assemble, armed, to discuss their grievances and resolve to right any wrongs being done unto them. We saw this occur in reaction to the imposition of the hated Poll Tax in 1381, in Jack Cade's rebellion of 1450, and the so-called 'Pilgrimage of Grace' in northern England in 1536, to name but a few examples. In 1450 it was the act of assembling as propertied citizens on Kentish village greens, sharing grievances and fears of further state repression, that led to Jack Cade's rebellion where thousands of peasants and military veterans formed an army that marched over London Bridge and attacked the royal palaces, slaughtering unpopular government ministers, while the king fled the city. Cade was himself part of the forces of law and order. His method of raising the revolt was through: (Müntzer 2010, 78)

> Commissions of array, which empowered those named as commissioners to summon the standards of all able-bodied men within their county. The evidence rather suggests that these commissioners, instead of being appointed ad hoc for a particular occasion, were given more long-standing powers of supervision over their potential forces. (Ross 1988, 206)

The people were thus rebelling in the name of law and order: as constables and as officials whose job it was to 'commission' others (i.e. to recruit them) into an armed body who would fight for justice. This was why popular leaders of riots and revolts were often called 'Captain'. They took it upon themselves to defend their interests in the name of the people, just as monarchs had defended their authority with armed forces. Later incarnations of those leaders chosen by the people to represent their cause were known as Captain Poverty, Captain Swing and General Ludd: the labels chosen provided a sense of continuity and customary right (rite) to acts of protest. Perhaps this is another origin of the term 'the mob'—coming from the people's act of mobilising. The propertied class learned to fear the potential power of the 'mobile' population when organised and welded together in a series of collective actions. The sheer speed with which the mass of English people had seized control of significant towns and surrounding areas in 1381, 1450 and 1536, using the method of assembling locally prepared to defend the community known as the muster (or 'wapentake' as it was known in the north), threatened to undermine their rule.

Popular law upheld common customs, especially around the common land which had traditionally been governed collectively rather than in the sectional interests of the new and growing class of property owners. Thus in 1524, the German radical preacher, Thomas Müntzer, proclaimed:

> The entire community has the power of the sword … princes are not lords but servants of the sword. They should not simply do what pleases them;

they should do what is right. So, according to good, old, customary law the people must be present if one of them is to be rightfully judged according to the law of God. (Müntzer 2010, 78)

And why? He maintains this is crucial because the peoples' presence is needed to ensure justice is done—and, when needed, to fight for that justice:

> If the authorities seek to render a perverted judgement, the Christians present should deny this judgement as wrong and not tolerate it, for God demands an accounting of innocent blood. It is the greatest monstrosity on earth that no one wants to defend the plight of the needy. The mighty ones do as they please as Job describes [the Leviathans]. (Müntzer 2010, 78)

Many acts of protest are often labelled as 'riots' by those in authority, but are also regarded as legitimate reactions to authority by the people concerned. As well as examples from the ancient world, I intend to examine actions from Europe between the thirteenth century and today, looking for common themes.

Here we have the rationale of the nineteenth-century English agricultural worker, described by Carl Griffin in *The Rural War: Captain Swing and the Politics of Protest*:

> This was a simple agrarian equipoise [balance]: to offer one's labour in exchange for a living wage and the support of the parish when needed. When the system broke down, those who had to labour for a living reminded their social 'betters' of their responsibilities, sometimes through protest. Such was E. P. Thompson's 'moral economy'. (2012, 47)

Yet, as social historian E. P. Thompson makes clear in his study of several hundred English food riots in the eighteenth century, this is not automatically what happens (Thompson 1971). Riots did not always occur at times of the greatest food shortages. They sometimes happened when food stocks were rising again. Moreover, they tended to happen around specific events, notably the transport of grain out of a locality. And when they occurred, people did not simply run off with produce. Rather, they tended to seize the grain, in order to sell it at a price seen as just, handing the money and often even the grain sacks back to the merchants. These actions, in other words, served a social purpose. As John Walter writes in *Crowds and Popular Protests in Early Modern England*, the rioters:

> certainly drew the attention of the authorities to their failings and set in motion the necessary exercise of authority designed to remove grievances which the crowd, by its own actions, could never hope to redress. Grain was kept within the local economy and purchased for distribution to the poor … In the long term, the riot's success lay in reminding the authorities of the crowd's slumbering existence. (2006, 42)

The phrase 'in the long term' is very important when considering whether riot or protest actions achieve anything for their participants. In the short term the likely result is often repression and condemnation, such as the trial and execution of Ann Carter after the 1629 riots in Maldon, Essex that Walter describes; however, governments have learned to respond to these actions across the centuries. Thus the Roman senators voted to provide a dole of grain after riots, and various public inquiries following riotous outbreaks such as in the USA in the 1960s or the UK in 1981, concluded that reforms were necessary. Contemptuous repression and failure to address the causes of distress can often cause their downfall, as Charles I himself was to learn within a few short years of the Essex riots when civil war broke out.

Although in many ways very different to these food riots, the English riots of 2011 shared a number of features with them. A popular sense of injustice flowed across London's poorer boroughs in the wake of the police killing of Mark Duggan in broad daylight on Ferry Lane, Tottenham Hale in early August. This was the borough whose MP, the late Bernie Grant, had famously claimed in 1985 that 'the police got a bloody good hiding' on the Broadwater Farm estate after Cynthia Jarrett collapsed and died in the midst of an illegal police raid on her flat—leading to a popular uprising where a policeman was killed with a machete. To many, Duggan's death felt like the police were continuing to operate in the same institutionally racist fashion that had caused the riots in 1981 and 1985—especially when the police failed to communicate with the family or even apologise for their actions. In the long term, society has responded to earlier anti-racist riots by becoming more accepting of multiculturalism and marginalising some of the more blatant racist practices of local authorities and schools. But at the same time the spark that ignited the 1980s riots—unjust and institutionally racist police 'stop and search' procedures which still continue—were undoubtedly the tinder that set off the Tottenham riots and which struck a chord in the many London neighbourhoods and provincial cities that rioted that week. The fact that Duggan's killing has been adjudged lawful following the January 2014 post-mortem only institutionalises the racial injustice at the heart of Britain's legal system. Rage at this victimisation, at the raw violence of the state, continually directed at black people, exploded in five days in August 2011 (Singh 2011; Briggs 2012). This institutional racism was confirmed by the actions of the Metropolitan Police and the Crown Prosecution Service within days of the lawful killing verdict of January 2014 when they charged Nicky Jacobs with the murder of PC Keith Blakelock in 1985. Jacobs's trial at the Old Bailey was farcical at times, as police-funded witnesses—one of whom admitted that 'all black people look alike' to him—claimed to have witnessed Blakelock's murder. The jury took just hours to acquit Jacobs, but the stain of racist intentions remained with the forces behind this malicious prosecution designed to shift the focus from the injustice of a black man killed to justice for a black 'killer'.

Further parallels could be drawn with other historical periods where the forces of law and order punish victims in public with extreme violence. When writing *The London Hanged: Crime and Civil Society in the Eighteenth Century*, Peter Linebaugh argued that 'the crime was well known, the culprit was selected as an "Example" … The agony of the hanging stirred various emotions—rage, glee, pity, terror and fear—with their own potentialities for action' (2006, xxii).

Many historians would agree that these are bloody and brutal matters, but would therefore conclude rather too quickly that they must be proof of the crowd's bloodthirsty and brutal nature. Crowd social psychologist Steve Reicher cites Gustave Le Bon's forthright conclusions:

among the special characteristics of crowds there are several—such as impulsiveness, irritability, incapacity to reason, the absence of judgement and others besides—which are almost always observed in beings belonging to inferior forms of evolution—in women, children and savages, for instance. (Le Bon 1895/1947, pp. 35–36 cited in Reicher 2011, 435)

Le Bon's comments sum up the problems with this demonisation of 'the mob', as Reicher explains:

Psychology has often been accused of sexism, of ageism and of racism. It takes a truly great psychologist to achieve all three in a single sentence. There are many grounds, both analytic and normative, on which to contest Le Bon's account. But perhaps the most fundamental is that it gives a profoundly misleading picture of what crowds do. It is simply wrong to suggest that crowd action is generically mindless and meaningless. Indeed those who have taken care to look at what people do conclude precisely the opposite. Crowd action is remarkable for just how meaningful its patterns turn out to be. (Reicher 2011, 435)

By contrast, the last 30 years of psychological research on group processes has been dominated by the notion that the self is not one dimensional but a complex system that encompasses different levels of abstraction. Thus we often think of ourselves in terms of what makes us unique as individuals compared to other individuals (personal identity). But we can equally think of ourselves in terms of what makes us unique, as members of one social category, compared to other social categories (social identity). Moreover, when we act in terms of any given social identity, our behaviour is not dominated by idiosyncratic beliefs and values but rather in terms of the beliefs and values associated with the relevant category. Reicher argues that 'social identity is the psychological mechanism through which social meaning systems come to structure the psychological field of the individual':

Is the intimacy, the solidarity and the cohesion of crowds a fleeting thing which evaporates as soon as the event is over? Or are these more long-lasting things and do crowds play a part in creating the everyday solidarities which allow social categories to achieve cohesion? Even if the former were true, it would still mean that crowds would have much to contribute to our understanding of the processes by which social solidarity can be produced. (Reicher 2011, 435, 440)

The inability of Le Bon's approach to crowds to account for, or even acknowledge, the socially meaningful patterning of events reflects a fundamental individualism in his core constructs. Le Bon considers a sovereign individual self to be the sole basis of reasoned action. The loss of the individual self in the crowd therefore leads to the supposition that crowd action is necessarily uncontrolled.

Despite today's rising inequality, it has become a commonplace assertion in social science that, although 'class' can be seen in social divisions, today's working class lacks 'consciousness', that is a political will to fight for its interests. Perhaps we need to look at this another way. Rick Fantasia writes in *Cultures of Solidarity* that:

> My concern was not to treat class consciousness as a fact to be uncovered, but to understand cultures of solidarity as active processes best understood in their oppositional context and their motion, with attention to the dynamics of group fusion and the institutional forms that generate and shape them. (1988, 229)

In other words, if we examine the events surrounding crowd actions, state reactions and provocations, we can begin to appreciate the way in which people are acting and thinking in a more useful way than simply demonising them. Nowadays this hydra monster has taken on a more orderly shape as a result of the work of George Rudé, Eric Hobsbawm, E. P. Thompson, Peter Linebaugh, Sam Cohn and others. We can observe these crowds as prompted by political and moral traditions which legitimise and even prescribe their violence. We may see urban rioters not as miserable, uprooted, unstable masses, but as men and women who often have some stake in their community; who may be craftsmen or of even higher social status; and who, even when poor and unskilled, may appear respectable to their everyday neighbours.

Finally, we may see their violence not as random and limitless, but aimed at defined targets and selected from a repertoire of traditional punishments and forms of destruction. Rioters often pull down the houses of the rich and powerful who oppress them such as when the Roman mob tore down Cicero's house after he had ordered the execution of rebels without trial when he was the city's leading minister in 63 BC. They replaced it with a temple of liberty—this was no act of mindless destruction. When London's Gordon rioters pulled down the houses of the likes of Chief Justice Lord Mansfield, who had presided over the trials that failed to punish the troops that shot rioters in St George's Fields in the previous decade, they brought along a water pump to ensure neighbouring houses were not damaged (Gatrell 2013). In riots where shops were destroyed, such as in St Paul's, Bristol in 1980, or Tottenham, London in 2011, it was notable that, whereas large chains were targeted, burnt and looted, local small traders' shops were often left alone.

There is of course a built-in opposition between these figurations, ruler and ruled, dominant and oppressed. Philosophers and communists have called this dialectics, and the struggle between them is a form of direct democracy or popular power in action. People governing together based upon collective decision-making processes were present in Athens and ancient Rome (Millar 1998). Marx's idea of communism draws upon the way of thinking of the commune that existed for thousands of years before him. To return to the fourteenth-century Tuscan example, Cohn describes how Highland peasants organise: 'the election of their own lay syndics [representatives] who negotiated with the city of Florence on tax relief and indebtedness' (Cohn 1999, 54). These 'communists' were asserting their right to control taxes and debts just as Syriza and other communists were attempting to do in Greece in 2015. Cohn outlines how:

> for understanding the formation of the modern state in Europe, perhaps it is time to re-evaluate 'class conflict' as a creative and not only a negative force in the formation of centralized states before the nineteenth century … notions of class, the periphery and the peasantry need to be brought back … not simply as the temporary obstacles that occasionally punctuated the modern state but as the positive 'driving forces'. (Cohn 1999, 7)

The shorthand for this statement is the famous phrase from *The Communist Manifesto* 'the class struggle is the motor of history'; and it is this explicitly Marxist dimension that has been largely either ignored or written out of much twenty-first-century analyses of riots and protest in sociology and criminology. The chapters that follow will develop various themes thrown up by protest movements.

- Chapter 2 examines the relationship between the birth of Athenian democracy and organised crowd resistance to tyranny (Ste Croix 1983):
- In ancient Rome we see how the people won their own representatives, the tribunes, and discovered their power to control their society by banding together as bodies of armed men (Wiseman 2003).
- In Chapter 3 we see how medieval revolts thrust merchants and the poor together in a struggle against the old order in movements to defend their rights to trade and gain a political voice or merely to survive the loss of land and the threat to wages (Hilton 1973; Cohn 1999).
- Notions of custom and community justice still underpin movements resisting land enclosures and reforming politics and religion from 1500 to 1800 (Bushaway 1982; Manning 1988; 2013, Linebaugh 2014), evolving through reformation, dispossession war and revolution, as the pattern of class struggle changes in the transition from feudalism to capitalism in England as discussed in Chapters 4 and 5.
- Riots grow into more organised forms in industrialising cities as the changing scale of industry changes the conditions and consciousness of the mass of the people—the making of the working class in need of economic, social and political justice in the midst of the terrifying industrial urbanisation that changed the poor from the oppressed to the collectively exploited, with all its associated subversive implications—both for those labelled the 'industrial proletariat' and their sisters and brothers in the reserve army of labour (Marx 1867).
- Riots often contained elements whose aims were not about improving the human condition, or rather believed the only way to advance the interests of one section of 'the people' was by using violence against what Virdee (2014) calls 'the racialized outsider'. Examples include US lynch mobs, British race rioters in 1919 and 1958, tsarist officials in the early twentieth century and of course fascist parties ever since. They are a product of a divide and rule strategy practised by governments, especially those with colonies, and promoted by the media in what Irish Marxist James Connolly christened a 'carnival of reaction'. However, Connolly also hailed the mob as the means of changing the world, and themselves, a new all-inclusive process of civilisation.
- These kinds of ideas, that protests and mass demonstrations—especially strikes—were crucial in achieving social and political change,

were much more prominent in the late 1960s (Berger 1968) and 1970s. For example, when the class struggle aspect of working-class relations with their employers was to the fore in countries like France, the USA, Italy and Britain, we saw mass strike waves that led to the overthrow of old military dictatorships in Greece, Portugal and Spain (Harman 1988). Chapter 6 explores how new set of ideas about how society worked were developing and, within criminology, the sociology of deviance and critical criminology revived this current of thinking and was itself a product of the shifts in consciousness caused by the struggles for civil and workplace rights—what Henri LeFebvre (2008) called 'the explosion'. I will review how this post-1968 movement grew and the subsequent authoritarian reaction, including a case study of 1970s Italy as described by Vincenzo Scalia. Many of the leading British criminologists called their approach Marxist at this time, epitomised by *The New Criminology* (Taylor et al. 1973). I will review their key findings about how to improve the criminal justice system and chart the process of its later adaptation into a more 'realistic' strategy.

For three decades, 1980–2010, the tide of struggle receded and the power of capitalism was resurgent. Since 2011 struggle has returned in forms that both differ and echo its ancestors. This has been called the 'rebirth of history' (Badiou 2012) and once again places the act of protest at the forefront of key political and economic phenomena. Anti-capitalism has moved from the margins to the mainstream of political actions and the agenda of parties and governments, partly through: new social movements like Occupy; movements of the squares such as the Indignados; new political formations challenging (and compromising) with capitalism such as Syriza in Greece and Podemos in Spain; and uprisings in 'neighbourhoods of relegation' (Wacquant 2008) from France to Brazil, from the UK to the USA. Besides the movements there is also a greater shedding of illusions in the once-supposed benefits of key social institutions whose roots can be seen in attempts to control society and fairly distribute goods and services, such as the police and welfare institutions, and above all in the whole machinery of contemporary democratic government where it exists. This study will conclude with a review of the rising tide of riot and protest since 2010 with examples from 2011:

Occupy, European anti-austerity movements and Tahrir Square in Egypt; from 2012: South Africa's Marikane Massacre of striking miners and their families; from 2013: the Rana Plaza riots in Dhaka, Bangladesh; from 2014: Hong Kong's umbrella movement. There also follows a more in-depth review of both the English riots of 2011 and the US mass movement against police killings of 2014–2015.

As people in Europe and the USA turn to anti-capitalist parties out of frustration at the elitist bias of traditional groupings, they are following a trend set in South America. Asia, the Arab world, India and Africa are, of course, also central to global riot, protest and social movements, but they only receive very limited comment in these pages. The question therefore once again arises of whether another world is possible, or whether the machinery of the capitalist system is just too powerful to be dismantled. The answer, I believe, lies in the very act of struggle that permeates human history. It is the sound of the crowd—its size, its ability to amplify and define its goals in the act of asserting humanity's right to achieve them—which makes the difference between the possible and the illusory.

References

Aldrete, G. (2013). Riots. In P. Erdkamp (Ed.), *The Cambridge companion to ancient Rome* (pp. 425–440). Cambridge: Cambridge University Press.

Badiou, A. (2012). *The rebirth of history: Times of riots and uprisings*. London: Verso.

Barker, J. (2014). *England arise! the great revolt of 1381*. London: Little Brown.

Becker, H. (1963). *Outsiders: Studies in the sociology of deviance*. London: Macmillan.

Berger, J. (1968). The nature of mass demonstrations. *New Society.* https://www.marxists.org/history/etol/newspape/isj/1968/no034/berger.htm. Accessed 23 May 1968.

Briggs, D. (Ed.). (2012). *The English riots of 2011: A summer of discontent*. Hampshire: Waterside Press.

Bushaway, B. (1982). *By rite: Custom, ceremony and community 1700–1880*. London: Junction Books.

Cohn, S. (1999). *Creating the Florentine state: Peasants and rebellion, 1348–1434*. Cambridge: Cambridge University Press.

Fantasia, R. (1988) *Cultures of Solidarity*. Berkeley: University of California.

Gattrell, V. (2013). *The first bohemians*. London: Allen Lane.

Goudsblum (1977) *Sociology in the balance* cited by Stephen Mennell 'Figurational studies: Some concepts, principles and major research areas' at http://www.norberteliasfoundation.nl/network/concepts.php

Griffin, C. (2012). *The rural war: Captain swing and the politics of protest*. Manchester: MUP.

Harman, C. (1988). *The fire last time*. London: Bookmarks.

Hilton, R. (1973). *Bond men made free*. London: Temple Smith.

LeFebvre, H.(2008) [1969]. *The explosion*. New York: Monthly Review Press.

Lenin, V. (1917). The state and revolution. https://www.marxists.org/archive/lenin/works/1917/staterev/ch01.htm#s2

Linebaugh, P. (2006). *The London hanged*. London: Verso.

Linebaugh, P. (2014). *Stop thief: The commons, enclosure and resistance*. Oakland: PM Press.

Macaulay, T. (1889). *History of England volume 1*. London: Longmans.

Manning, R. (1988). *Village revolts*. Oxford: Oxford University Press.

Marx, K. (1867). Capital. https://www.marxists.org/audiobooks/archive/marx-engels/capital-vol1/

Matza, D. (1969). *Becoming deviant*. New York: Prentice Hall.

Matza, D. (1990) [1964]. *Delinquency and drift*. New Brunswick: Transaction.

Mennell, S. (1990). Decivilisng processes: Theoretical significance and some lines of research. *International Sociology, 5*(2), 205–223.

Millar, F. (1998). *The crowd in Rome in the late republic*. Ann Arbor: University of Detroit.

Müntzer, T. (2010). *Sermon to the princes*. London: Verso.

Powell, R.(2013). The Theoretical Concept of the 'Civilising Offensive' (Beschavingsoffensief): Notes on its Origins and Uses. *Human Figurations 2*(2), http://hdl.handle.net/2027/spo.11217607.0002.203

Reicher, S. (2011). Mass action and mundane reality: Crowd analysis and the social sciences. *Contemporary Social Science, 6*(3), 433–449.

Ross, C. (1988). *Richard III*. London: Methuen.

Singh, D. (2011). Five Days in August: An Interim Report on the 2011 English Riots available at. http://webarchive.nationalarchives.gov.uk/20121003195935/http:/riotspanel.independent.gov.uk/wp-content/uploads/2012/04/Interim-report-5-Days-in-August.pdf

Ste Croix, G. (1983). *The class struggle in the ancient Greek world*. London: Duckworth.

Taylor, I., Walton, P., & Young, J. (1973). *The new criminology: For a social theory of deviance*. London: Routledge/Kegan Paul.

Thompson, E.P. (1971). The moral economy of the English crowd. *Past and Present, 50*(1), 76–136.

Virdee, S. (2014). *Racism, class and the racialized outsider*. Basingstoke: Palgrave Macmillan.

Walter, J. (2006). *Crowds and popular protests in early modern England*. Manchester: Manchester University Press.

Wacquant, L. (2008). *Urban outcasts: The comparative sociology of advanced marginality*. Cambridge: Polity.

Wiseman, T. (2003). The political vacuum. In T. Wiseman (Ed.), *Classics in progress*. Oxford: British Academy/OUP.

Wood, A. (2013). *The memory of the people*. Cambridge: Cambridge University Press.

Žižek, S. (2012). *The year of dreaming dangerously*. London: Verso.

2

Democracy and Protest in the Ancient World

What has happened to democracy in the twenty-first century? The ancient Greek word *demokratia* meant two things: the people (*demos*) and power (*kratos*). To understand why people don't have power in modern so-called democracies we need to look at how the institution has changed since it was first expressed in fifth-century BC Athens. Ellen Wood explains:

> Citizens in modern democracy have been converted from 'actors' to 'electors' ... democracy has been replaced by representation ... intended not to give the demos a voice but to speak in its stead ... election became the essence of representational democracy, not as a means of transmitting the vox populi, but rather as a means of tempering democracy with oligarchy. (Wood 1996, 124)

The result of this shift from direct democracy to representative democracy not only removes the mass of the people from the control of their affairs, but also limits the areas that democracy is allowed to effect. As Aristotle wrote in *Politics* about Athenian democracy, 'the freeborn and the poor control the government—being at the same time a majority'. He was clear about what this meant, stating 'the true difference between

© The Editor(s) (if applicable) and The Author(s) 2016
M. Clement, *A People's History of Riots, Protest and the Law*,
DOI 10.1057/978-1-137-52751-6_2

democracy and oligarchy is the difference between poverty and wealth' (Wood 1996, 126).

In a direct democracy the people are the state. They carry out its functions as they see fit: 'in Athens there was no such clear distinction between the state and civil society, no distinct and autonomous economy not even a concept of the state as distinct from the community of citizens. There was no state of Athens or Attica, only the Athenians' (Wood 1996, 128). To the modern reader this can sound idealistic—a naïve and unrealistic view. Can ordinary people really do the job that modern states employ a corps of experts to carry out? Kurt Raaflaub explains how the people exercised their democratic power:

> By being paid for political functions, they gained the leisure necessary for involvement in politics and running a polis. For this very reason equality could not be limited to occasional elections and votes, nor delegated for extended periods to a small number of representatives. This democracy had to be lived actively and intensively, its equality realised to the fullest by involving the highest possible number of citizens from all classes in government and power, by ruling and being ruled in turn. (Raaflaub 1996, 158)

There were major flaws in Athenian democracy, not least the fact that women and slaves were not admitted. Slavery is, of course, itself a denial of human rights and democracy, so it was far from a complete or universally inclusive system. Even so, it represented a massive advance upon what went before, and shows the kind of active direct democracy that could form an alternative to today's tragically limited version where Athenians are forced to strike for democratic rights they are denied by a European imposed austerity (Clement 2013). What a contrast with the ancient model:

> By enabling all citizens, even the poorest and lowliest, to participate in communal affairs, the concept of democratic equality encouraged perhaps even compelled them to be active and involved … the readiness of these citizens continually to devote themselves to the affairs of their city, both politically and militarily in remarkable intensity and consistency, without slackening, over an extraordinary period of time … unique in world

history, these men understood that their job and responsibility—their 'metier'—was to be citizens. (Raaflaub 1996, 159)

Of course, Athenians had had to fight to win their control of society from the aristocratic rule of the tyrants before they could make democracy. The word itself had other meanings beyond 'people's power'. Spivey calls it 'the peoples' grasp, implying that the *demos* had physically to seize control through their actions. Paul Cartledge argues that one translation that makes sense is that '*demokratia*' equals 'dictatorship of the proletariat' (Ober and Hendrick 1996, n. 24, p. 183). The Athenian world overall was far from democratic, as only citizens of the city state had an input into its workings, and the countryside population outnumbered that of the city by 10 to 1 according to Ste Croix, making the city economically parasitical upon its rural neighbours. This was far less true for ancient Rome in the last century or so of its republic, when hundreds of thousands flooded into the city as they were thrown off their lands (Brunt 1971). 'Proletariat' is a Latin, not an ancient Greek, word, and there is more to learn about how riot, protest, democracy and law come together by looking at what happened in the republic of Ancient Rome.

The crude caricatures painted by Marx's political opponents and, it has to be said, occasionally by those who consider themselves his disciples, describe Marxism as a belief in a rigid preordained theory of history which is convinced of the inevitably of the victory of socialism as its final phase. In order to demonstrate his disagreement with this perspective, Marx reminded his readers of the fate of republican Rome's plebeians.

They were originally independent peasants, cultivating their own plots of land. In the course of Roman history they were expropriated. The same development which separated them from their means of production and subsistence, also gave rise to large landed property and large financial capital. Thus, at a certain moment, there were on the one hand free men stripped of everything except their labour power, and on the other hand, the owners of all this accumulated wealth, ready to exploit their labour. But what happened? The Roman proletarians did not become wage earners but an idle mob, more abject even than the erstwhile 'poor whites' of the southern states of the USA. Beside them grew up a system of production which was not capitalist, but was based upon slavery. (Bottomore et al. 1961, 37–38)

If the course of history is always decided by economic circumstances then capitalism would have first appeared in ancient Rome over 2000 years ago because, as Marx has pointed out here, the preconditions were in place. In fact, there was a period of intense class struggle between the plebeians and their rulers over whose interests should prevail as I outline below, but eventually the Roman revolution was defeated and the Emperor Augustus succeeded in establishing imperial rule. The bourgeois class would rather not remember how riotous were the revolutions that brought their ancestors to power. Thus much crowd action is muffled and revised into other motivations when historians discuss revolutions in England, America or France in the seventeenth and eighteenth centuries. A similar 'ideological vacuum' (Wiseman 2003) affects twentieth-century readings of 'the class struggle in the ancient Greek world' (Ste Croix 1983). This interpretation denies agency to the people in the mass upheavals in the century after the defeat of Carthage in 145 BC. According to mainstream classical scholars, the democracy of the forum is a sham operated by powerful men who control their clients so they vote in the interests of that powerful few. The vast bulk of the evidence for this period is the speeches and letters of Cicero, an advocate and politician who made his name defending the people's interests—particularly in the trial of the corrupt senator Verres in 70 BC—only to desert their cause as he took his turn as consul several years later, a year which climaxed with his ordering the public execution of several Roman citizens without trial. This is scarcely impartial evidence, although as Millar (1998) shows it is possible to use it to uncover some significant facts about how 'the people' had a controlling influence on much of government.

The case of Rome in the late republic will be examined more closely because here was a society where events played out in the open with the crowd playing a crucial role in their direction and legitimation. The Roman forum was the state. The people's vote decided issues on welfare and warfare. Trials were held in public—the jail was beneath the forum.

Even the treasury, the spoils of war, sat in a temple in the forum. Whilst the nobles had their senators, the rest of the people had their tribunes to represent their interests and block their rulers' use of violence to achieve their ends. If you controlled the forum—the space where laws were made and voted upon, the *res publica*—you held the power.

Who Are the Mob?

To begin with there were the nobles and the rest—the plebeians, established as outsiders in terms of political rights. The plebs seceded—assembled and withdrew from the city in protest at their exclusion from the political process. According to legend they moved to a nearby hill – demonstrating by their action that Roman society could not function without them. This 'strike' led the nobles to create a new form of representation, the tribunes of the people, who would act on their behalf in the public arena of the Forum where decisions were made—won their tribunes.

Society became more complex. Some plebs were traders/businessmen (*equites*), some farmers, some artisans; many citizens were propertyless (*cense capite*); and of course there were the slaves. Those without property were the *proletarii*—they were mobile, unattached to property. They came to win increasing rights to vote in the tribal assembly once their labour as soldiers was required for Rome's expansion. Those who wished to rule now called upon their support—they represented their interests.

In this chapter I aim to provide insight into the key events that affected the Roman masses in the last century of the republic. Rome had reached new heights of imperial conquest with its comprehensive defeat of the Carthaginians (North-East Africans) in 145 BC. Their army was becoming the ancient world's most powerful industrial organisation—allowing it to vanquish its enemies but also generating an expectation of reward in greater and greater masses of its citizens. The leadership of the army was the state's key source of power: 'transfer of the right of appointment to be in the gift of the people was put forward as a bill in 145, and achieved in 103' (Millar 2002a, 127).

The city of Rome grew to a million inhabitants, with much of the Mediterranean supplying its food through taxes, rents, and trade. By the 130s BC an agrarian crisis gripped Italy; with so many men in the legions, aristocrats made rich by their victories could buy up the land and work it with millions of slaves captured in the wars, growing food for the city, and leaving dispossessed farmers little choice but to move to Rome, expanding the urban market still further, or to join the army. Some ancient historians call this the 'war-slave-war loop': it created a feedback process enriching the aristocracy and driving the Italian free peasantry into ruin. But as dispossession accelerated, fewer men met the property qualification for military service, starving Rome of soldiers and bringing on a crisis. (Morris et al. 2005)

At the forefront of this demand were the soldiers themselves, so it is hardly surprising that it was a great noble general, Tiberius Gracchus, who found himself the 'people's champion' when he raised the demand of land for his victorious soldiers to be taken from the spoils of the senatorial ruling class. Here is his speech to the crowds in the forum as described by Plutarch:

The wild beasts of Italy have their caves to retire to, but the brave men who spill their blood in her cause have nothing left but air and light. Without houses, without settled habitations, they wander from place to place with their wives and children; and their generals do but mock them when, at the head of their armies, they exhort their men to fight for their sepulchres and the gods of their hearths, for among such numbers perhaps there is not one Roman who has an altar that has belonged to his ancestors or a sepulchre in which their ashes rest. The private soldiers fight and die to advance the wealth and luxury of the great, and they are called masters of the world without having a sod to call their own. (Plutarch 75 AD)

Plutarch says this speech by Tiberius Gracchus 'filled the people with enthusiastic fury, and none of his adversaries durst pretend to answer him' (Plutarch 75 AD) For his audacity in championing the popular cause, he was assassinated, though he was succeeded as the people's tribune by his brother Gaius in the 120s. Despite courting the equestrian business class as allies in his campaign for popular land reform, Gaius too was cut down in the forum by the paid assassins of the senators. He and his 2000 or so supporters tried to hold out but were massacred on the order of the nobles, who then erected a Temple of Concord (Peace!) to commemorate their victory.

Ever since the defeat of Gaius Gracchus's land reforms late in the second century BC, the old and new money had been heavily invested in land. Smallholdings were devastated as vast slave plantations, *latifundia*, created super profits for the rich and drove the peasants off the land, creating the swollen headcount in Rome's slums—the first proletariat. Fergus Millar, following on from research by Lily Taylor, traces how these men were slotted into the 35 tribes in the tribal assembly, bringing their interests to bear on what was legally the sovereign decision-making power in the state (Millar 1998; Taylor 1963).

The proceedings of the assemblies bear some relation to the evolution of other institutions of citizens' power in modern revolutionary times, such as Chile's *cordones* of the early 1970s and the popular neighbourhood assemblies established in a wave of popular protest in Argentina in 2001 (Schaumburg 2015). Tribunes of the plebs were representatives of the people, recallable at annual election: they brought laws before the public at the forum, calling for *contios* (public meetings), where they would make addresses from the rostra. Other tribunes could be put up by opposing factions to debate or even veto the legislation proposed, the crowd subsequently separating into tribes and voting on the amended proposals. The process of developing from ex-peasants into an 'idle mob', synonymous with the Roman historian Juvenal's famous description of their consciousness as one addicted to bread and circuses, had begun in Rome's late republic in the second and first century BC; although it was not until the first century AD that this condition was institutionalised by the erection of the city's coliseum.

Before this, politics and entertainment had occurred in the same place, on the **arena** (sand) of the great public square at the heart of the city. Mass gatherings of citizens, freed men and slaves assembled in the forum to hear orators address them in *contios*, to divide and vote on laws, and to attend public trials of criminals and enemies of the people, as well as being entertained by the banquets and games laid on by competing politicians. American scholar Lily Ross Taylor says: 'voting at Rome was, as in our national election for president and vice president, entirely by units' (Taylor 1963, 1). But before the division 'there was always at Rome a preliminary public meeting in which the citizens appeared unsorted. Such a meeting, held often for other purposes besides voting, was known as a conventio, a 'coming together' (Taylor 1963, 2). So anyone in the forum could be part of the democracy, even women and slaves. Taylor also points out the root of the Roman word for 'voting' (*suffragium*) is *frangere* (to break), and means 'to break into sound'. Therefore we can infer that voting was at first done by people gathered together, shouting, acclaiming or denouncing, as they chose how to act and who would lead their actions. As if THE SOUND OF THE CROWD is the sound of democracy.

> The mob were the 'mobility'—those without property—in ancient Rome they were comprised of freed men, women and slaves—peoples with a shared heritage of oppression by the higher orders of society. In the case of the freed men they were now classed as citizens, entitled to free grain dole from 58 BCE onwards, and often ganging together in clubs known as collegia—associations of various localities and trades. (Brunt 1966, 3)

This group clearly had their own interests—their own sense of what they expected their city and society to value. As the world's first truly global city their mass presence represented a demand that these interests be respected. However, Brunt reminds us that 'the true governing organ of the Roman Republic was the senate … dominated by a few noble families and on the number of their dependents' (Brunt 1966, 4–5). With the massive migration to the city, as Italians were forced off the land and people from other lands seeking work and trade flooded in, Rome now numbered almost one million people, and the relatively democratic structure of the republic gave all male citizens the vote, exercised not once every five years but at regular public assemblies, where all were entitled to vote on policies and make laws. There was clearly a growing tension between the people's aspirations and the reality of government. The masses in Rome had learnt a bitter lesson:

> Unorganised and unarmed, the followers of the Gracchi could save neither their leaders nor their own interests; men of the same class, with arms in their hands, were the essential instruments for bringing down the Republic. (Brunt 1988, 241)

The traditional rulers of the Roman elite, established for hundreds of years, no longer found it easy to convince the 'lower orders' of society to leave them in charge. As it grew from a city-state to a regional power dominating the Italian peninsula, Rome had hegemonised its rule by granting many cities *civitas sine suffragio* (citizenship without the vote). What this meant in practice was that many cities in Italy, Southern France, Spain and Portugal had their own places of assembly where citizens elected magistrates to propose law in Roman fashion: these citizens did not have the vote in Rome, but did exercise some form of democratic participation locally. As these regions increasingly supplied the soldiers who fought Rome's wars of expansion, and many were drawn into Rome through land enclosure, they brought an expectation of citizenship rights with them (Brunt 1971; Sherwin-White 1973, 69).

Rome's ruling class were next challenged by the military prowess of those leaders who claimed to represent the people's *populares* cause, especially Gaius Marius, the general re-elected as consul seven times in the voting assemblies, whose recruitment of the propertyless proletariat, the *censi capite* (the headcount), had given the urban poor a real stake in this military imperial state. Not only did they, as proletarian soldiers, provide the 'sinews' of Rome's wealth from imperial plunder, especially in the east through the army's occupation and continued domination over 'tribute nations', but the propertyless also now asserted their own theoretical property rights in order to legitimately feel a part of the public interest within Roman society, the *res publica*. If they could gain representation as new Roman citizens within more of the voting districts or 'tribes' into which the electorate was divided for counting the tallies in the legislative assemblies held in the forum (Taylor 1990), then the growing populations of ex-soldiers, ex-slaves or 'freed men' could join forces with the city's artisans and shopkeepers and assert the popular interest.

The senatorial oligarchy had maintained control of legislation and elections up to now by enlisting the bulk of the Roman masses into only 4 of the 35 tribes. Marius's triumph had served time on the nobles' right to rule, and he savoured his victory in one of his speeches that, according to the contemporary historian Sallust, 'fired the spirit of the commons':

> I shall encourage my soldiers; I shall not treat them stingily and myself lavishly, nor win my own glory at the price of their toil. Such leadership is helpful, such leadership is democratic; for to live in luxury oneself but control one's army by punishment is to be a master of slaves, not a commander. (Sallust 86.2, 85.34–5 in Rolfe 1921, 323, 321)

Up to the end of the second century BC military veterans had received allocations of land upon retirement. As the army's size grew the senators increasingly vetoed and suppressed the land reform programmes designed to bring this about: after assassinating the Gracchus brothers they repressed a series of popular leaders calling for land for the people and cancellation of debts (the original meaning of the word 'jubilee') over the next 30 years. Then the blatant corruption of the noble senators, accepting bribes from the African leader Jugurtha, fired the commons into electing Marius—therefore recognising their own, popular interests were opposed to the oligarchs and must be contested. This is why Sallust argues that 'the institution of parties and factions, with all their attendant evils, originated at Rome':

> For the nobles began to abuse their position and the people their liberty, and every man for himself robbed, pillaged and plundered. Thus the community was split into two parties, and between these the state was torn to pieces. (Sallust ibid. 41.1, 41.5)

He is referring to the way in which the people's cause emerged as a distinct interest group, wielding their influence within the machinery of the Roman republic's political body. In the last decade of the second century BC the people's party (*populares*) leader Marius was re-elected as consul (leading minister) seven times by mass assemblies of citizens gathered in the forum. Re-election of leaders was against the rules of the constitution as maintained by the mostly noble oligarchy, though the strength of the popular movement ensured his victory. These votes took place in the tribal assemblies where each of the 35 districts elected delegates who cast votes in mass secret ballots in the great urns erected on the rostra raised up in the arena where proceedings could be observed. The popular interest could be more easily exercised in this assembly, rather than the alternative body, the centuriate assembly, where voting was 'classified' with those of the rich being counted first and the popular interest being far more marginal.

For the vast majority of urban citizens—the shopkeepers who eked out a precarious existence alongside the non-voting freed men, women and slaves of the city—this exercise of their interests was vital in a period of increasing lawlessness across the Italian peninsula. The once publically owned lands were enclosed by the rich, in defiance of the regulation that stipulated that no one should own more than 500 *iuegera* of land. Indeed this was why the poor districts of the city were swollen with the new proletariat forced off their smallholdings turned into vast *latifundia*—plantations run by slave labour. Marius's inclusion of those without property in the legions promised them a stake in society, just as their votes kept him in power.

In the end, after compromising with senators and giving them the head of popular guerrilla leader Saturninus who led an urban uprising against the nobles, Marius himself was defeated by his own former lieutenant Sulla—a pro-noble general who marched on Rome in 88 BC and massacred thousands of the *populares* supporters at the Colline Gate. 'Lucky' Sulla suspended the powers of the tribunes—those men who for the previous 60 years had called public meetings and initiated the passing of new laws in the assemblies held in the Roman Forum next to the Senate House where the oligarchy presided.

But the mood of revolt was still there upon Sulla's death in 78 BC: the great Roman historian Theodore Mommsen, contemporary of Marx and Bismarck who wrote his *History of Rome* as a vindication of the revolutionary wave so savagely repressed in Germany in 1848, describes the scene:

> The proletariat of the capital, which equated free bread to true freedom was likewise discontented … the entire families and freedmen of those democratic chiefs who had lost their lives … the whole body of ruined men, all the rabble high and low … aristocratic lords whose only mark of quality was their debts: the Sullan troopers whom the regent could make into landholder but not into farmer … All these awaited only the unfolding of the banner which invited them to fight against the existing order, whatever else might be inscribed upon it. (Mommsen 1959, 204–205)

For the next two decades or so the crowd often went to the Forum, Rome's central city square, where they met together, demonstrated, witnessed public trials, voted and even rioted in order to establish welfare rights through the establishment of the corn dole, create allotments for veterans and other deserving families and extend Roman democracy by giving the vote to all ex-slaves, the freed men or *libertini*.

Their case is important for our understanding of the role the crowd can play in shaping society today because it was their votes that made laws and elected the city's officials. As the eminent classical historian Fergus Millar reminds us, 'a crucial fact cannot be repeated too often; the Senate was not a parliament'. Those men of noble families thought of themselves as the rulers of Rome, but this was not the constitutional position:

> That rule belonged to the populus Romanus (Roman people) or rather to those citizens who were present in the Forum when the moment came for them to form themselves into the thirty five voting units, or tribus, that constituted the normal form of the legislative assembly. (Millar 1998, 7)

The parallels with twenty-first-century mass demonstrations in Tahrir Square or in the streets of Madrid are interesting. It is those active citizens who wield the power to make decisions, change laws and elect representatives. Of course, this ability to shape their world was contested by the rich and powerful. Millar states how 'the sovereign power of the people … was the subject of the most intense controversy'. Nevertheless 'in this brief period we can catch the echoes of a level of open public debate that is not common in human history' (Millar 1998, 12).

In 70 BC the people's champion was the young Julius Caesar, nephew to Marius, who had decorated his statues in defiance of Sulla: Caesar later won favour amongst his legions by championing the efforts of Rabirius to force through reforms from 67 BC, though two far more ambiguous figures won the consulship in that year. Pompey, known as the 'teenage hangman' when lieutenant to Sulla, and Crassus, the billionaire, were the leaders of the *populares* who restored the rights of the tribunes. Both men had recently combined to defeat the heroic slave revolt in 72 BC: 'why Spartacus threw away the opportunity to try to seize Rome is one of the great mysteries of history … 100,000 slaves died in the crushing of the revolt' (Harman 1999, 80).

Because Roman citizens abhorred the state of slavery many classical historians have chosen to believe they would rather side with their noble masters than revolting slaves. However, in Sicily previous revolts 'received support from the local population who were delighted to see the suffering of the rich' (Harman 1999, 78). We will never know whether Rome's mass of poor citizens, freed men and the legions of private slaves who serviced the capital's rich families would have defended 'their' city from this mortal threat: could it have heralded a new civil war, less than 20 years after the 'social war' that won Italians Roman citizenship, where the body politic divided along different lines?

In 70 BC the power of the tribunes of the people was restored, by order of the two consuls, Pompey and Crassus. They could see that the path to political power was to become populist or *populares*, but as oligarchic rulers they also wanted to bring more and more of Rome's growing wealth and property into their grasp. That process was the motor of the social changes which were dragging hundreds of thousands into the city and the army. This in turn gave the masses a potential power that in itself demonstrated what Millar calls 'the highly exposed position of the Senate when popular feeling was aroused' (Millar 2002a, 177). One recent fictional account describes how elections were run at the Field of Mars—the great arena known today as the Circus Maximus:

> It was packed right down to the river's edge, for there was a census in progress, and tens of thousands had come to the city to register. You can imagine the noisy roar of it. There must have been a hundred candidates for those thirty-four offices, and all across the vast open field one could see these gleaming figures passing to and fro, accompanied by their friends and supporters, trying to gather every last vote before polling opened. (Harris 2006, 196)

Our principal source for the history of Rome's late republic is Marcus Tullius Cicero. His letters, speeches and accounts of how the republic governed itself in the wake of the civil wars and Sulla's dictatorship of the 80s and 70s BC describe a period when the ongoing Roman revolution threatened finally to overturn the political rule of the senators: once the powers of the tribunes were restored, the public interest was served by a public trial of one of the city's most corrupt politicians—the ex-governor of Sicily, Verres. Harris's description gives a flavour of the public and participatory nature of these great public trials. The jury may be from the elite and specially selected, but the proceedings will take place in front of 'the eyes of the people'—meaning these decision-makers must pay heed to the masses:

> Hundreds of spectators, determined to have a decent vantage point, had slept out in the forum overnight. By dawn there was nowhere left to stand that offered any shade. By the second hour, there was nowhere left at all. In the porticoes and on the steps of the Temple of Castor, in the forum itself and in the colonnades surrounding it, on the rooftops and the balconies of the houses, on the sides of the hills—anywhere that human beings could squeeze themselves into, or hang off, or perch on—there you would find the people of Rome. (Harris 2006, 204)

It is interesting to observe how Cicero reported this conflict in his account of his prosecution speech. His dramatic oratory would have taken place from the rostra in the Forum, Rome's premier public arena. *Arena* is Latin for 'sand', and derives from the open public space where politics, and entertainment, were enacted. Thousands of citizens, freed men and slaves would have heard his powerful denunciation of this rich and powerful noble exploiting and corrupting the people of Sicily as governor. Cicero claimed he would 'pin him down, in your hearing and before the eyes of the world, as a thief and a criminal. He sees the many senators and knights who can bear witness to his misdeeds. He sees the crowds of Romans and allies whom he has grievously wronged' (Grant 1972, 39–40). At this time he spoke for the people's cause, emphasising their power:

> This crowd from all over Italy, which has gathered at a single moment from all directions, for the elections, the games and the registration in the census … this trial will bring you either great popularity or great discredit … it should also provide the entire population with a chance to understand the procedure, and to memorize what each speaker will be saying … if things go wrong with this court … the general conclusion will be that our judges must be sought from another order altogether. (Grant 1972, 55–56)

Verres was found guilty in what appeared to be a manifestation of the will of the people. Cicero had dramatically recreated the scene where Verres had a man executed in public, despite him claiming his rights as a

Roman citizen, that is to a fair trial. This had struck a real chord with the masses who were fed up with the arbitrary abuse of their human rights by the powerful few. Seven years later, Cicero would make the same mistake when he was Consul (leading minister) and pay the price by being exiled and having his mansion above the Forum burnt down and a Temple to Liberty erected in its place. Cicero was subsequently courting Pompey who at this time was also parading himself as the people's champion—in 67 BC—organising wars against the pirates threatening Rome's corn supply and claiming mass allotments of land for his soldiers as the honour due to victorious veterans.

Now the power of the tribunes, formally suppressed during Sulla's dictatorship, was regained, the many-headed hydra of the urban proletariat continued to contest for their interests. For example, in 67 BC the tribune Cornelius 'told a public meeting' that the provinces 'were being bled dry by the interest charged by Roman profiteers'. Emboldened by the crowd, he

> now widened the range of his attack on the Senate with a bill restating the old principle that the individual should be exempted from the operation of the law except by a popular vote … The people assembled to vote, the crier began to read out the terms of the bill [another tribune] … Globulus forbade both crier and clerk to speak. Cornelius himself then read the text. (Wiseman 1994, 333)

This is direct democracy, the people's representative, their tribune proposing a law that the citizens wish to pass, asserting their control over the oligarchs, the ruling class of senators. Wiseman relates what happened next:

> Cornelius Piso, the consul, protested firmly that Globulus' right of tribunician veto had been improperly infringed, but the assembly knew which of its tribunes was doing the obstructing, and shouted him down. Some made as if to grab him; Piso ordered his lector [official] to arrest them; the crowd seized the lictor's fasces [the bundle of rods that symbolised the city's power] and smashed them; stones were thrown. (Wiseman 333)

Cicero was still portraying himself as a *populares* and relying upon Pompey to endorse his rise through the political career ladder (*cursus honorum*). As a result, his first appearance on the rostra (*templum*) addressing the masses took place in 66 BC where he was championing the bill of this same Manilius which endorsed Pompey, the vanquisher of the Mediterranean pirate fleets, as the new military commander in 'Asia' (present-day western Turkey). His tone is unashamedly populist, acclaiming the dignity and political maturity of the masses he was addressing, in contrast to their noble 'betters':

> The Roman people can now of its own right, defend its own authority … if you [the crowd], in spite of their resistance, by yourselves conferred dignity on the empire, safety on the whole world; then at last let those noble men confess that both they and all other men must obey the authority of the Roman people. (Cicero 1898, 171)

However, this was Cicero's last 'popular' speech. He had to choose sides, and he chose to back the oligarchs, the senators who he wished to join by winning office as a Consul. His contempt for the poor was legendary and he was hated by the *populares* all the more because he had started out portraying himself as a 'man of the people' before selling out; maybe this is why Tony Blair was nicknamed Cicero by some critics. As Millar comments, 'we should read his judgements as reactions to a political system and not as descriptions … Cicero's conception of the Roman state … has had far more success with posterity than it ever had in his lifetime. (Millar 2002, 148).

In 66 BC, Asconius tells us that 'C. Manilius as tribune of the plebs, supported by a gang of freedmen and slaves, was passing an utterly immoral law to allow freedmen the vote in all of the tribes, and was pursuing this aim with rioting and was blockading the climb to the Capitol'—before they were scattered and killed by the senators' henchmen (Lewis 2006, 91, 282–283). 'The Senate, with a clear conscience, declared the law invalid' (Wiseman 1994, 338). Rome's nobles were convinced of their divine right to rule and refused to respect the people's rights:

> There were too many checks and balances in the constitution, which operated in practice only in the interests of the ruling class. Reformers had to use force, or at least create conditions in which the senate had to fear its use. This was the first factor which favoured the growth of violence in Rome. (Brunt 1966, 8)

The class struggle in the ancient world (Ste Croix 1983), often called the conflict of the orders, was hotting up in the 60s BC. Citizens' associations, *collegia*, were often actively campaigning, demonstrating and rioting in the forum: these groups often included masses of slaves as well as the urban poor, the *proletariat*. Like the Parisian clubs established in the years before the French Revolution, and the corresponding societies that helped form 'the making of the English working class' at the end of the eighteenth century, they allowed collectives to organise and agitate for their share of the *res publica* (public interest).[1] In 64, the senators banned the *collegia*. This illegal act was in the midst of their desperate attempt to remain in power. From 65 until 62 their regime was seriously under threat by the attempt of the popular leader, Catiline, to win the consulship. Sallust's history, *The Conspiracy of Catiline*, retells this story through senatorial lenses—and vindicates the actions of the consul of 63, Cicero, in the suppression of the revolt. From the popular point of view, it would be better described as the conspiracy against Catiline: Cicero was the figurehead of a sustained campaign to deny 'the people of Rome' their legal right to associate, campaign and elect a popular leader to address the calamitous growth of poverty, hunger and debt that was killing off the poor at a frightening rate.

Reversing the oligarch's land seizure and declaring a jubilee, where debts would be cancelled and land ownership democratised, was imperative for their survival. Catiline was the leader of the popular party at this time, following Pompey's departure. Many historians have argued that there were no political parties in the late republic, pointing out that there was not a named organisation with official members and a defined programme. Earlier writers, such as Theodore Mommsen or Edward Beesly, do not agree—indeed, the latter asserts that at the time of Catiline's candidature:

> There was a large political party, numbered in the tens of thousands, and its leaders were in correspondence with the insurgents [of Catiline] in Etruria. An exact parallel is to be found in our own revolution with Pym and Hampden. (Beesly 1878, 8)

---

[1] The public laws, the *res publica*, was the central concept for Roman society at the time. The senatorial oligarchy saw it as their goal to maintain it, but saw popular measures as undermining it. Their opponents saw the oligarch's desertion of the *republica mixta* as described by Polybius as similarly fatal to their understanding of it.

Like the English Revolution, this was an opposition broad enough to include 'respectable' and 'popular' elements, and which believed itself entitled to legislate and was driven by those '"friends of order", the nobles or *optimates*, into revolt against intolerable practical evils. No government has been such a scourge to the governed' (Beesly 1878, 8, 4). Patiently and diligently, Catiline renewed his candidature in 64 and 63 as the senate manouevred to keep him out of office.

The senators' greatest coup was persuading Cicero to become their candidate. As we have seen, this 'new man', like Marius from the provincial town of Arpinium, had been a leading orator for the popular cause. When he failed to secure the *populares* nomination for the consulship in 63, he announced his desertion of the people's cause in his famous candidate's speech '*In toga candida*' where he accused Catiline of beheading a popular politician and displaying his head on the street as well as sleeping with a mother and her daughter. He aimed to raise a moral panic over Catiline, wore a breastplate in the forum whilst declaring he feared he would be assassinated, and then demanded his exile. Although the people felt they had a right to assemble and elect their own leaders, elections were in practice a much dirtier business. Brunt describes how:

> Candidates for office seldom stood on programmes and organized parties did not exist. Men were returned to office … by reason of their munificence and lavish bribes, in general because of their family and connections … They used their power to grow richer from the profits of war and empire, and to oppose every measure to relieve the poor [which] could be rejected on the ground that they were more than the treasury could bear, the treasury from which the senators drew handsome allowances for themselves. (1966, 5)

As a result Cicero won the election and became Consul, that is the leading minister for one year. He later presented 'proof' of a terrible conspiracy by Catiline to burn down Rome and slaughter the rich whilst declaring all debts cancelled. Soldiers were sent out to crush the rebel army at its base in Tuscany, but what really damned Cicero in the eyes of the people was when he organised the public execution of his so-called co-conspirators in the prison below the Roman Forum as a warning to all future rebels. These he executed without trial, in the interests of homeland security. '*Vixere*,' he announced, in a chilling understatement, as he emerged from the prison where he had overseen their punishment: 'They have lived.' That is: 'They are dead' (Beard 2015). This violent act was to recoil upon Rome's rulers because, as Sallust explains, all of the plebeians were initially on Catiline's side due to rising inequalities:

> They hate the old order and yearn for a new; in detestation of their own lot they work for total change; to them turmoil and riots are a source not of anxiety, but of nourishment; for the destitute cannot easily suffer any loss. (Rolfe 'Catilina' Book 37, Brunt 1966, 22)

The senators attempted to repeat the trick by a show trial of the leading tribune of the plebs, Clodius, in 61. The charges were clearly manufactured, as proven by the fact they weren't even raised until seven months after his alleged 'offence' of violating the Vestal virgins ceremony (Beesly 1878, 8). However, the Senate whipped up a storm of scandal as they sought to liquidate the increasingly popular opposition forces. Panicked, Caesar—who was allied with the *populares*, but feared for his safety after his life had been threatened when he spoke up against the execution of the Catiline conspirators the previous year—temporarily retreated by divorcing his wife, signalling his fear of further oligarchic reaction capturing him in its web. But he had calculated wrongly: the *optimates* had overreached themselves. The popular feeling was increasingly intolerant of this latest senatorial attempt to behead their movement, so much so that even the consul, Piso, tried to withdraw Clodius's prosecution which he had himself instigated. Cicero wrote:

> The Right … are keeping clear of the whole affair; gangs are being collected; I myself who at first showed a draconian severity am daily cooling down … I'm afraid this lack of interest from the respectable, and warm support from the disreputable, may lead to much political trouble. (Wilkinson 1959, 41)

The show trial became a spectacular own goal for the *boni* or 'good men'. 'The Forum was packed with slaves', reported Cicero, concluding that

Clodius's acquittal graphically demonstrated the strength of the popular cause; 'there were more who thought about poverty than probity'. During the trial Cicero had intervened to attempt to destroy Clodius's alibi, claiming to Atticus that 'I thought I saw a chance of using the surgeon's knife on immorality and curbing youthful excesses … in the hope of purging or even curing the body politic'. His failure left him full of gloom: 'but a great blow has been dealt to the state through the corruption and debauchery of the jury … a single year … has thrown away the prestige of the Senate and broken up the harmony of the two orders' (Wilkinson 1959, 43, 45). Of course, Cicero's harmony was precisely that undemocratic senatorial grasp on power, the Roman yoke holding down popular organisation and aspirations.

The breakthrough year for the popular cause was Caesar's consulship of 59, when he initiated the successful land reform legislation which finally met the aspirations of the *censi capite* proletariat, providing some of them with allotments, as well as a substantial proportion of the prized land of the neighbouring province of Campania that had been seized by the state and allocated to larger poor families. The previous years had seen attacks on the rights of citizens to organise themselves in associations or *collegia*. Now the popular forces counter-attacked: 'Clodius' law of 58 reasserted and perhaps extended the right of association', so Brunt speculates; 'men could have become aware that the right was part of their freedom, once they had been deprived of it' (Brunt 1988, 306). The introduction of public welfare in the form of the grain dole was pushed through and, according to Brunt, put the city's ex-slaves (freedmen) and current slaves in the centre of the struggle:

> The urban plebs consisted preponderantly of freedmen, and particularly after Clodius made grain distribution free in 58 masters were very ready to manumit [free] slaves, who could still be required to work for them while obtaining rations from the state … Slaves were employed in every trade, craft and profession. Freedom was a necessary incentive to good work … granted … or bought by the slave from the wage or share of the profits he was allowed. (Brunt 1966, 8–9, 15)

This practical solution to the rising tide of impoverished citizens was bitterly resented by the senatorial class, outraged at this legal usurpation of their privileges. Now their control of the state machinery was under-mined, they sought their own dictator to champion the optimate cause, namely Pompey, whose cooperation Caesar also required. He, in turn, vacillated between representing himself on the one hand as a popular politician, vanquisher of the pirates and administrator of the corn dole, and on the other hand as a military strongman in the Sullan tradition who could 'save' the republic from its people. When he appeared as a 'man of the people' in the forum Pompey was heckled—labelled a 'teenage hangman' for his bloody role in aiding Sulla's march on Rome back in the 80s. In the mid-50s, the rivalry between Caesar and Pompey, both describing themselves as *populares*, led to Pompey's construction of a great stone theatre—completed in 52:

> The question was whether Pompey meant to have contiones and comitia transferred to his splendid theatre. If he did, Caesar countered his action by starting in 54, the year after Pompey's still uncompleted theatre was dedicated, a permanent marble building in the Campus Martius for the elective meetings of the tribes and for all meetings of the centuries. (Taylor 1990, 31)

Many historians have underestimated the social significance of the experience of popular power in the late republic. They have taken at face value the very low estimation accorded by written sources to the public meetings, trials and legislation passed, describing this process as the product of rival aristocrats employing large client groups of poorer citizens to clap and cheer for their causes. Richard Evans addresses these themes in his conclusion to his review of the period *Questioning Reputations*:

> namely that what we feel about Saturninus, Glaucia, Drusus, Sulpicius, Clodius and Milo is heavily influenced by the bias and propaganda in the source material. This colouring of the portrayals has not always been revealed to its fullest extent in modern treatment, allowing ancient misconceptions even deliberate designs to remain unquestioned and dominant. (Evans 2003, 194)

Taylor, Brunt and Millar have offered a more neutral interpretation which recognises the validity in many of the popular claims: Taylor has described the voting assemblies' decisions as often reflecting legitimate concerns, and demonstrated how the Tribal Assembly method of voting often allowed for a higher degree of participation by poorer citizens than assumed by traditional accounts.

Millar (1998) has argued that many Roman citizens who came originally from other parts of Italy would have retained their membership of 1 of the 31 'rural' tribes and thus exercised some influence in popular votes on legislation in the forum. This would explain how laws granting land reform and grain doles, as well as trials acquitting popular leaders like Clodius—so despised by the *optimates*—could come about: Caesar's champion Clodius pursued during his tribunate an ultrademocratic policy. He gave the citizens free grain. He then fully legalised the *collegia* and 're-established the "street clubs" which with their almost military street by street set up were nothing less than the formal organisation of the whole free and slave proletariat of the capital' (Evans 2003, 328). If the state proceedings were merely the act of puppets manipulated by politically ambitious masters then why the popular fury when Clodius, in 52, and eight years later Caesar himself, were assassinated? On both occasions the Senate House was burnt down. All this took place in the 50s while Caesar was away campaigning in Gaul. Mommsen is emphatic about the popular character of political life at the time:

> The rabble never had a merrier time. The number of little great men was legion. Demagoguery became quite a trade … the tried tricks of the theatre were much in demand. Greeks and Jews, freedmen and slaves, were the most regular attenders and the loudest shouters in the public assemblies where frequently only a minority of those voting consisted of citizens constitutionally entitled to do so. (Mommsen 1959, 327)

With Caesar's death in 44 a bloody reaction was instigated by an oligarchy who, for all Cicero's fine words about preserving a democratic republic, only believed in the rule of the *bona dea*, the good men, the democracy of the few that reminds us of the bourgeois 'democracies' of the modern world. Rather than concede to the people, these reactionaries preferred the one-party tyranny of Rome's counter-revolutionary empire under Augustus.

Millar argues that the public political struggle played out in the assemblies 'were not a sign of weakness but ultimately of strength'(Millar 2002b, 74). Following Machiavelli he is convinced that the accountability exercised by a cross-section of the population, including women and slaves, in the mass meetings, demonstrations and public ballots in the huge public squares of the city gave a strength and dynamism to this city state as it expanded across the Italian peninsula.

Eventually it came to civil war: Julius Caesar led the *populares* cause in a battle to the death with Pompey's and Cato's oligarchic forces. Those backing direct democracy fought—and won—then lost all but its semblance through Caesar's assassination and the degeneration of the army into a genuine paid-off 'labour aristocracy'. Without the lifeblood of accountability that flowed through the act of democratic assembly, the people lost their sovereignty. His successor as dictator, Octavian, named himself Augustus so he could symbolically follow Julius Caesar in the calendar his uncle had instituted. Like those later 'Augustans' in 1688 he hailed his permanent dictatorship as a 'glorious revolution', and retained much of Caesar's planned building programme of public works.

The dynamism acquired by this burgeoning imperial power came from the revolutionary era which had forged it, just as the social revolutions in England and France were later to lead to the evolution of powerful military states that invaded their neighbours. We should not let the fact that the success of the people's cause led to a dictatorship blind us to the popular measures achieved through mass participatory events in the arena of the forum where the 'mobile population'—those without property—fought for their interests. Cicero provides something of the flavour of these occasions when recounting to his brother what Brunt calls 'a relatively peaceful scene in the 50s', where 'Publius Clodius, the patrician leader of the urban proletariat, had indicted his enemy, Titus Annius Milo, on a charge of seditious violence before the popular assembly':

> Clodius asked his followers who was starving the people to death. The gang replied: 'Pompey'. Who wanted to go to Alexandria? 'Pompey.' Whom did they want to go? 'Crassus' ... At about three o'clock, as if at a signal, Clodius' people began to spit in unison at ours. A crescendo of anger. They began to shove our people out. We charged: the gangsters fled. (Brunt 1966, 3)

Clodius not only ensured Cicero's exile in 58, but remained the people's champion against the optimates' mob leader, Milo. Asconius tells us, when commenting upon Cicero's speech in defence of Milo, that in 53 BC, 'there was a battle on the Via Sacra between the retinues of the candidates Hypsaeus and Milo, and, many of the Milonians were surprised and killed' (Lewis 2006, 97). A year later Clodius was murdered by Milo and popular *resistance* looked to Caesar and his soldiers rather than the Roman proletariat to rule in their interests.

Because Greek and Roman history has been a staple of the elite schools of the West for centuries, intended as a guide to the rules of 'good government' for the ruling class of the future, it has often been interpreted in a conservative way. In the case of the Roman republic this has meant endorsing Cicero's viewpoint and seeing 'the mob' who filled the forum as a blind destructive force that could only be controlled by the dictatorship of the Emperor that followed the end of the republic in 31 BC.

A contrasting view comes from Michael Parenti's account, *The Assassination of Julius Caesar*, who says 'the optimates come down to us through the filter of gentlemen's history as men of the highest principles', but in fact, 'they opposed land reform, rent control, and debt cancellation. More for the many meant less for the few. They opposed the secret ballot and all forms of popular input' (Parenti 2003, 141).

On the other hand, the mob saw Caesar as a leader who had championed their interests and defeated the noble leaders to prevent them extending slavery and tyranny still further. He was a dictator but he was 'the people's dictator' (Canfora 1999) who had fought a revolutionary war to defeat the old regime of privilege. This explains why Caesar was such a role model for the leader whose dictatorship prevented a reactionary return to monarchy and absolutism in France—Napoleon:

> He was also extremely conscious of Caesar's special relationship with 'the people': (Marat's newspaper had the title L'Ami du people); the word denoted the politically active part of the lowest social strata that actually shaped political life and influenced the holders of power. (Canfora 1999, xiii)

We can see what the people thought of those so-called liberators who had assassinated their hero. According to Plutarch's account of events at the funeral:

> Some called out to kill the murderers and others, as formerly in the case of Clodius the demagogue, dragged from the shops, the benches and tables, piled them upon one another, and thus erected a huge pyre; on this they placed Caesar's body and … burned it. Moreover, when the fire blazed up, people rushed from all sides, snatched up half-burnt brands, and ran round to the houses of Caesar's slayers to set them on fire. (Canfora 1999, 339)

Thus the tradition of rioters targeting the property of their oppressors goes back thousands of years in human history. The other obvious analogy to draw is that once again the popular uprising was a reaction against the violent actions of their rulers. 'No justice, no peace' would have been a slogan well understood on the streets of ancient Rome. The people's anger at Caesar's death would not abate. They killed a man who they mistakenly thought had condemned Caesar the day before and 'set his head on a spear and paraded it about the streets'. An ex-slave calling himself Amatius—meaning the false Marius, to link him with the former popular leader—'collected a band of reckless men and made himself a perpetual terror to the murderers', according to the Greek historian Appian (Canfora 1999, 342).

References

Beard, M. (2015, October 2). Why ancient Rome matters to the modern world. *The Guardian*.

Beesly, E. (1878). *Tiberius, Catiline and Clodius*. London: Kessenger Reprint.

Bottomore, T., & Rubel, M. (1961). *Karl Marx selected writings on sociology and social philosophy*. Harmondsworth: Pelican.

Brunt, P. (1966). The Roman mob. *Past and Present, 35*, 3–28.

Brunt, P. (1971). *Social conflicts in the Roman republic*. New York: Norton.

Brunt, P. (1988). *The fall of the Roman republic*. Oxford: Oxford University Press.

Canfora, L. (1999). *Julius Caesar: The life and times of the people's dictator*. Berkeley: University of California.

Cicero (1898). In defence of the proposed Manilian law. In Cicero (Ed.), *Select orations* (trans: Yonge, C. D.). New York: Harper & Brothers.

Clement, M. (2013). Manufacturing austerity in the Eurozone. *Human Figurations, 2* (1). ISSN: 2166-6644. http://hdl.handle.net/2027/spo.11217607.0002.106

Evans, R. J. (2003). *Questioning reputations essays on nine Roman republican politicians*. Pretoria: University of South Africa.

Grant, M. (1972). *Cicero selected works*. Harmondsworth: Penguin.

Harman, C. (1999). *A peoples' history of the world*. London: Bookmarks.

Harris, R. (2006). *Imperium*. London: Arrow.

Lewis, R. G. (2006). *Asconius: Commentaries on speeches by Cicero*. Oxford: Oxford University Press.

Millar, F. (1998). *The crowd in Rome in the late republic*. Ann Arbor: University of Michigan.

Millar, F. (2002a). *Rome, the Greek world and the East*. Hanover: University Press of New England.

Millar, F. (2002b). *The Roman republic in political thought*. Hanover: University Press of New England.

Mommsen, T. (1959) [1854]. *A history of Rome*. New York: Meridian.

Morris, I., & Manning, J. G. (2005). The economic sociology of the ancient Mediterannean world. In N. Smelser & G. Swedberg (Eds.), *The handbook of economic sociology*. London: Sage.

Ober, J. & C. Hedrick (Eds.) (1996). *Demokratia: A conversation on democracies ancient and modern*. Princeton: Princeton University Press.

Parenti, M. (2003). *The assassination of Julius Caesar*. New York: The New Press.

Plutarch (75 A.D.). Tiberius Gracchus. http://classics.mit.edu/Plutarch/tiberius.html.

Raaflaub, K. (1996). Equalities and inequalities in Athenian democracy. In J. Ober & C. Hedrick (Eds.), *Demokratia: A conversation on democracies ancient and modern*. Princeton: Princeton University Press.

Rolfe, C. (1921). *Sallust*. London: Heinemann.

Schaumburg, H. (2015). Argentina's 2001 crisis: The lessons for Greece. *Socialist Review, 405*, 20–22.

Sherwin-White, A. N. (1973). *The Roman citizenship*. Oxford: Oxford University Press.

Ste Croix, G. (1983). *The class struggle in the ancient Greek world*. London: Duckworth.

Taylor, L. R. (1963). *Voting districts of the Roman Republic*. Berkeley: University of California.

Taylor, L. R. (1990). *Roman voting assemblies*. Ann Arbor: University of Michigan.

Wilkinson, L. (Ed.). (1959). *Letters of Cicero*. London: Arrow.

Wiseman, T. P. (1994). The senate and the populares, 69–60 B.C. In T. Wiseman et al. (Eds.), *The Cambridge ancient history volume IX*. Cambridge: Cambridge University Press.

Wiseman, T. (2003). The political vacuum. In T. Wiseman (Ed.), *Classics in progress*. Oxford: British Academy.

Wood, E. M. (1996). Demos versus "We the people": Freedom and democracy ancient and modern. In J. Ober & C. Hedrick (Eds.), *Demokratia: A conversation on democracies ancient and modern*. Princeton: Princeton University Press.

3

Medieval Riots

Rebellions and riots are deeply abnormal occasions. English society in the Middle Ages was normally pacific. The majority of the people lived and died without ever becoming involved in any form of violent or civil disturbance. Whilst there were clearly tensions between the commons and elite groups, whether landlords and tenants, clergy and laity, or the 'county community' and the Crown, the number of occasions on which the normal bonds of deference dissolved into violent or mass action is very small (Hoyle 2001, 18). A rebellion in which the commons are mobilised in a disciplined fashion on the instructions of their social superiors, with authority concentrated within a small elite group, is obviously a relatively simple matter provided the rank and file are compliant with their instructions. A rising launched by activists drawn from outside the local elites is more complicated. It allows for the possibility of disputes amongst the activists over objectives; but it also has implicit the possibility of conflict between the activist cadre and the displaced elite as the latter try and claw back their grip over society (Hoyle 2001, 20).

Many of the events condemned as riotous and destructive are themselves the products of the bloody process of what David Harvey has called 'accumulation by dispossession'—that is the normal business of states

© The Editor(s) (if applicable) and The Author(s) 2016
M. Clement, *A People's History of Riots, Protest and the Law*,
DOI 10.1057/978-1-137-52751-6_3

and corporations involving crimes such as stealing property or violently assaulting other persons in organised warfare (Harvey 2003). If we want to understand what motivates people to gather together in acts of mass protest, often labelled as riots by those whose authority they are contesting, we need to see them in this context.

In this chapter I will look back at historical riots, principally in England, between 1000 and 500 years ago, in order to illustrate some of the key themes and concerns of those protesting and those in authority. One key focus here will be through the lens of justice and the law. The powerful have often used the law to establish their control, whilst those not in power have sought justice in the name of the law. For both groups, or figurations, their interpretations about property, community rights and customs have upheld their sense of entitlement to act as fermenters or repressors of riot and protest.

Even today, people continue to believe they are entitled to freedom of movement—the right to cross the barriers erected at the frontiers of states. An Ethiopian woman, interviewed during the attempt by hundreds of migrants to cross the French border in Calais in August 2015, was adamant that her human rights included that of seeking a means to live wherever she could, in this case by entering the UK. The barrier was preventing her doing this. As a lawyer, she demanded to know what entitled the authorities to prevent her access. Sometimes barriers can be targets for political protest, such as during the 2000s when states erected 'secure estates' to house world leaders gathering for international summits that prevented effective demonstrations by the public (Fernandez and Scholl 2014). The momentum for these political protests was sparked by the successful Seattle anti-globalisation protest in the USA in 1999 when hundreds of thousands of demonstrators flooded the city in a spectacular display of people power. The barriers of the next decade were the worlds' rulers response.

It is impossible to understand history without including migration as a key factor in how states developed. We are used to the idea of America as a nation built on migration, but it is also true for Europe. For example, those people we know as 'Normans' were originally 'Norse men', that is from Scandinavia. They settled in north-western France, named it Normandy, and from there invaded England in 1066, establishing a new regime which controlled the land and sanctifying the dispossession of the old Anglo-Saxon nobility in the Domesday Book. Its purpose was stated as 'to bring the subjected people under the rule of the written law'; but it was an evolution rather than a break with the past and 'could not have been made without the Anglo-Saxon organisation of shires and hundreds, and the habit of settling property disputes at meetings of the county court' (Clanchy 1998, 38).

So the new Norman law was grafted upon the old forms of social organisation which contained strong elements of local control over the agenda and practice of keeping the peace. The popular memory of this time being one of annual parliaments and community control meant that for hundreds of years rebels regarded the new regime as a 'Norman yoke'—a dictatorship forced upon a reluctant people. This chimed with the reality that as society advanced people tended to lose their day-to-day control over land held in common, and that the law—rather than being an expression of the popular will—was becoming more of a machinery of repression and social control wielded by an expanding state: 'modern legal vocabulary is primarily of French origin (agreement, burglary, court, debt, evidence … justice, police, fines, constables, arrests' (Clanchy 1998, 35–36).

We should not romanticise the Anglo-Saxon past: their rulers fought continuously and often made slaves of those they defeated. But the Norman yoke was real. A string of fortresses provided bases for armies to repress local communities. Only the ability to use violence kept those at the top in power, continually in fear of their bloody rivals. For example, in the 1100s King Rufus was 'killed while hunting in the New Forest … the future Henry I, who was also hunting in the forest, moved fast … took control of the treasury at Winchester within hours of Rufus' death and he was crowned at Westminster three days later' (Clanchy 1998, 44). The chronicles that record events such as these are of course commissioned and overseen by the monarch, so we cannot tell from the source whether Henry plotted to have Rufus killed, killed him himself, or just took advantage of a favourable situation.

To stay in power you had to look after one group whose loyalty could help defend you in this dog-eat-dog society. Rufus had created a class of knights who had power but also the privilege of paying no taxes. Inheritance became a right they could pass on; these were the laws of Edward the

Confessor (Clanchy 1998, 45). All these concessions to the equites (meaning horsemen) were part of the process of instituting a greater share of power amongst the class of people known as 'Nobles', which extended beyond the original grouping of Norman leaders who had initially monopolised the land of England and Wales. Inheritance secured property rights and led the knights or equites—towards greater appreciation of its value— the status to be gained in the greater exploitation of people and resources under their control, as part of the process of civilisation. Limiting the absolute power of the monarch in this fashion meant sharing power with those classes ruling and rising towards governing England. But Henry ensured that '"the royal forests were to be retained"' (Clanchy 1998, 45).

This brief summary makes it sound as if the developing society was one in which there was more interdependency between different groups or classes and the raw violence of the conquest was being softened; but this was not the case. The ruling figurations of nobles (a Roman term), or aristocrats (ancient Greek), controlled the lives of their tenants, exploited their labour and demanded their loyalty as retainers in their private armies when so required. Things were far from stable, with the principal threat of revolt against the Crown likely to come from the king's appointed rivals. In the time of Henry III, rebellions in both Normandy and England were common among the barons, as they manoeuvred for new positions in case Henry's power collapsed, or, as the Anglo-Saxon Chronicle puts it, '"those who troubled him most were his own men, who frequently deserted and betrayed him and went over to his enemies and surrendered their castles to them to injure and betray the king"' (Clanchy 1998, 46). In turn, Henry 'blinded the Count of Mortain who had fought against him at Tinchbrai … In 1125 all the Moniers (minters of coin) in England were sentenced to have their right hands cut off and to be castrated'. Henry seemed to recognise the madness of these policies, saying '"if I make men fear me, then I'll end up living in fear"' (Clanchy 1998, 46).

In 1196, London citizen William Fitzosbert, known as Longbeard, launched a protest movement against the unfair distribution of taxation. According to the chroniclers his aims were unworthy, as:

> he plotted great wickedness in the name of justice, a conspiracy of the poor against the rich. By his fiery eloquence he inflamed both the poor and the

modestly well-off with a desire for limitless freedom and happiness and with a hatred for the arrogance of the rich and noble which he painted in the blackest colours. At public meetings he proclaimed himself the king of the poor and their saviour … he kept a list of 52,000 supporters, claimed sanctuary in St Mary Le Bow. But Chief Justice and Archbishop of Canterbury Hubert's troops set fire to the church … he and 9 friends were tied to horses' tails and dragged to Tyburn and hanged. (Danziger and Gillingham 2003, 63–64)

Although we cannot take all these accounts by the chroniclers to be accurate—for example, London had a population of considerably less than 52,000 at this time, so there is clearly some exaggeration—they are another reflection of the reality of riot and protest in medieval Britain.

A new status of people who were essentially controlled by their masters was created post Magna Carta in 1215. The Normans had ended Anglo-Saxon slavery, but the nobles made serfs of their tenants and called them *Villeins*. This is where the pejorative term villain originates, reflecting the fact that for those of high status these lowly people were inherently evil. This legalised control of the persons and the labour of around half the population, continued until essentially overthrown by the Peasant's Revolt of 1381. The Normans saw nothing wrong with this unequal and exploitative treatment. One proverb at the time stated, 'the churl should always be well plucked for he is like a willow that sprouts better the more often it is pollarded' (Danziger and Gillingham 2003, 41). This injustice was institutionalised, since being unfree meant you and your family had no rights that your master could abuse: you had no legal freedoms. The result was to 'disbar half the population of England from access to the public courts … Unfree and legally classified as serfs or villeins' (Danziger and Gillingham 2003, 42).

Not surprisingly, given all this exploitation and inequality, the majority of the population sought to win freedom and justice for themselves. Monarchs and nobles recognised the benefits of trade and sought to create towns where market exchange could take place. One way to encourage urban migration was to promise that any serf who lived in a town for a year and a day as a burgess (trader) could win their freedom. This policy was written down as part of 'the great charter' Magna Carta.

No free man should be taken or imprisoned or deprived or outlawed or exiled or in any way ruined, nor will we good send against him, except by the lawful judgement of his peers or by the law of the land. To no one will we sell, to no one will we deny or delay right or justice. (Danziger and Gillingham 2003, 5)

By 'free men' the nobles meant themselves, and they were reluctant to grant any notion that these rights would be universal. If serfs or tenants wanted to have rights they needed to escape the judicial power of their lord by migrating to the towns and cities, where they gained important civil rights.

free to sell, sublet, mortgage or pass on their burgage to heirs. They were to be free from having to pay servile dues or perform labour services … Burgesses could have their own oven and handmill … a serf who managed to live in a borough as a burgess for a year and a day was thenceforth to be regarded as a free man." (Danziger and Gillingham 2003, 53)

The monarch and the nobles saw the growing towns as a source of revenue through trade which they could profit from by controlling monopolies and taxes, so they also encouraged these economic and social changes. The growth of villages and centres to exchange, the market towns, were the engine of expansions at this time. Magna Carta had institutionalised a certain character to this process of civilisation: a solution was held in check—the absolute power of the monarch degraded, and in turn the noble monopoly on riches, compromised by their need to form commercial relations with the rising figuration of the gentry.

The thirteenth century was also when the nobility was compelled to follow the laws of profit by more efficiently exploiting the great estate. The franchising process created the gentry. This figuration, the bourgeoisie of the future, ran the managerial revolution that put the quest for efficiency at its heart; they oversaw the transplantation of peasants from smallholding to the village. By encouraging the artisan/yeoman figuration below them to cooperate in enhancing the agricultural use of technology—such as the horse-drawn plough—they were managing greater resources and controlling more wealth.

How could the minority of those in authority succeed in triumphing over the needs of the majority? Only by employing forces to threaten and enact violent repression to ensure the people respected their rule. Medieval knights had been recruited by lords; and for both these groups power was glorified by the church. In secular terms the aristocrats became the magistrates, setting up groups of men as their constables. To police was their policy. Below them were the workers, and sometimes they combined to seek their freedoms on such a scale that people's justice and liberties seemed within their grasp, for example the Peasants' Revolt and the cloth workers of Florence.

The key legal documents in medieval Britain were of course drawn up on the orders of the ruling powers. The Domesday Book recorded who owned what, validating the Norman conquests where they comprehensively appropriated the lands of their Anglo-Saxon predecessors. But by implicitly validating the social relations of 1089, they became a tool in the hands of peasants and small landowners with which to resist future noble demands to enclose lands, ban the taking of game and throw the 'common man' off the common land. Magna Carta was drawn up to guarantee the lords' civil rights from being overruled by the monarch. However, it also became, in the hands of the people, a 'Manifesto' for their liberty (Linebaugh 2008):

> There is much to be said for the protesters' view of Magna Carta. Although there is not a word in it about the right to protest, there is a sense in which Magna Carta in its entirety represents protest. It was in origin the product of direct political action, of negotiation after rebellion. As a symbol of the struggle against tyranny it will always retain its value. (Danziger and Gillingham 2003, 284)

A good place to begin understanding this process is to look at the core provisions of the important 'Statute of Winchester' which instituted a system of police in England in 1285, which can be summarised as follows:

> That every man between fifteen years and sixty be assessed and sworn to arms according to the amount of his lands and chattels … And in each hundred [district] and liberty let two constables be chosen to make the

view of arms: and the aforesaid constables shall, when the justices assigned to this come to the district, press before them the defaults they have found in arms, in watch-keeping and in highways … And the justices assigned shall present again to the king in each parliament and the king will provide a remedy therefore. (Harding 1984, 166)

As Harding comments, 'it is easy to see how the Statute of Winchester might have come to represent an ideal of communal self-policing', under the exclusive lordship of the king, who was confining the privileges of the magnates within narrow limits (Harding 1984, 167). This meant all citizens would be bound by the same rules, rather than the nobles/magnates believing they were free from all restraint. Under the statute, communities were mandated to elect their own constables, turn out whenever a hue and cry was raised against criminals, and assemble on the village green when summoned, ready to fight— whether in time of war for the king or nobility, or for themselves and to right injustice. This legislation implicitly recognised the truism of 'No justice, no peace'.

Despite the fine words of the Statute, the King still relied upon the nobles to govern locally, allowing them to maintain the disciplinary power in their hands as justices of the peace. The aristocracy, and the layer of gentry that carried out their orders in return for their favour, remained in control of the land, the forests and the fields and now had control of the law through being appointed justices of the peace: the accountable framework of the Statute of Winchester was twisted to suit their own purposes. 'The strains of war made the king resort to special criminal commissions, almost punitive expeditions, in the hands of the magnates' (Harding 1984, 169).

But if those nobles in power were themselves committing crimes, they could face protest and rebellion. One legendary English outlaw was Robin Hood, and tales of his deeds can be traced back to the 1300s. Conservative historians have reacted against the claims of the Left, particularly social historians like Hilton, Thompson, Hobsbawm, Hill and Rudé, who have explored the history of revolt and revolution. They are accused of having a simplistic or romanticised view of rebellion. Apparently they ignore its violence, such as when Hood beheaded the Sheriff of Nottingham.

'Violent death is accepted with almost casual brutality', according to Sir James Holt when describing Hood's actions:

> Violence takes two directions. One is towards rebellion: not rebellion against authority for the outlaws are at one in their veneration of the king, but against the local exercise of that authority by the Sheriff. (Holt 1981, 11)

This twists the sense of the legendary outlaw. Robin Hood demands justice and will fight the unjust forces that repress him and his community. This is rebellion against authority—in the name of a higher authority, justice itself—represented, in the legends of this time, in the person of the monarch. In the modern age of nation states ruled by a governing bureaucracy, with a president or monarch as its symbolic head, rebellion would naturally be anti-royal. Holt compounds his partiality by telling us that 'the other route is criminal. The most realistic early tradition of Robin is that he extorted money from travellers who he waylaid on the Great North Road. They are forced to disgorge under duress' (Holt 1981, 11).

Holt seems to forget that the wealth shows their guilt—the reason that justifies the outlaws' seizure and redistribution. Earlier Holt claims that Hood 'has no practical scheme for improving the human condition' (Holt 1981, 10). But clearly the legendary appeal of taking goods from the few who have far too much, for the benefit of the many who have too little, makes a lot of sense to the story's many fans over the centuries. Holt misses the point that pirates and bandits will always be able to justify robbing the rich, because this echoes the organised violence that past generations of nobles, kings and empires have employed in the process of acquiring their positions and possessions. However, if they go on to serve the monarch, like Drake and Raleigh, they will become national heroes!

So when Holt argues 'in Robin Hood the criminal is made heroic', the same could have been said that in Elizabethan England, or in the actions of the British forces in China and India as they heroically carved out a profitable opium trade in the nineteenth century. All states and many businesses have 'heroic leaders' with criminal records. To recognise this is not to romanticise everyone who rebels against or robs the representatives of the status quo, but it does provide more context for a richer, more appreciative, understanding of bandits and primitive rebels, ancient and modern (Hobsbawm 1959). Robin Hood's cause is that of popular justice and his enemies are the criminal ruling classes of the English nobility. They retained gangs of thugs and conducted protection rackets where they threatened to contrive lawsuits and false indictments 'bribing corruptible jurors and browbeating honest ones in the process' (Harding 1984, 170). For example:

> When a great lord, or man of power, wished to ruin an enemy he alleged an enormous trespass by him … The sheriff and his bailiffs would be brought into the plot, to make sure the dependant was summoned too late, or summoned to appear in his opponent's territory where he dared not go for the peril of his life, with the consequence that enormous damages were awarded against him … many were condemned to perpetual imprisonment … or they were outlawed and driven into exile. (Harding 1984, 171)

The case of late medieval England in the fourteenth and fifteenth centuries illustrates this well. The Hundred Years War between England and France was succeeded by the decades-long Wars of the Roses: the whole period from 1350 to 1485 was marked, not just by these dynastic battles between states in the process of their formation, but also regular protests, riots and revolts from groupings below the level of the ruling class. It is impossible to appreciate the true sense of actions like the 1381 Peasant's Revolt without recognising how the oppression and injustice meted out by the powerful cliques around the monarch made life so hard for everyone else. A further turn of the screw occurred in 1351, when the state legislated to prevent people from raising their wages. The statute set a maximum wage for labourers that was commensurate with wages paid before the Black Death, specifically in the year 1346. It also mandated that all able-bodied men and women work, and imposed harsh penalties for those who remained idle. By the Statute of Labourers, the Justices of the Peace gained the power 'compelling the service and regulating the wages of all sorts of workmen' (Harding 1984, 182). It stated:

Each and every man and woman in our realm of England, of whatever condition, free or servile, who are strong in body and under sixty years of age; if they are not living by trade or exercising a special craft, do not have property to live from or land to cultivate and are not already in the service of others, shall be bound to serve anyone who requires their services to work suitable to their status. (Harding 1984, 185)

Being forced to take the wages paid five years ago was felt to be a form of wage slavery. Those without property were to be made to serve, and if they refused their master they were liable to imprisonment. It was a crime not to work as directed by the propertied, who were your masters. Thus class oppression was the seedbed for the revolt.

Across the continent in the area we now know as Italy, then split into many city-states and regions, the *popolo* (people) showed amazing organisation in resisting the domination of the powerful local lords, known as the magnates. In Pavia, near Milan, the leader of the *popolo* Iacopo Bussolari 'choosing 20 men representing each neighbourhood ... These 20 the ordered to choose 100 men, Centuriones, for the 22 neighbourhoods of the city' and 'sent his Centuriones against the head of the ruling Beccharia Family' (Cohn 2006, 114). Terrified he fled, and Bussolari told the people that as long as the tyrant's palaces and mansions remained he would return. They 'dismantled the Beccharia's palaces, according to the chronicler Villani, without "leaving a stone atop another ... it was awesome; all the people, men, women, the rich and the poor, like ants, removed the buildings leaving the squares entirely bare"' (Cohn 2006, 114–115). Thus the medieval occupy movement went one stage further than their equivalents in New York and Hong Kong!

Meanwhile, in 1378, when the members of Florence's lowest status guilds—that is associations of tradesmen—revolted, they began by assembling in the city's main squares, San Pietro Maggiore and San Stefano: 'their number exceeded 6000', according to the history of Machiavelli:

> They took possession of the palace [demanded] three new companies of the arts; namely one for the wool combers and dyers, one for the barbers, doublet makers, tailors and such like, and the third for the lowest class of people ... [and] that the Signory [government of the city state] should provide a suitable place of assembly for them. (Machiavelli 1960, 133)

They wanted financial reform—the cancellation of the debts of less wealthy citizens. No debt under 50 ducats would have to be settled, and banks should only take back what was owed—no interest was to be paid. These measures strike a chord with those workers suffering from the threat of unemployment and the cuts associated with austerity today, with its emphasis on the need for the rich to settle debts rather than the poor. Then as now, those most powerful financial institutions had often built their wealth on the exorbitant rates charged for lending money, whilst demanding favours of 'bailouts' when their books didn't balance. Machiavelli continues:

> When the plebeians entered the palace, the standard of the Gonfalonier of Justice was in the hands of Michael de Lando, a wool comber … [who] turning to the multitude announced, 'You see this palace is now yours, and the city is in your power; what do you think ought to be done?' (Machiavelli 1960, 135)

He proposed a new settlement granting some new officers from the lower guilds as candidates, and he also 'gave to Salvestro de Medici the revenue of the shops upon the Old Bridge'. For the plebeians this was not enough, they 'had not a sufficient share in the government … again took up arms, and coming tumultuously into the court of the palace' de Lando 'advised them to lay down their arms … The multitude enraged at this reply, withdrew to Santa Maria Novella, where they appointed eight leaders for their party … so that the city possessed two governments, and was under the direction of two powers' (Machiavelli 1960, 136). The prominent city merchants began to see that they had made too many concessions to the wool workers. De Lando 'mounted on horseback, and followed by crowds of armed men, proceeded to Santa Maria Novella … drove part out of the city and compelled the rest to throw down their arms' (Machiavelli 1960, 137).

The parallels with how the English authorities dealt with Wat Tyler and the Peasant's Revolt when it reached London are striking. De Lando now went back on his earlier agreements to represent the lower trades, just as Richard II and his advisers abandoned their promise to grant charters of rights to the peasants and artisans. The most advanced economies at the time, Florence, England and that other future harbinger of republicanism, the Netherlands, all shared trading ties:

From England and the Low Countries, as well as from the hills and valleys of Tuscany, vast quantities of wool had for generations come into Florence to be refined, dyed and re-exported. Before the Black Death the industry was believed to have supported as many as 30,000 people. (Hibbert 1974, 33)

It was a mini industrial revolution. Many of the poor were more like workers in a trade than peasants tied to a smallholding. Their grouping together into workshops bred a consciousness of their entitlement to representation and social justice. Although Machiavelli, as a representative of the merchant class, is contemptuous of this more humble figuration, the words he puts into the mouth of the wool workers' leader show how their aspirations and motivations were sharpened by their keen awareness of the injustice of their exclusion from the democracy and responsibility of governing the city:

> If the question now were, whether we should take up arms, rob and burn the houses of the citizens, and plunder churches, I am one of those who would think it worthy of further consideration, and should perhaps prefer poverty and safety to the dangerous pursuit of the uncertain good. But, as we have already armed and many offences have been committed, it seems to me that we have to consider how to lay them aside, and secure ourselves from the consequences of what is already done. (Machiavelli 1960, 128)

This is a crucial question for protestors. How to continue with the struggle—to retreat or to advance? The worker's logic shows how being in the new situation changes the perception of what is necessary; in a way it broadens the range of possibilities way beyond the common sense of 'poverty and safety':

> We … have two things to consider; the one is, to escape with impunity for what has been done during the last few days, and the other, to live in greater comfort and security for the time to come. We must, therefore, I think, in order to be pardoned for our old faults, commit new ones; redoubling the mischief, and multiplying fires and robberies; and in doing this, endeavour to have as many companions as we can; for when many are at fault, few are punished; small crimes are chastised, but great and serious ones rewarded. When many suffer, few seek vengeance; for general evils are endured more patiently than private ones. To increase the number of misdeeds will, there-

fore, make forgiveness more easily attainable, and will open the way to secure what we require for our liberty. (Machiavelli 1960, 129)

This inspiring speech contains some important home truths about crime in general. It is the crimes of the powerless that society tends to punish—just look at the class of people who fill the world's jails. Either only the poor commit crime, or the rich go unpunished and—indeed, as the wool worker claims—are rewarded with further wealth. The worker's class consciousness certainly seems to have been sharpened in the concluding section:

> Our opponents are disunited and rich; their disunion will give us the victory, and their riches, when they have become ours, will support us. Be not deceived about that antiquity of blood by which they exalt themselves above us; for all men having had one common origin, are all equally ancient, and nature has made us all after one fashion. Strip us naked, and we shall all be found alike. Dress us in their clothing, and they in ours, we shall appear noble, they ignoble—for poverty and riches make all the difference. (Machiavelli 1960, 129)

One is reminded of the verse attributed to the radical priest of the English Peasant's Revolt John Ball: 'When Adam delved and Eve span, who was then the gentleman?'.

Recent research by Sam Cohn has revealed the vast extent of social revolt in medieval Europe. He lists:

> the peasants who stormed the city walls of Parma in 1385, the wool workers in the Ciompi revolt who broke into the Palazzo Signoria on 20 July 1378, or the throng in Paris who in March 1382 broke into the Châtelet, stole the hammers, and rioted against Charles VI's taxes on commodities. The Flemish revolts of 1297–1304 and 1323–1328 were the largest and most widespread rebellions of the Middle Ages. (Cohn 2006, 7)

He describes their tactics of 'forming assemblies and village alliances, electing their own leaders, and defending their rights by attacking their class superiors' (Cohn 2006, 35). They were not purely peasant revolts; 'commoners and to some extent burghers from the cities formed alliances with the peasants … since the 12th century many in the countryside had

the status and the right of urban burghers … and many weavers and full-
ers resided in small towns and villages' (Cohn 2006, 32–33).

The so-called idyllic age of chivalry upheld the myth that lords had
kept their obligations to their tenants and servants, thus buying their loyalty by services performed and protection offered. But by the fourteenth
century we are in the era of 'bastard feudalism' where, according to a
parliamentary debate of 1390, those who wore livery [uniform of their
noble master] 'inflicted great and unbearable oppression and extortions
on the common people' (McKelvie 2015).

Throughout the ages, a precondition for an uprising has been a crisis
in government. As McFarlane explains, 'in medieval England the form of
government was monarchical and the first condition of its political health
was that the king should rule' (McFarlane 1952, 25). Following the Black
Death, the king's senility set in in the 1360s, 'a period of royal minority,
in which the childhood of Richard II immediately followed the second
childhood of his grandfather, Edward III. In the only sense that mattered,
the country was without a head' (McFarlane 1952, 25). The failures of
the French wars, and the constant clamour for more taxes to fund them,
were fuelling resentment, as was the blatant injustice of the poor paying
a higher share of their income than the rich. Anyone who resisted paying
was to be arrested and imprisoned (Barker 2014, 138).

The Peasants' Revolt, according to Hilton (1973), resulted from their
belief that they could mount a public challenge to their lords and bishops.
They could make their own charters and destroy the feudal monopolistic
culture. The harsh terms of the Third Poll Tax provoked many to revolt
in 1381. The Poll Tax may have been the spark that set the fire, but class
injustice was the fuel. Wat Tyler, the leader of the revolt, demanded 'no
man should serve another except at his own will and by a proper covenant'
(Harding 1984, 187), which meant that the main struggle was for civic
freedom: a fourteenth-century civil rights movement. Just like all such
movements, a number of grievances came together to bring it into life:

> The rising in the eastern counties was caused by a general explosion of the
> suppressed grievances of class: villeins who disliked manorial customs,
> townsfolk who wanted a charter, artisans oppressed by municipal oligarchs,

clergy who felt the sting of poverty, discontented knights and squires, all took part in it. (Oman 1989, 103)

It is remarkable just how radical were the events of 1381. Bury St Edmunds in Suffolk was one town where people felt sorely oppressed by the monopoly on trade and privileges held by their abbey. A major uprising had occurred there earlier in the 1300s (Cohn 2013), and by 1381 it was in the vanguard of the uprising:

> the time of insurrection seemed favourable for the humbling of the mon-archy and the winning of the charter ... the rebels appeared in great force, and were welcomed with open glee by the poorer classes, many of whom joined them. The wealthier burgesses affected to hold themselves aloof from the movement, but secretly gave both encouragement and advice to the invaders. (Oman 1989, 106)

The Prior John Cambridge, and the Chief Justice of England, also Chancellor of Cambridge University, Sir John Cavendish, were both beheaded by the mob of villeins, townsfolk, artisans and lower clergy: 'it seemed an excellent jest to the mob to parade the two heads side by side, sometimes placing the judge's mouth to the prior's ear, as if he was mak-ing his confession, at others pressing dead lips together for a kiss' (Oman 1989, 107).

Rebel leaders were in charge for over a week—the town's monks 'were made to surrender their deeds and muniments into the hands of a commit-tee of burgesses; their jewels and plate were taken from them to be held as a pledge for their good behaviour'. The people's contempt for the church's greed for gold and power was blatant: 'a great charter of liberties for the town was drawn up, which the sub prior was forced to seal' (Oman 1989, 107–108).

These were the acts of the whole group of rebels, the mob, who called themselves 'magna societas' (Oman 1989, 115), the 'big society'—in a version of the social movement that would give David Cameron night-mares, as the people asserted their civil rights and took justice into their own hands by tearing up aristocratic privileges and tearing down the oli-garchs and legal authorities who had upheld their monopolies of power.

They were to seek from the king 'a charter more special than all the other charters' (Oman 1989, 119).

It appears that nearby, in another town dominated by an abbey—St Albans, the residents believed the 'urban myth' spread about a lost charter, as explained by the town's chronicler, Thomas Walsingham:

> What chiefly instigated the townsmen to rebel and to seek liberties were the lies of certain old men of the said town, who led the younger people on to this by false stories so that they believed that they had once had liberties and privileges granted by King Offa but that afterwards these had been taken away by force by the abbot and monks, and unjustly made void. (—Gesta Abbatium Monasterii Sancti Albani iii 365, quoted in Faith 1984, 64)

They believed that such a charter existed 'with initial letters decorated alternately with gold and azure, that was kept somewhere in the abbey, [and which] played a crucial part in the rising' (Faith 1984, 64). Once emboldened into action, more symbolic acts of defiance followed at St Albans. Walsingham describes the solemn procession 'with great pomp' of an armed crowd to Faunton Wood setting off to break the fences and gates enclosing land. At a mass meeting of '2000 or more' (Faith 1981, 58) townsmen and peasants 'joining their right hands' they swore an oath to stick together. Then they took a live rabbit, fixed it on the common punishment spot, the pillory, 'as a sign of the free warren they had won' (Faith 1984, 66). The power of symbols is also evident in the repression in the aftermath of the revolt: 'some of the offenders against the Church's property were drawn through the same fields and hanged on a scaffold cut from these same woods' (Faith 1981, 58).

The crowd even sanctified their actions by giving them an air of religious endorsement. A previous abbot had preserved the church's monopoly on grinding corn—and the accompanying profits—by confiscating the millstones from his tenants' illegal hand-mills and cementing them into the abbey floor. There had been previous struggles over this issue in 1274 and 1327. In the latter case the townspeople besieged the abbey, demanding the right to use hand-mills and claiming the Domesday Book authorised their civic rights. The hard-pressed abbey authorities issued a charter, but later retracted it; 'the townsmen's seal was broken up and the metal used to repair the shrine of St Alban in the Abbey Church' (Faith 1981, 56). Now the rebels symbolically righted the wrongs done to them half a century earlier; they:

> Took up from the floor of the parlour doorway the millstones which had been put there in the time of Abbot Richard … and handed them over to the commons, breaking them into little pieces and giving a piece to each person, just as the consecrated bread is customarily broken and distributed in the parish churches on Sundays, so that the people, seeing these pieces, would know themselves to be avenged against the abbey in that cause. (Gesta Abbatium Monasterii Sancti Albani iii 309, quoted in Faith 1984, 66)

The rebels' actions are an interesting comment upon their religious outlook. In a society still drenched with religion, their reaction is not secular, but rather one that condemns how 'worldly' the church authorities have become with their power and wealth and their ruthless exploitation of the poor.

Early heretics such as the Cathars or Albigensians in France 'took poverty as its doctrinal basis … the Roman church was a product of the forces of evil … Christ's Church should tread the road taken by the apostles, preferably barefooted'. New movements such as the Fransiscans reflected this change: no longer isolated in their country monasteries they 'lived close to towns, addressing themselves to works of charity or preaching in the open air' (Vale 1988, 330). This movement in turn split between the 'conventuals' who saw owning property as necessary, and the 'spirituals' who rejected it and were therefore seen as a threat to be suppressed by clerical and state authorities. In England, two years before the 1381 rising erupted, John Wycliffe demanded reform of a corrupt church:

> The clergy, he asserted, must be made to live, like the Levites of old, on their tithes and whatever the faithful were moved to offer them by the way of alms, surrendering all else to the laity [secular society] as having been acquired without scriptural authority. (McFarlane 1952, 79)

One year later Wycliffe was to be prosecuted for his denunciations of papal power and calls for a reformation that would amend the corruption of the Church—which stands as testament to the fear his ideas generated by empowering the commoners:

> 'God cannot give civil dominion to man for himself, and his heirs, in perpetuity ... Charters of human invention concerning perpetual civil inheritance are impossible' ... it was nothing if not easy to read into Wycliffe's philosophy ideas for a programme of devastating revolution. (Aston 1960, 2)

The logic of Wycliffe's arguments dictated that 'the people could lawfully remove the possessions of kings, dukes and their lay superiors, whenever they habitually offended'. The Dominican Roger Dymoke, in his 1395 rejoinder to Wycliffe, argued:

> Removal of ecclesiastical possessions, if not carried out by legal means, which, he said, was impossible, could only damage the whole land by ending in insurrection or tyranny. For if the commons took action 'it is probable that they would also usurp for themselves the lordships of others, and thus civil war would arise'. (Aston 1960, 9)

His warnings probably struck a chord with the authorities who had been shaken by the scale and depth of the 1381 rising which had targeted prominent state and church officials for punishment and organised many actions designed to gain new rights and freedom.

The rising in Norwich, England's second largest city at the time, was led by Geoffrey Litster of Norfolk, a dyer:

> Litster and his men at once betook themselves to plunder, and were eagerly aided by the rabble of the city. Their first act was to arrest, maltreat and finally behead Reginald Eccles, a justice of the peace, one of a class which everywhere bore the brunt of the wrath of the multitude ' ... the insurgents saluted their leader as King of the Commons' who 'superintended the burning of an infinite number of deeds and court rolls, dispossessed many persons'. (Oman 1989, 116–118)

In Cambridgeshire, messengers rode up and down the county proclaiming that the king had freed all serfs and that no one for the future owed suit or service to his lord. In a score of villages there were bonfires of charters. Essex sent a deputation 'with a demand for the ratification of the promises made at Mile End'. Richard told them the pledges made during Tyler's reign counted for nothing, having been extorted by force, announcing: 'Villeins ye are still, villeins ye shall remain' (Oman 1989, 84). A last stand at Billericay in Essex saw 500 slaughtered and routed, the rebels fleeing to Suffolk. Another band escaped to Ramsey Abbey near Huntingdon where 'they were suppressed, 25 slain, the rest dispersed' (Oman 1989, 85).

Over the next few decades, society was modernising, as described by Bernard Guenée:

> After the feudal state, the territorial state came into being, [the king] imposing his laws and his tax system with increasing effect, thanks to the growing number of his agents, controlled from the capital by an ever-expanding network of services … placing the governors opposite the governed and the prince opposite his country. (Guenée 1985, 20)

The English King Henry V defeated the French nobility at Agincourt in 1415 and set in train the bloody conquest of Normandy and the neighbouring provinces to create the English kingdom of France, which in turn dispossessed many French people and was eventually itself vanquished at the end of the 1440s. This reconquest of France by the French King Charles VII then had the effect of dispossessing the thousands of English settlers who had fought and gained lands in Normandy, Brittany and Maine. What was to happen to these men and their families, often used to soldiering themselves and therefore habituated to making a living through the exercise of arms? Some of the soldiers of both France and England, made unemployed by the Truce of Tours in 1444, quit their barracks and banded together to commit crimes in order to seize the means by which to live. According to 'A Parisian Journal 1405–1449', French soldiers gathered on the outskirts of Paris:

A great gang of robbers and cut-throats ... limbs of Antichrist every one, for they were all thieves and murderers, incendiaries, ravishers of women ... When people complained to the rulers of Paris, they were told: 'They've got to live. The King will be seeing to it very soon.' (Barker 2009, 331)

As for the English soldiers, the governor of Normandy, the Duke of York, ordered them 'to the furthermost marches between Normandy and Maine, living there under their chiefs and leaders in an orderly fashion, taking nothing except reasonably adequate victuals for men and horses' (Barker 2009, 333). The fact that these orders were given betrays the reality that when not turning their fighting skills to the cause of their respective monarchs and commanders, soldiers would employ them as groups acting in their own interests. For example, in 1447 the English noble, Roger Lord Camoys,

> gathered around him 'a great assembly of soldiers' [and] made the fortified abbey of Savigny his base and lived off the land, indiscriminately pillaging and ransoming both in enemy territory and his own. (Barker 2009, 362)

In this way, groups, or figurations, of armed people are transformed from a weapon to enforce the king's peace to a dangerous threat to public order. In the latter case Thomas Hoo, chancellor of English Normandy, had to hire more unemployed soldiers to 'suppress his damnable enterprise' (Barker 2009, 362).

Ending wars without securing a sustainable living for the soldiers who fought them is always dangerous, and has been throughout history. The most notorious case in the twentieth century was that of Germany in 1918, where 400,000 soldiers were left without occupation after the end of World War I. They formed the 'Freikorps' who were called in to suppress the German revolution at the end of World War I. Led by disillusioned officers of the Kaiser's old regime they were the first to wear the swastika emblem on their uniforms and formed the basis for the later rise of the Nazi party (Broué 2006). In the twenty-first century, Britain and America's experiment of disbanding, training and equipping new armies, following their occupations of Afghanistan and Iraq, resulted in the breakdown of the very public order they were supposed to ensure. In the case of Iraq, the West has ended up supplying its enemy, Islamic State, with an arsenal of military hardware as its proxy, the Iraqi army, fled from the the battlefield.

In both the cases cited above, the end of a war posed the question of the direction that society would now take. The German Communist Rosa Luxemburg described the choice as between 'socialism or barbarism', by which she meant either a revolution of the masses or an authoritarian counter-revolution. With her murder and the eventual defeat of the German revolution of 1918–23 (Harman 1983), the road was clear for Nazism and the Holocaust. Currently, with the defeat of the mass popular movements that made up 2011's 'Arab Spring', we see the rise of the counter-revolution in the form of the Egyptian military and Islamic State. In neither case was counter-revolution inevitable. Mass protest can win concessions from the powers that be, especially when the example set by the initial revolt threatens to generalise into wider struggles with the power to overthrow rulers, making them realise how narrow is the base of their support. These examples illustrate that the only way to appreciate fully events labelled as riots or uprisings is not to see them as something undesirable that needs to be alleviated by the correct mix of policies, but rather as the necessary response to actions taken by powerful institutions that undermine peoples' very existence. Riots have been caused by hunger, war and regime change as well as in response to crimes that go unpunished: the justification for protest in all of these cases can be summed up as the demand for justice.

Evidence of the crimes of the powerful is well illustrated by the case of the gang of nobles authorised by King Henry VI to control the county of Kent. This 'garden of England', just next to London, was one of the wealthiest parts of the country, encouraging 'a particularly sophisticated body of abuses and corruption in local government and justice' (Harvey 1991, 36). By cataloguing their crimes Harvey makes a powerful case for the rebellion that was to follow: James Fiennes, titled as Lord Say, in 1446 'became steward of all the Duke of Warwick's Sussex and Kentish lands … a justice on every commission of the peace in Kent between 1436 and 1447, Henry VI's chamberlain, constable of Dover Castle and warden of the county's Cinque (Five) Ports. In 1449 he also became Lord

Treasurer'. In 1447 'he and Stephen Slegge, sheriff of Kent 1448–9 … expelled a man from his 250 acres' (Harvey 1991, 37). In 1448 he 'threatened a Reginald Peckham with imprisonment, death, drawing and hanging' to make him hand over his property. In 1449 Fiennes and Slegge raised their tenants' rents by 50% per acre. A political poem survives that describes how he was viewed:

> The lorde Say biddeth holde them downe
> That worthy dastarde of renowne
> He techithe a fals loore. (Harvey 1991, 38)

Stephen Slegge also became MP for Dover in 1449, seeing his political influence as a licence for 'extortion, oppression and fraud', working with Fiennes's son-in-law William Crowmer backing local household 'raiding parties taking livestock and goods' (Harvey 1991, 40). It is easy to see why the legend of Robin Hood fighting for justice against the evil sheriff of Nottingham was so popular in the centuries that followed. Even the nobility were not safe, as Slegge 'with a great gang, two hundred strong … looted the granary of Edward Neville, Lord Abergavenny, and assaulted his servants' (Harvey 1991, 39). According to the court records this was not the first time.

Another man on the raid with Slegge was Robert Est. He also was accused of manufacturing faked warrants to seize and ransom some of the tenants of the Archbishop of Canterbury. He was employed as the keeper of Maidstone Jail in 1448 and 'imprisoned a man for a week for ransom' (Harvey 1991, 41). With Est running the jail, Slegge as sheriff, along with Fiennes as constable, injustice ruled: 'the royal courts of law were used as vehicles for exploitation … the county returning officer for the parliamentary elections was the sheriff himself' (Harvey 1991, 42)!

These men were the true gangsters of Kent, whose thieving and violence provoked Jack Cade's 1450 rebellion. The fact that they were also appointed and openly favoured by King Henry VI meant that the whole regime was seen as contrary to justice and should therefore be opposed. St Augustine had famously pronounced, 'What are states without justice but robber bands enlarged?' (Green and Ward 2004, 1). According to Guenée:

Justice remained the dynamic and the purpose of the State. Everyone saw justice in a hundred guises from the streets to the palace. They were all familiar with the Augustinian tag and repeated it more or less accurately. And they were all convinced, like an advocate in the Paris Parlement, that 'no power endures without justice'. (Guenée 1985, 41)

Two popular influences in this period were Thomas Aquinas and the scholar of law, Ulpian. Their maxims regarding justice would be familiar to the more educated sections of the population, but also understood by many others. Aquinas declared 'the first duty of a ruler is to govern his subjects according to the rules of law and justice with a view to the common good of the whole community', whereas Ulpian defined justice simply but effectively as 'the constant and ceaseless will to render each his due' (Guenée 1985, 41). Both the royal-licenced robbery of the 1381 Poll Tax, and the legally sanctioned crimes of the local ruling class in the 1440s described above, were clearly criminal and immoral acts in the eyes of the bulk of the population on whom they were inflicted. It is possible to appreciate more fully the process of protest and resistance that ensued using the concept of the 'moral economy' as pioneered by E. P. Thompson.

The moral economy was employed to discuss the mechanisms of food riots, but it is not about there being no food, rather a sense of injustice about the market and its operations, namely engrossing and price setting based on monopolistic control. Thompson was unpicking the idea of riot, not in terms of the actions of a mindless mob, but in terms of motives, negotiation, outrage and intervention to ensure 'fair play' (Thompson 1991). According to Patel and McMichael, Thompson 'used the term moral economy to point to the cluster of political and pre-political ideas circulating within society that governed the natural and desirable means of the distribution of common wealth … the word riot is too small to encompass all this' (Patel and McMichael 2014, 240). Maybe this was the sense in which Thompson saw the law and its enactment closely bound up with the English people and their causes, that is, as popular struggles.

As far as constables saw their cause as serving the community and felt a sense of solidarity with their neighbours then the law could be seen as a potential ally against royal tyranny. But at this time the king's soldiers were feeling betrayed rather than empowered as their colonies in France were overrun. When the capital of the English Kingdom of France, Rouen, fell in October 1449 the government desperately contracted an army to ship across the channel and stop the French advance. One reason they had not acted sooner was the national debt. The previous month the Bishop of Carlisle, one Marmaduke Lumley, had resigned as Lord Treasurer 'with a balance in the treasury of £480 five shillings and three pence' (Harvey 1991, 61). His replacement 'had to pawn the crown jewels to raise loans for the expedition because "we be not as yet purveyed of money"' (Barker 2009, 392). Another disgraced politician, Adam Moleyns, also Bishop of Chichester, was notorious for leading a large gang of several hundred men in another attack on a Suffolk manor house. In January 1450, he attempted to deliver the back-pay to the troops waiting to embark for France at Portsmouth. But the men rioted, denouncing him as 'the traitor who sold Normandy', and he was murdered by army captain Cuthbert Colville (Barker 2009, 393).

The following month saw a small but historic event: for the first time the red flag was raised in rebellion on English soil. At Bishops Waltham, a village on the road between Portsmouth and Winchester, an ex-soldier marshalled a small group of troops, appointing captains and officers, to threaten war and an uprising against the monarch. They displayed a mock oriflamme, the red battle flag of the French, most recently carried by their knights at Agincourt, where these soldiers or their fathers may well have been part of the English victory. When soldiers revolt, there is much reason for rulers to fear, as those they rely upon to 'keep the peace' are merging with the rebels whom the rulers regard as the public enemy.

A few months later it was the peacekeepers themselves who rose up: the June 1450 assembly of constables in the villages of Kent shared the soldiers' grievances and feared a bloody royal reaction after the death of the Duke of Suffolk. They resolved to march on the king to demand justice, burn down London Bridge and challenge a monarchy already on the brink of civil war. As far as the constables were concerned, they saw their cause as serving the community and felt a sense of solidarity with their neighbours: for them the law could be seen as a potential ally against royal tyranny. Jack Cade's rebellion of 1450 was further dominated by citizens with deadly weapons and extensive experience of armed conflict.

In fact, the king could not rely on the support of his own regiments to quell the rebels: 'on Friday 19 June some of the retainers of the king … began to agree amongst themselves that Cade had a genuine cause; and to threaten that unless the king did execution upon the "traitors" about him they themselves would go over to Cade's side' (Harvey 1991, 85).

Under pressure, Henry VI put Lord Saye in the Tower of London. He planned secretly to let him escape, but the constable of the Tower refused the king's orders and kept him under lock and key. The royal party fled the capital and panicked citizens drew up London Bridge to try and prevent the rebel invasion. While Cade and his main force entered London via the south bank of the river at Southwark, Essex men were joining the rebellion in the east at Mile End—where Richard II had diverted the rising less than 70 years previously. Cade threatened to set fire to London Bridge, thereby winning the freedom of the city for his men—taking the keys to the gate beyond the bridge and cutting the ropes at the southern end so it could not be drawn up again (Harvey 1991, 91). The enemies of the rebels were denounced at the city guildhall, including the prisoner Lord Saye and his son-in-law, the sheriff of Kent, William Crowmer. Both were beheaded and Saye 'publicly degraded by having his naked corpse dragged by a horse through the streets' (Harvey 1991, 93). Following a pitched battle at the Tower of London between London citizens and Cade and his rioters, whose numbers had been strengthened by opening up the Marshalsea Prison in Southwark and enlisting the prisoners to the cause of the rising, negotiations were held in a nearby church between Cade and the Archbishops of York and Canterbury and the Bishop of Winchester. On 7 July a general pardon was offered to Cade and his followers, guaranteeing that all crimes and participants would go unpunished by the king or his officials (Harvey 1991, 97). The rising went beyond London with stories of mobs in Salisbury, Colchester, Romsey, Southampton and the Isle of Wight as well as throughout Kent and Essex.

The victories of these popular revolts are remarkable. Cohn lists over 1000 in Europe between 1200 and 1425, of which at least 700 were successful. Britain can add hundreds more for the same period (Cohn 2006, 155; Cohn 2013). Another reason for the word 'mob' raising moral panic amongst the powerful is the reality of people 'mobilising'; especially when the call-up has not come from their masters but emanates from their own sense of an injustice requiring righting. The 'mob' reduced taxes, curbed noble power and prevented even greater violence and oppression. If it appears that peasants, artisans, tradesmen, labourers and soldiers often went to war with authority, this was because their very existence was continually threatened by the violent actions of the noble class. Moreover they 'brought to power heretofore disenfranchised social classes'. Successful revolts 'were both the cause and the fruit of this shift in the balance of power' (Cohn 2006, 156).

References

Aston, M. (1960). Lollardy and sedition, 1381–1431. *Past and Present, 17*, 1–45.

Barker, J. (2009). *Conquest: The English kingdom of France*. London: Little Brown.

Barker, J. (2014). *England arise: The people, the king and the great revolt of 1381*. London: Little Brown.

Broué, P. (2006). *The German revolution*. Chicago: Haymarket.

Clanchy, M. (1998). *England and its rulers* (2nd ed.). Oxford: Blackwell.

Cohn, S. (2006). *Lust for libery: The poliics of social revolt in medieval Europe 1200–1425*. Cambridge, MA: Harvard.

Cohn, S. (2013). *Popular protest in late medieval English towns*. Cambridge: Cambridge University Press.

Danziger, D., & Gillingham, J. (2003). *1215: The year of Magna Carta*. London: Hodder & Soughton.

Faith, R. (1981). The class struggle in fourteenth-century England. In R. Samuel (Ed.), *People's history and socialist theory*. London: Routledge and Kegan Paul.

Faith, R. (1984). The "great rumour" of 1377 and peasant ideology. In R. Hilton & T. Aston (Eds.), *The English rising of 1381*. Cambridge: Cambridge University Press.

Fernandez, L., & Scholl, C. (2014). The criminalization of global protest: The application of counter-insurgency. In V. Eick & K. Briken (Eds.), *Urban (in) security: Policing the neoliberal crisis* (pp. 275–299). Ottowa: Red Quill.

Green, P., & Ward, T. (2004). *State crime: Governments, violence and corruption*. London: Pluto.

Guenée, B. (1985). *States and rulers in later medieval Europe*. Oxford: Blackwell.

Harding, A. (1984). The revolt against the justices. In R. Hilton & T. Aston (Eds.), *The English rising of 1381*. Cambridge: Cambridge University Press.

Harman, C. (1983) The Lost Revolution Germany 1918-23 London: Bookmarks

Harvey, I. (1991). *Jack Cade's rebellion of 1450*. Oxford: Oxford University Press.

Harvey, D. (2003). *The new imperialism*. New York: Oxford University Press.

Hibbert, C. (1974). *The rise and fall of the house of Medici*. London: Penguin.

Hilton, R. (1973). *Bond men made free*. London: Temple Smith.

Hobsbawm, E. (1959). Primitive rebels. Manchester: Manchester University Press.

Holt, J. C. (1981). *Robin Hood*. London: Thames and Hudson.

Hoyle R.W. (2001) The pilgramage of grace and the polittihces o1f5 30s. Oxford: Oxford University Press

Linebaugh, P. (2008). *The Magna Carta manifesto*. Berkeley: University of California.

Machiavelli, N. (1960) [1515]. *History of Florence and of the affairs of Italy*. New York: Harper.

McFarlane, K. (1952). *John Wycliffe and the beginnings of nonconformity*. London: English Universities Press.

McKelvie, G. (2015). *Bastard Feudalism: A new perspective*. Paper to the University of Winchester Medieval Research Conference, 30 Apr 2015.

Oman, C. (1989). *The Great Revolt of 1381*. London: Green Hill.

Patel, R., & McMichael, P. (2014). A political economy of the food riot. In D. Pritchard & F. Pakes (Eds.), *Riot, unrest and protest on the global stage*. Basingstoke: Palgrave Macmillan.

Thompson, E. P. (1991). 'The moral economy of the English crowd in the eighteenth century' and 'The moral economy reviewed'. In E. P. Thompson (Ed.), *Customs in common*. London: Penguin.

Vale, M. (1988). The civilization of courts and cities in the north 1200–1500. In G. Holmes (Ed.), *The Oxford illustrated history of medieval Europe*. Oxford: Oxford University.

4

Artisans and Citizens: Riots from 1500–1700

Roger Manning argues that 'no clear and unqualified definition of "property" can be found in any legal dictionary before the eighteenth century' (Manning 1988, 5), which means that in previous centuries many aspects of life were 'held in common', that is in villages operating the common-field system: 'the time of ploughing, sowing, and harvesting … would be subject to community decisions and husbandry by-laws made in the manorial court or village assembly' (Manning 1988, 18). People made their laws together, locally, acting in their collective interest. They also had what were known as use-rights over wasteland and the right to gather fuel for their fires and material to make their houses and barns. These traditions applied in towns as well as the countryside. Many events labelled as riots came about as a result of the systematic attack on these communal rights by property owners. Often, these attacks were seen as unlawful in the eyes of those working and living on the land. The three charges levelled at the lords of the land were that they were encroaching, engrossing and enclosing either land held by tenants in common or wasteland used by commoners.

Even today, around one and a half million acres of common land survive in England and Wales for the use of all. Attempts to enclose it for commercial purposes are still resisted, for example when Newcastle

© The Editor(s) (if applicable) and The Author(s) 2016
M. Clement, *A People's History of Riots, Protest and the Law*,
DOI 10.1057/978-1-137-52751-6_4

United Football Club proposed building a new stadium on the Town Moor in 1997 and fans threatened to camp out on the moor to prevent it. Past protests over enclosure have been more powerful and emphatic: the sixteenth-century chronicler Edward Hall related how Londoners reclaimed the commons in Islington, Shoreditch and Hoxton in 1513 after land had been enclosed by hedges and apprentices and citizens had been told to stay off the common:

> This saying sorely aggravated the Londoners, and suddenly a great number of the city assembled themselves in a morning, and a turner (barrel maker) in a fool's coat came crying through the city, 'shovels and spades!' and so many people followed that it was a wonder and within a short space all the hedges about the towns were cast down, and the ditches filled, and every-thing made plain the workmen were so diligent. ('Hall's Chronicle' in Manning 1988, spelling modernised)

Five hundred years later, much of London's common land is gone. Nowadays it is buildings and land used for public purposes such as social housing, school playing fields and hospitals that are being engrossed by the powerful. Working-class Londoners face being made outcasts in their own city. The dynamic is the same as that described in the Chicago School study 'Black Metropolis', where 'the city's outcasts of every type have no choice but to huddle together where nobody else wants to live' (Cayton and Clair 1946, 206):

> The conflict over living space is an ever-present source of potential vio-lence. It involves not only a struggle for houses, but also competition for school and recreational facilities … Race prejudice becomes aggravated by class antagonisms, and class feeling is often expressed in racial terms. (Cayton and Clair 1946, 114)

In another case of then and now, John Stow in his Elizabethen *Survey of London* yearned for a better past when the excesses of the rich were less evident:

> We now see the thing in worse case than ever, by means of enclosure for Gardens, wherein are builded many fair summer houses, and as in other places of the suburbs, some of them [are] like Midsummer Pageants, with towers,

turrets and chimney tops, not so much for use or profit, as for show and plea-sure, betraying the vanity of men's minds, unlike the disposition of the ancient citizens, who delighted in the building of Hospitals, and Alms houses for the poor, and therein both employed their wits and spent their wealth in prefer-ment of the common commodities of this our City. (Manning 1988, 23)

The excesses of capital in the twenty-first century are at their sharpest in contemporary London where the oligarchs burrow under their streets to create underground carparks and networks of service tunnels to keep them apart from the rest of the city. This was a part of the context of the 2011 London riots, where inner city residents are all too aware of the endless pressure of precarious employment and housing conditions on their sense of wellbeing. The paranoia of the rich in this context may be well-founded and invites another historical comparison. In January 1582, Elizabeth I was riding through Islington when she found her carriage surrounded by hundreds of beggars. Immediately she ordered William Fleetwood, the recorder of London, to organise a sweep of masterless men. In 1589, sev-eral soldiers were pulled from a crowd of 500 menacing the royal palace in Westminster—and hanged (Manning 1988, 169, 181). During the 2010 student riots against the new £9000 tuition fees, Prince Charles and the Duchess of Cornwall found their Rolls Royce surrounded by protestors (*Daily Telegraph* 2010); and London Mayor Boris Johnson has since been promising water cannon will be trained at future protestors.

Enclosures, ancient and modern, are about the dispossession of the common people. It is a crime, hence the title of Peter Linebaugh's collec-tion *Stop, Thief! The Commons, Enclosures and Resistance*, which opens by quoting the anonymous poem:

The law locks up the man or woman
Who steals the goose from off the common
But lets the greater villain loose
Who steals the common from the goose. (2014, 1)

However, the current 'law of the land' is a more definite statement emphasising the exclusive rights of the property owner:

the theory of the common law is that all land is held of the king who is the supreme feudal lord … a holder of land is entitled to a number of legal rights in respect of his landholding, and these rights are crystallised into one thing. This is the tenant's 'estate' … such estates are 'real property' or 'realty'. (Burn 2004, 3–4)

In the great grain riot, or Grande Rebeine, of Lyon in France in 1529, the crowd met on the grounds where municipal assemblies were ordinarily held under the slogan 'The commune is rising against the hoarders of grain', where they decided that if the justices of the peace failed to do their legal duty in guaranteeing the food supply, then they would carry out the provisions of the assize for them. The assembled people then went about opening the municipal granary and seizing grain from the wealthy with ample supplies, actions which the city council had undertaken in the past, but had failed to do promptly during the current crisis. In the grain riot of Provins in 1573, the artisans seized grain that had been sold at a high price to non-residents of the city because the civic authorities had failed to provision the town at an honest price (Davis 1973, 61). Clearly these are the actions of people taking their affairs into their own hands. Despite the fact that the powerful will always view these as a challenge to their authority and implicitly therefore as subversive, that is undermining the social order, we should not automatically understand actions labelled as riots as necessarily unlawful.

Once an individual tenant or property owner has gained control by vanquishing the old common rights through enclosure, all the rights were with the new and exclusive possessor—'the appearance of the enclosing hedge in the landscape served notice that henceforth the commodity of one individual was to be preferred' (Manning 1988, 25). Resistance was not to be tolerated, in the opinion of Justice of the Peace Michael Dalton writing in 1622 in 'The Country Justice':

> When an actual hedge was broken, the law assumed that force was required, and the act was said to be done 'vis et armis'—with force of arms. If three or more people, having made menacing gestures or speeches, destroyed an enclosure, the trespass was considered a riot. (Manning 1988, 27)

The reign of Henry VIII from 1509 has been called 'the age of plunder', citing the famous quote from Sir Thomas More's *Utopia*: 'so God help me, I can perceive nothing but a certain conspiracy of rich men procuring their own commodities under the name and title of a commonwealth' (Hoskins 1976, 1). It produced the greatest change in the pattern of land ownership since the Norman Conquest of 1066. The religious reformation was thus accompanied by an economic reformation which saw the already rich aristocracy joined by a new class of wealthy tradesmen determined to exploit the land more efficiently than the previous great landowner, the church. As ever, it was a question of the rich getting richer and the poor becoming poorer still. The 1522 valuation of wealth stated that in London 80% of the population owned just 6% of the wealth, whilst the top 5% owned 80%. Even more obscenely the top 0.5% owned 32% of the capital's wealth. This scale of inequality has seldom been matched in British history, but it may be returning today judging from the findings of Piketty's recent 'Capital in the 21st Century'. Of course these figures reflect only those actually assessed: 'unfortunately one of the wealthiest Londoners was not assessed in 1522 as he was then resident in Spain' (Hoskins 1976, 38, 39). Just like today's 'non-doms' and tax exiles, the wealthiest of all appear to have evaded any fiscal responsibility.

As we have seen, this process had begun much earlier as the new rich tried to turn the screw on the poorer classes, sometimes allied with monarch or the church. The poorer mass of society had gained more traction over their masters following the Black Death of the mid-1300s as shortage of labour strengthened their bargaining position. They had thus negotiated working conditions that were far freer from their masters' control than the old arrangements of serfdom. Now in Henry VIII's reign they were determined to resist the threat to their means to making a living and their relative autonomy over their communities represented by the common field system, for example 'the time of ploughing, sowing, and harvesting … would be subject to community decisions and husbandry by-laws made in a manorial court or village assembly' (Manning 1988, 18). Gentlemen and merchants, many from outside the locality, meant to extend their commercial control, converting tenure into leases. The poorer peasants and artisans sought to assert themselves collectively against these enclosures and land-grabs.

Thus, the so-called Pilgrimage of Grace rebellion in 1536 was not about simple country folk clinging to their old allegiance to the church and its monasteries, but rather an occasion for the poor landless labourers to defend their interests against the rising class of gentry who stood to claim all the church lands for themselves:

> The 1536 movements were, in the first days, activist movements in which the local bonds of deference were severed or, perhaps it is truer to say, inverted: the activists expected the gentry to do their bidding. When he was captured, Sir Stephen Hamerton was told that where he had ruled his captors, now they would rule him. (Hoyle 2001, 19–20)

One of the reasons for this attitude was that the vast scale of the land-grabbing by the rich forced smallholding peasants off 'their' land:

> Since few among the surplus population could find tenancies, numbers of landless wage-earners swelled. These artisans and labourers—rather than smallholders—constituted the bulk of the crowd during the riots and rebellions. (Manning 1988, 33)

As Hoskins states, 'not much land was available … except the commons and wastes which were vital to the agrarian economy of the peasant husbandry [process of farming] itself … It is not true that England consisted of islands of cultivation in a sea of waste, but rather the reverse: precious islands of commons in a sea of cultivation, certainly in the lowland commons' (Hoskins 1976, 64).

On 2 October 1536, the labourers of the Lincolnshire town of Louth were expecting the arrival of the bishop's official, Dr Frankish, who they suspected would confiscate the silver plate and goods of their church, a place they held dear, as in those days 'all the colour of life lay in the church not in the home' (Hoskins 1976, 2):

> To prevent their seizure, a group of men barricaded themselves in the church overnight. There were no such plans … Frankish narrowly escaped being beaten up by his own clerical colleagues and saw his books and papers publicly burnt … [A] group of Louth townspeople travelled to Caistor on the following morning. Their aim was to seek confirmation from the gentry present there that their church goods were not threatened, but the subsidy commissioners, seeing their approach, scattered, and what

might have been a meeting where they defused the rebellion became a
fiasco as the commons rode after and captured some of their number.
(Hoyle 2001, 6–7)

Rumour of the uprising spread and a 'copycat rising' at the neighbouring town of Horncastle led to gentry being captured and the bishop's
chancellor, Dr Rayne, was lynched by his own priests. Perhaps as many
as 10,000 commoners marched on Lincoln and sent demands to the king
(Wall 2000, 171). They dispersed a week later, so Henry disbanded the
army he had been gathering to repress the revolt, only to learn that the
Lincolnshire rising had spread into the neighbouring county of Yorkshire.

> In October 1536 they set about capturing the gentry of the district and
> then, after a meeting in Richmond when letters calling for a general rising
> were circulated in the name of Captain Poverty, the movement sent out
> three raiding parties to spread the word and capture additional gentry. One
> penetrated through the Dales to Skipton; another went into County
> Durham, where they held musters and sacked the bishop of Durham's pal-
> ace at Bishop Auckland; and a third travelled into Ryedale towards
> Scarborough … The Richmondshire men appear to have advocated social
> revolution: their risings had a radical anti-landowning edge not generally
> found elsewhere. (Hoyle 2001, 8)

The rebels' methods of gathering the people together emphasised the
supposed legality of doing so. As with Jack Cade's rebellion in 1450 in
Kent, discussed above, local constables and village figures of authority
organised the assemblies in the villages using the traditional methods for
call-up to military service (Wall 2000, 171). The letters sent by 'Captain
Poverty' led to men mustering across Cumberland and Northumberland,
Westmoreland and into Lancashire: 'the magnitude of the Crown's problem was that by the last weekend of October it had lost control of virtually the whole of the North from the rivers Don in Yorkshire and Ribble
in Lancashire to the borders of Scotland' (Hoyle 2001, 9).

It is interesting to examine the way in which the commons were
organised. When being assembled they would divide into 'wapentakes', a
northern variation on the Anglo Saxon word 'hundred' which, according
to the *Oxford English Dictionary*, means *vápnatak* in Old Norse, from

vápn 'weapon' + *taka* 'take', perhaps with reference to voting in an assembly by a show of weapons. The record of Thomas Moigne, one of the gentry, describes how they tried to use their higher social position as justices of the peace to push the commoners into backing down from their rebellion. It shows they were not easily fooled:

> When the common bell was rung and the commons reassembled in large numbers, the gentlemen sought to muster them in the fields outside Louth, 'to the intent that every gentleman might resort to his wapentake and so to do the most good amongst his own neighbours in [the] staying of them … every one of us went to our own wapentakes and persuaded them that they should not go forward but to depart home unto their own houses to such time as they had answer from the king's highness, but that they would not do in no means, but cried to go forward out of hand or else they would destroy and slay us and choose other captains. And then when we did see them in such obstinate and wilful opinions, we determined ourselves for to follow their minds and to stay them when we came to Lincoln by such policies as we could in our minds invent, to the intent to weary them and make them spend their money and so by such policy compel them to go home again'. (Hoyle 2001, 148)

One group—the commons—was led to rise in opposition to the Crown, pulling along with it those higher social groups whose instinct was to comply with and perhaps implement unpopular government policies. This is an activists' or commons' rising. In this model the rising can properly be called popular, but it is also sectional within that society: 'of the 100 Lincolnshire men indicted, tried, and executed, then the preponderance of poorer urban trades is striking' (Hoyle 2001, 136) (see Table 4.1).

Artisans launched the action and the clergy 'were ready recruits to the project':

> The priests were sworn to ring their common bells … 'and assembled the commons of that parish, moving them to take the common's part for they did enter a commonwealth … and further said that if they did not assent, they should be hanged and burnt at their own doors and their houses burnt and destroyed'. (Hoyle 2001, 138–139)

Table 4.1 Occupations of men indicted for rebellion at Lincoln, 6 March 1537

	Louth	Horncastle	All other places	Total
Urban trades				
Butcher	3		1	4
Carpenter			2	2
Cooper	1			1
Labourer	4	4	10	18
Mercer			3	3
Miller			2	2
Plumber	2			2
Potter			1	1
Sawyer	2			2
Shoemaker	5	4	3	12
Smith	1			1
Tailor	1		1	2
Thatcher	1	1		2
Tinker			1	1
Weaver	1	1	3	5
Clergy				
Seculars	3		4	7
Regulars			14	14
Rural status groups				
Fishermen			2	2
Yeoman	1		9	10
Husbandmen			7	7
Gentleman			2	2
Total	25	10	65	100

Source: PRO, KB9/539 mm. 1–6; (Hoyle 2001, 136–137).

Once the commoners were on the move, it was their intention to compel their social superiors, known at the time as the gentry, to go along with their movement. Once again, Hoyle describes how they did this:

> The form of address used is to 'you, the king's true subjects and their faithful friends'. The recipients were 'to prepare yourselves forward' to meet the senders at Ancaster Heath on Sunday afternoon and 'raise the country, swearing every man as well gentleman as other, to be true unto God, to the king and the commonwealth'. It was, then, not addressed to the justices, head constables, or constables but to the commons. The result was a rising without noble or gentle leadership which compelled the gentry to be its

captains ... The threat had been made by the commons that the goods of any gentry who had fled or refused to be sworn would be seized for the maintenance of the army. (Hoyle 2001, 140–141)

The gentry (i.e. the rising class of property owners) did not want to do this, but were intimidated: 'the failure to comply with their demands was to invite the commons to seize and destroy property and perhaps person' (Hoyle 2001, 142):

> The gentry, on their own account, sought to control the movement to delay the common's offensive whilst using the petitions as an excuse for procrastination ... In January the activists in some quarters, convinced that they had been sold out by their notional leaders, attempted to reconstruct the alliances of October. (Hoyle 2001, 153 17)

What were the commoners demands?

> The first demand was that the church was to have all its traditional privileges restored, meaning that the status quo of 1529 was to be revived. Secondly, all suppressed religious houses were to be restored except for those which the king had suppressed for his own power. Thirdly, a roll-call of royal servants and bishops, starting with Cranmer and including the trio of Cromwell, Wriothesley (Master of the Rolls), and Rich (Chancellor of Augmentations), were either to be delivered to the rebels or banished. And finally, the king was not to demand further taxes of his subjects except in time of war. (Hoyle 2001, 155)

By the time the gentry had reformulated the commons demands into their petition, it was severely watered down:

> The articles sent to Henry had ceased to be a series of demands but were transformed into a set of grievances which the rebels drew to the king's attention, and to which was annexed a request for a pardon. Hence, the demand circulating in Holland that the king should demand no more taxes except in time of war was transformed into a request that the subsidy should be rescinded, and finally became an observation about the impossibility of paying the fifteenth due to be collected a year hence. The demand that the

liberties of the church should be re-established became first a request that suppressed religious houses should be re-established, and then an observation that because of the dissolution, the service of God was less well performed and hospitality had decayed. The king was not asked to reverse the dissolution. The demand that the king send to the rebels Cromwell and others to be lynched was replaced by some gentle chiding about the king surrounding himself by counsellors of low birth and reputation who were suspected to be corrupt. The petition only sought the repeal of the Statute of Uses. Every other clause was explanatory. It had ceased to be a platform from which the rebels could negotiate. (Hoyle 2001, 156–157)

The Pilgrimage of Grace was a full-scale rebellion, even though it began as a local protest. But the 1500s were littered with riots which were mostly very local and on a much smaller scale. Manning has looked at 75 riots that occurred after 1530 and notes that 'in 32 instances the number of persons participating was 30 or fewer … larger-scale enclosure riots were the work of peers, gentry and townsmen' (Manning 1988, 46). In these larger cases this was the gentry using violence against their rivals—poaching their game and harassing them in the courts. Manning notes: 'Apparently, it did not occur to the early-Tudor aristocracy that they might be setting a bad example for their social inferiors' (Manning 1988, 39). The use of violence to secure their interests was also employed by the church against rebellion when it suited. In Derbyshire, 'when the Over Haddon tenants levelled the abbot's hedges and poached fish from his millpond, his servants fired volleys of arrows at them'. Rioters 'retaliated by drowning a number of the abbot's cattle' (Manning 1988, 46).

As European society grew more complex and the pace of social change accelerated, the threat of the crowd was becoming ever more apparent to those in power. Roger Manning reports that in England by later in the sixteenth century, 'it would have been considered imprudent to muster companies of the county militia without the presence of a provost-marshal appointed by the lord Lieutenant' (Manning 1988, 179). This new group of state officials were to be the 'iron fist' of authority that would discourage those people mobilised from taking affairs into their own hands once they assembled and aired their grievances. The emergence of this group indicated that the rulers of the state were recognising the need to employ extra people to maintain their monopoly of the use of force, thereby undermining resistance from the countervailing power of the people. The leader of the 1917 Russian Revolution, Lenin, described the state simply as 'special bodies of armed men', and these were the bodies that the modernising English state was recruiting in order to maintain their control. The authority of the Elizabethan provost marshals—'Martial law'—was a military form of social control that was meant to override that 'common law' which was so often being interpreted by the common people as serving their interests:

> Popular rumour had depicted provost martials such as Sir Ralph Ellerker, Sir Anthony Kingston and Sir George Bowes as travelling about the countryside with wagon-loads of halters for dealing out summary justice to rebels. (Manning 1988, 179)

It was supposed to be only an emergency measure, to be used when the state was threatened by rebellion, but this relied upon the rulers of the state deciding whether there was such a threat, and they could be trusted only to act in their own interests. The British state has a long history of first trying out the most brutal forms of violent suppression of human rights in its colonies, rather than at home, but then importing them where necessary; and Martial law was first declared in 1556 in Ireland to suppress vagrants and the poor generally, rather than rebels. In the 1580s the marshals hanged several soldiers pulled out of a crowd gathered outside the royal palace at Westminster, vagrants were frequently jailed or beaten and in 1596 they impressed 1000 men for military service. Here there was a direct clash with the 'common law', represented by the local forces selected by communities to keep the peace, as 'constables were fined and imprisoned for disobeying or abusing the marshals or allowing prisoners to escape' (Manning 1988, 181,184).

Clearly, the ruling institution in society is the state. Marx's collaborator Engels recognised and defined it as 'the establishment of a public power which no longer directly coincides with the population organizing itself as an armed force' in *The Origins of the Family, Private Property and the State*:

> This special, public power is necessary because a self-acting armed organization of the population has become impossible since the split into

classes … This public power exists in every state; it consists not merely of armed men but also of material adjuncts, prisons, and institutions of coercion of all kinds, of which gentile [clan] society knew nothing. (Engels 1884)

The process of state formation had been going on ever since 'the split into classes' many millennia ago. In the medieval world of thirteenth to fifteenth-century Europe, the classes below the ruling nobility were often 'a self-acting armed organisation' capable of advancing their interests as they did in England in 1381 and 1450, and in France and Italy very frequently. As a result states built up their institutional capacity to maintain order by advancing their power and control over those below them. Sam Cohn describes how 'the growing imbalance in power between rulers and the ruled can be seen more graphically from the perspective of the prince':

> Changes in the repressive forces at his disposal, and changes in his attitudes and willingness to oppress, torture and destroy his own subjects … Instead of capital punishment issued to a select number of popular ringleaders, monarchs by the mid 15th century engage in massacres of the innocents, sacks of cities, with the rape, pillage and murder of thousands of women and children. (Cohn 2015, 432)

He compares the, probably exaggerated, figure of 6000 peasants killed after the 1358 Paris Jacquerie with the 50,000 slaughtered at Frankenhausen in Germany in the key battle of the Peasant War in Germany in the 1520s 'with nearly twice that number of peasants facing death during the two-year rebellion' (Cohn 2015, 433). This was not just because the state had a more powerful machinery of repression—it also reflects changes in the class structure. Up until the mid-1400s in Europe, the lesser gentry and merchant classes had been allied with craftsmen and richer villagers against the noble few. Now a modernising society sought to incorporate many of the former in the ruling order, thus weakening the coalition of resistance to authority. The sixteenth-century Elizabethen Poor Law and Book of Orders redefined the origin of popular disturbances and riots as the problem of 'masterless men' and began to devise policies that combined the use of force for repression with welfare measures:

> A determination to protect property rights but also positive remedies such as the regulation of food supplies, and prices, housing for impotent paupers and other forms of poor relief ... The livery companies laid on stocks of grain and coal, sent the aged and the sick to St Barts and St Thomas's, the insane to Bedlam, the beggars and orphans to Christ's Hospital and Bridewell Hospital for correction of unruly apprentices and sturdy beggars. (Manning 1988, 200)

Of course, this was all occurring after the religious reformation of the 1520s. Although Protestantism was, literally, a protest movement against the power and corruption of the organised church, Protestant rulers such as the princes in Germany had used brutal violence against revolting peasants led by Thomas Müntzer, with a more radical vision of how religion and society should be reformed, and indeed who the real criminals within society were:

> Behold, the basic source of usury, theft and robbery is our lords and princes, who take all the creatures for their private property ... And then they let God's commandment go forth among the poor and they say, 'God had commanded Thou shalt not steal'. But this commandment does not apply to them since they oppress all men—the poor peasant, the artisan, and all who live are flayed and sheared ... But as soon as anyone steals the smallest thing, he must hang ... The lords themselves are responsible for making the poor people their enemy. They do not want to remove the cause of insurrection so how, in the long run, can things improve? (Müntzer 2010, 78–79)

In England, Henry VIII massively consolidated the state and his level of control over church and people, and by the time of Elizabeth I there was a growing opposition to aspects of her rule out of which developed a movement looking for a more reformed religion that suited the needs of both the rising commercial classes and the tenants and artisans who feared for their futures as their old patterns of living changed and much common land was enclosed. This movement—Puritanism—wanted a church that maintained its break with the authoritarian 'High Church' style that naturally sought to put a distance between believers and their priests, who threatened to replicate the ornate ceremony and worship of images associated with Catholicism. As Elizabeth's successors, the Stuarts, showed more sympathy with Catholicism and developed ideas of the divine right of kings, a clash loomed between the English people and their parliament and their monarch who was increasingly determined to rule without their input (Gregg 1981). Religious and social movements mushroomed to defend Parliament and some control over their lives, turning the world upside down in the process (Hill 1973).

Iconoclasm is the breaking of images deemed unholy and disrespectful and it was central to the seventeenth-century English Revolution. The twenty-first-century 'Occupy' movement shared some of these characteristics in its symbolic demonstrations in New York and London, seeking to demystify the power of commodities and challenge the common sense of the rule of oligarchic capitalism (Chomsky 2012). The statue of the Bull of Wall Street, New York, and London's Bank of England were the locations chosen for protest. The injunction to 'occupy'—to claim the space for the people and their values rather than allowing their owners to control their use—is an assertion of democracy whose roots go back to the agora in Athens and the Roman Forum.

The state was doubtless the most violent body. Hoskins estimates that Henry VIII had 72,000 hanged during his reign (1976, 2). In fact, given the scale of repression, Hoskins asks 'why there was no massive uprising of the poor against the rich … There were it is true, small disturbances in 1549 and 1553, but no general movement in the Midlands until the famous rising of 1607' (Hoskins 1976, 50, 72).

These rioters had no choice but to resist the enclosure of their common lands. Marx described them in *Capital* as the beginnings of the proletariat, or working class, that was to supplant the peasants; 'suddenly dragged from their wonted mode of life, could not as suddenly adapt themselves to the discipline of their new condition. They were turned *en masse* into beggars, robbers, vagabonds, partly from inclination, in most cases from stress of circumstances' (Melossi 2015, 6).

Shakespeare's *Coriolanus* was written between 1607 and 1608, and 'is designed to remind his audience of the Midlands peasant uprising' (Siegel 1992, 145). One of its key ideas is the relation of the ruler to his or her people—'a public that Shakespeare brilliantly labels "worshipful mutineers" (I.i.249). Within the moral landscape of the play, what the People receives by virtue of its membership in a republic is not so much a special capacity to be heard and make decisions, but a special opportunity to supervise, inspect, and otherwise survey its leadership' (Green 2009, 134). In other words, the popular belief was that rulers should rule, but must listen to the people who will assemble to judge them. Coriolanus's mother sends him to face the amassed People with the words 'Go, and be rul'd' (III.ii.90), implying that in some senses the people have a right to rule their leaders. Perhaps this is what the Warwickshire peasants meant when they proclaimed themselves the king's 'most true hearted community', that is they would respect his rule if he respected their customs and community rites (Manning 1988, 230). The play opens with a senator berating a citizen: 'you slander/The helms of the state, who care for you like fathers, when you curse them as enemies'. The citizen's reply is a forthright defence of the peoples' right to revolt:

> Care for us? True indeed! They ne'er cared for us yet. Suffer us to famish, and their store houses crammed with grain; Make edicts for usury, to support usurers: repeal daily any wholesome act established against the rich, and provide more piercing statutes daily to chain up and restrain the poor. If the wars eat us not up, they will; and there's all the love they bear us. (Act 1 Scene 1) (Wiseman 2009, 25)

The centre of the Midlands revolt was Northamptonshire and involved areas of the neighbouring counties of Warwickshire and Leicestershire, 'once the heartland of the classic common-field system of agriculture and one of the great corn-growing regions of the Midlands' (Manning 1988, 241). The Warwickshire protestors had begun a few days earlier with between 1000 and 3000 gathering to dig up the enclosures. They produced a 'Digger Manifesto' claiming they would 'manfully die' rather than 'be pined to death for want of that which these devouring encroachers do serve their fat hogs and sheep with'. They 'do feel the smart of these encroaching Titans which would grind our flesh upon the whetstone of poverty' (Manning 1988, 232, 230). In Leicestershire 5000 assembled and began levelling hedges—a Royal Proclamation denounced them as 'levellers'—a name they had begun to use themselves. The Warwickshire magistrates were intimidated by the size of the crowd and pleaded with them to return home. This angered the state authorities like Gilbert, Earl of Shrewsbury, who thought it 'very strange to expostulate with such insolent, base and rebellious people'. The magistrates should have 'used force … and set upon them and used them as rebels and traitors' (Manning 1988, 131). This was an approach they would take a few days later in Northamptonshire.

The revolt there sprang up after many decades of land-grabbing and exploitation by the notorious Tresham family, headed by Sir Thomas Tresham of Rushton. In the 1570s he had increased his tenants rents by 500 %. In the next two decades he continued engrossing and enclosing over 1000 acres of tenants' holdings and depopulated 11 farms. One of the protestors' targets was his cousin, also called Thomas Tresham, who had converted 150 acres of land held in common into pasture for dairy yet engrossed a mere four farms (Manning 1988, 240, 238). They arrived at his estate armed with stones and bows and arrows, determined to cast down his enclosures. The authorities fought back brutally. A band of armed men confronted the protestors the next day, 8 June 1607. The Earl of Shrewsbury narrated the result, claiming they:

> first read the proclamation twice unto them, using all the best persuasions to them to desist that they could devise; but when nothing would prevail, they charged them thoroughly both with their horse and foot … The first charge they stood, and fought desperately; but at the second charge they ran away, in which there were slain some 40 or 50 of them, and a very great number hurt. (Manning 1988, 232)

Determined to set an example, so that others would be discouraged from revolt, many were taken prisoner, publically hanged and their quarters displayed in county towns. Once again the violence of the masters, both in their ruthless exploitation, some would say robbery, of common property and livings from their tenants, and their savage repression of the ensuing revolt, was most notable. No wonder the English common people remembered the names of their resistance movements and the Levellers and the Diggers were revived in the revolt of the 1640s, which led on to civil war and revolution. The long-term trend of social movements from below contesting for power was also remarked by monarchs. When Charles I answered Parliament's 19 propositions in 1642 he warned of the danger that:

> At last the common people … [will] set up for themselves, call parity and independence liberty … destroy all rights and properties, all distinctions of families and merit, and by this means a splendid and excellently distinguished form of government end in a dark, equal chaos of confusion … in a Jack Cade or a Wat Tyler. (Hill 1978, 51)

This was more than an English phenomenon. In his analysis of social change across Europe, Kamen argues 'the accumulated problems of governments and the grievances of their subjects exploded in a continent-wide outburst of revolution' (Kamen 1971, 330).

Barbara Ehrenreich's *Dancing in the Streets: A History of Collective Joy* explains the way people gathering together in groups, celebrating, dancing, singing and feasting, had been central to religion in ancient times. Taking the example of Christianity, she demonstrates how it was rooted in these actions, which provided meaning to peoples' experience: it justified their participation and belief, and anticipated a better world to come. As the church hierarchy developed in the twelfth and thirteenth centuries the priests sought to control behaviour in church and banish dancing, singing and feasting. They would be the sole preachers, singing would be usurped by the choirs and 'the communal meal shrivelled into a morsel that could only tantalize the hungry' (Ehrenreich 2008, 76). The method by which they could transform what happened in church was to deflect these activities onto the streets: 'the dancing, drinking and other forms of play … became the festivities that filled up the late medieval and early modern church calendar … the Church, no doubt inadvertently, invented carnival' (Ehrenreich 2008, 78). Carnivals were very significant events. Every country had dozens of holy days where work was banned and the people celebrated together. In fifteenth-century France one day out of every four was an official holiday. No longer under the control of the church, the people made their own entertainment. Goethe wrote, 'it is a festival not given to the people, but one the people give themselves' (Ehrenreich 2008, 95). In the seventeenth century, throughout Europe, cities were expanding as the migrating poor flooded in. The sheer scale of their presence meant that festivals organised by the church now led to so many assembling on the streets that they feared losing control: 'during the Shrove Tuesday celebration in 1529, gangs of armed men overran the city of Basle'. No wonder the authorities started to see these celebrations as 'vulgar and, more important, dangerous' (Ehrenreich 2008, 104, 102):

> Imagine … if the London of 1600, with its approximately 250,000 disparate and often desperate residents, declared a several-day-long, citywide carnival, in which pickpockets and wealthy merchants were to revel together in the streets. (Ehrenreich 2008, 104)

Just as people made their own entertainment, with carnivals that inverted traditional hierarchies, with low-status people playing king and queen, and the powerful encouraged to act as servants in a theatrical role-reversal, so the authorised translation of the Bible into English in 1611 (the King James version) helped people to criticise the actually existing religious institutions by comparing their behaviour and values with those upheld in the Bible. This, of course, justified rebellion against many types of religious and political authority by giving it divine authority. No wonder then that Christopher Hill calls his chronicle of radical movements and ideas *The World Turned Upside Down*, because that idea of literally overturning society so that the low govern the high is both a definition of revolution and also a description of the climate of the early seventeenth century.

The effect of the English Revolution of the 1640s was so powerful, so profound in terms of changing people's sense of what was right and indeed what was possible, that even after the monarchy was restored in 1660 a profound sense of unease remained. Ruling by resort to force was James II's maxim: 'I will make no concession' was a catch phrase of his, followed by 'my father made concessions and he was beheaded' (Macaulay 1889, 358). Macaulay's conclusion was the wise maxim which could be applied to any number of riots and acts of protest: 'if he attempted to subdue the Protestant feeling of England by rude means, it was easy to see that the violent compression of so powerful and elastic a spring would be followed by as violent a recoil' (Macaulay 1889, 350). In May 1686:

> At Bristol the rabble, countenanced, it was said, by the magistrates, exhibited a profane and indecent pageant, in which the Virgin Mary was represented by a buffoon, and in which a mock host [i.e. representation of the Holy Spirit] was carried in procession. Soldiers were called out to disperse the mob. The mob, then and ever since one of the fiercest in the kingdom, resisted. Blows were exchanged and serious hurts inflicted. (Macaulay 1889, 377)

The magistrates who connived at this 'riot' were the class of gentry—the rising 'middling sort' whose interests were not being served by the king and would tolerate it no longer. By the 1680s there was a feeling that the court was corrupted, poverty had deepened and the people may rise up again in rebellion. The brutal suppression of the 1685 Western Rising or 'Monmouth's Rebellion' in Somerset saw hundreds of peasant farmers and artisans—named 'club men' after their primitive weapons—massacred by troops. The respectable fears of revolt in the capital were palpable:

> All those evil passions which it is the office of government to restrain ... were on a sudden emancipated from control: avarice, licentiousness, revenge ... the human vermin, which, neglected by ministers of state and ministers of religion, barbarous in the midst of civilisation, heathen in the midst of Christianity, burrows, among all physical and all moral pollution, in the cellars and garrets of great cities, will at once rise into a terrible importance. So it was now in London. (Macaulay 1889, 601)

Macaulay's vision is of 'thousands of housebreakers and highwaymen, cutpurses and ... thousands of idle apprentices who wished merely for the excitement of a riot' (Macaulay 1889, 601). Many of the young men of the city were compelled by the law to serve for seven years as apprentice to a trade and Macaulay's 'respectable fears' represent the perennial moral panic of the elder generation. He goes on to complain that 'even men of peaceable and honest habits were impelled by religious animosity to join the lawless part of the population' (Macaulay 1889, 601). This is in many ways the definition of a riot, where the generally law-abiding 'cross over'—or transgress or make a transition. For Macaulay, a so-called Liberal Lord, these rebels are a reactionary force, they are 'barbarians in the midst of civilisation', rather like the way Prime Minister David Cameron decried the behaviour of the rioters in 2011 as symptomatic of a 'slow motion moral collapse'.

The rising bourgeois class themselves needed a change of monarch to ensure their interests dominated, therefore Macaulay called 1688 the 'Glorious Revolution' by which the last of the Stuart kings, James II, was overthrown by William of Orange. He describes this mass action in a much more favourable tone. James had demanded the Bishops read out the 'Declaration of Indulgence' in their churches, granting toleration to Catholicism. When they refused 'he had no choice but to send them to prison':

> A great multitude filled the courts of Whitehall and all the neighbouring streets … All down the river, from Whitehall to London Bridge, the royal barge passed between lines of boats, from which arose a shout of 'God bless your Lordships' … Thousands of humbler spectators constantly covered Tower Hill. (Macaulay 1889, 505)

A mass demonstration was ushering in regime change by force of arms, but, for its chronicler, this is a story of the restoration of harmony, sanity and control:

> In a very few days the confusion which the invasion, the insurrection, the flight of James, and the suspension of all regular government had produced, was all at an end, and the kingdom wore again its accustomed aspects. There was a general sense of security. (Macaulay 1889, 620)

References

Burn, E. (2004). *Maudsley and Burn's land law* (8th ed.). Oxford: Oxford University Press.
Cayton, H., & St. Clair, D. (1946). *Black metropolis*. London: Jonathan Cape.
Chomsky, N. (2012). *Occupy!* London: Penguin.

Cohn, S. (2015). Authority and popular resistance. In H. Scott (Ed.), *The Oxford handbook of early modern European history 1350–1750 volume II: Cultures and power.* Oxford: Oxford University Press.

Daily Telegraph (2010, December 9). Tuition fees protesters attack car carrying Prince Charles and the Duchess of Cornwall.

Davis, N. (1973). The rites of violence: Religious riot in sixteenth century France. *Past & Present, 59,* 53–91.

Ehrenreich, B. (2008). *Dancing in the streets: A history of collective joy.* London: Granta.

Engels, F (1884) The origin of the family, private property anthde state. https://www.marxists.org/archive/marx/works/1884/origin-family/ch09.htm

Green, J. (2009). *The eyes of the people: Democracy in an age of spectatorship.* Oxford: Oxford University Press.

Gregg, P. (1981). *King Charles.* London: Dent.

Hill, C. (1973). *The world turned upside down.* London: Temple Smith.

Hill, C. (1978). From lollards to levellers. In M. Cornforth (Ed.), *Rebels and their causes: Essays in honour of A.L. Morton* (pp. 49–69). London: Lawrence & Wishart.

Hoskins, W. G. (1976). *The age of plunder: King Henry's England, 1500–1547.* London: Longman.

Hoyle, R. W. (2001). *The pilgrimage of grace and the politics of the 1530s.* Oxford: Oxford University Press.

Kamen, H. (1971). *The iron century: Social change in Europe 1550–1650.* London: Weidenfield and Nicholson.

Linebaugh, P. (2006). *The London hanged.* London: Verso.

Linebaugh, P. (2014). *Stop thief! The commons, enclosures, and resistance.* Oakland: PM Press.

Macaulay, T. (1889). *History of England volume 1.* London: Longmans.

Manning, R. (1988). *Village revolts: Social protest and popular disturbances in England 1509–1640.* Oxford: Oxford University Press.

Melossi, D. (2015). *Crime, punishment and migration.* London: Sage.

Műntzer, T. (2010) [1524]. *Sermon to the princes.* London: Verso.

Piketty, T. (2014). *Capital in the twenty-first century.* Cambridge, MA: Harvard University Press.

Siegel, P. (1992). *The gathering storm—Shakespeare's English and Roman history plays: A Marxist analysis.* London: Redwords.

Wall, A. (2000). *Power and protest in England 1525–1640.* London: Arnold.

Wiseman, T. P. (2009). *Remembering the Roman people: Essays on late-republican politics and literature.* Oxford: Oxford University Press.

5

Custom, Law and Class

The law is an expression of whoever, or whatever grouping of individuals, controls the state. The state—what Lenin termed simply 'bodies of armed men'—is society's governing institution which also holds the monopoly on the legitimate use of violence for the purpose of defending itself—defending society's rulers and the status quo that they have established.

As a Dutch criminologist put it:

> The state is not an institution for the public well-being; it is chiefly a means of maintaining the external order in the disorder which results from the complicated and muddled systems of capitalistic production; it is before all a system of police. (Bonger 1969, 9)

In seventeenth and eighteenth-century France, where monarchy wielded absolute power, the state was clearly the handmaiden of royalty. Louis XIV, known as the 'Sun King', in order to remind his subjects that they would perish without the benefit of his rule, put it bluntly when he said: '*L'état, c'est moi*'.

When absolute power is challenged by an act of protest, or faces revolt, particularly when it is overthrown, then the old rulers have lost control of

© The Editor(s) (if applicable) and The Author(s) 2016
M. Clement, *A People's History of Riots, Protest and the Law*,
DOI 10.1057/978-1-137-52751-6_5

the law. New legal experts can claim authority and make their interpretation. On 13 November 1792, Louis Antoine Leon Sainte-Juste, just 25, a fervent Jacobin, stood before the French Legislative Assembly to demand the death of Louis XVI because he was an 'enemy of the people':

> Today, respectfully, we conduct a trial for a man who was the assassin of a people, taken in flagrante, his hand soaked with blood, his hand plunged in crime … monarchy is an outrage, every king … a rebel and a usurper. (Bloom 2010, 39)

How had the mighty fallen! In this situation of a developing French Revolution, not only is the king no longer the master, he is judged by others, and found to be a violent criminal, indeed a traitor to the nation. Saint Juste continued:

> Louis waged war against the people … you have seen his army; the traitor was not a king of the French, he was a king of a band of conspirators … he regarded the citizens as his slaves … this man must reign or die. (Bloom 2010, 39)

Legal experts were to the fore in the French Revolution, and it was another lawyer, Robespierre, who spelt out the unshakeable logic of the new situation that the Revolution had brought about. Social relations were turned upside down: 'Louis was king and the republic is founded … Therefore Louis has been deposed by his crimes'. There is no longer room for compromise with such a defeated enemy:

> Louis denounced the French people as rebels … Victory and the people have decided that he alone was a rebel. Therefore Louis cannot be judged; he has already been condemned, else the republic is not cleared of guilt. (Bloom 2010, 41)

The act of revolution emerging out of uprising and popular protest had changed the world. The French Revolutionary Lafayette called it 'the most sacred of duties' (Carlyle 1889, 218). What is this phenomenon that is sometimes described as rioting? How should we understand acts of protest? The obvious response to these questions is to begin by examining their legitimacy. Is the action legal? Is it based upon applying the principles of justice in the eyes of its participants—indeed, is the assertion of their rights the very reason the act takes place at all?

This study examines all these factors, looking at cases from the past and the present in order to discuss the relationship between riot, protest and the legal institutions of a society—whether we mean rules and policies imposed by government, or acts carried out by agents of social control in their employ.

Protesting is an active process, involving conflicts between real people, some judged to be more powerful than others. It is not static. Those phenomena that make up society are constantly in motion: it is a struggle between different social forces. Perspectives on a riot, a demonstration or act of protest vary according to the point of view—the actual physical position within one grouping or another. The participant may be inspired to become more involved in helping the action to grow, whilst a more 'detached' observer may be equally convinced of the senseless nature of such a counter-productive action. Those whose perspective is shared with those in authority are more likely to take the latter view, often denouncing the protest in moral terms using phrases such as 'criminality pure and simple' or deploring the 'rule of the mob'.

The realisation of the act itself tends to amplify and polarise these contrasting opinions. In trying to get to the bottom of this conundrum it is important to recognise how the 'sound of the crowd'—the discourses of those protestors whose voice is so often unheard—is crucial to gaining a true appreciation of what is going on in a world ever more full of riot and protest. Sociologists and social psychologists have drawn attention to the way in which people assembled in a united action often think and act in ways which they would not do 'normally', that is in a different, more everyday situation. It is as if there is a shift in people's consciousnesses—a broadening of the horizons of possibility taking place. Thomas Carlyle expressed this very well in his *The French Revolution*:

> Few terrestrial Appearances are better worth considering than mobs. Your mob is a genuine outburst of Nature … here once more, if nowhere else, is a Sincerity and Reality. Shudder at it; or even shriek over it, thou must; nevertheless consider it. Such a Complex of human forces and Individualities hurled forth, in their transcendental mood, to act and react, on circumstances

and on one another; to work out what is in them to work. The thing they will do is known to no man; least of all to themselves. It is the inflammablest immeasurable Firework, generating, consuming itself. With what phases, to what extent, with what results it will burn off, Philosophy and Perspicacity conjecture in vain. (Carlyle 1889, 218)

The group of people he was referring to was the famous insurrection of women who marched to the royal palace of Versailles to demand bread: 'how could anyone die of hunger when so much corn was on the move? They were taking it away from the people to hoard it up in shops … How could they resist the temptation to lay hands on the corn when it was constantly trailed forth before their hungry, desperate eyes?' (Lefebvre 1973, 25). Carlyle is attempting to capture the sense in which they transformed themselves through the act of daring to do something they would not previously have contemplated. Their 'common sense' of what was possible, ethical or vital to them was challenged and undermined by the new circumstances in which they found themselves. For these women marching to Versailles, these humble subjects demanding welfare from the figure who had up until recently been their absolute ruler, this was a prime example of a class of people acting for itself. To a certain extent this phenomenon occurs in every act of protest which manages to draw in enough numbers: the world around the mob is changing; other people's heightened emotions and notions of outrage at authority combine with an augmented sense of popular justice. This process of transformation reflects and reverberates upon each person's psyche and collectively raises the threshold of their sense of the possible.

Edmund Burke, in his *Reflections on the Revolution in France*, had pronounced that this event was epoch making, saying 'the age of Chivalry is gone'. To this, Carlyle added:

And could not help but go, having produced the still more indomitable Age of Hunger. A set of mortals has arisen, who believe that truth is not a printed speculation, but a practical fact; that Freedom and Brotherhood are possible in this Earth … Who will say that Church, State, Throne, Altar are not in danger; that the social strongbox itself, last Palladium of effete Humanity, may not be blasphemously blown away, and its padlocks undone? Old Europe and new France could not subsist together. A Glorious Revolution, oversetting State, Prisons and Feudalism. (Carlyle 1889, Vol. 2, 192)

In summary, rioting or protesting in large numbers can change the mood of those involved. Within this process a general acceptance of authority and their laws can seem inappropriate. A different set of morals can appear to place people up against the state and the law; rather than benefiting from the status quo they may believe their real interest lies in overthrowing the existing state of affairs.

Social Crime

This is a difficult category to define. It has been 'loosely described as acts proscribed by law, but thought neither immoral nor warranting punishment by considerable sectors of the community, notably poaching and the theft of articles historically embraced by crumbling customary rights, especially waste and woodland products' (Wells 1992, 136). Karl Marx began his political life commenting on such matters. As editor of a Rhineland newspaper he reported how a deputy to the Provincial Assembly objected to a proposal which would treat the gathering of berries as theft, 'an activity which has been permitted by the owners *since time immemorial* and has given rise to a *customary right* of the children. This fact was contested by another deputy, who recorded that in his area these berries have already become articles of commerce and are dispatched to Holland by the barrel'. He concluded that 'in one locality, therefore, things have actually gone so far that a customary right of the poor has been turned into a monopoly of the rich' (Marx and Engels 1975, 234–235).

This observation is at the heart of a Marxist understanding of crime. He believed the crime committed is the act of robbing the poor of their customary entitlements. The so-called 'theft' of wood by the Rhine peasant is in fact the theft of the right to gather wood for fuel, which for Marx is a human right, but which had been abolished in the name of property ownership. In 1822, William Cobbett reminded his readers that the phrase 'by hook or by crook' referred to the tools used by the poor to take wood from the forest, 'that old and expressive saying, which is applied to those cases where people will have a thing by one means or another' (Bushaway 1992, 118). The idea that these are 'crimes' was one that should and would be contested by those whose rights were threatened and whose resistance is labelled criminal. Therefore, in these cases, considerable sectors of the community simply do not believe that these acts are criminal: 'open and secretive modes of protest were widely supported especially by working people, in response to factors over which they had little, if any, control'. These were not simply moral judgements, they were also practical as well as just. Wells calls them 'legitimate expressions which regularly succeeded in achieving some redress of grievances' (Wells 1992, 136). The struggle between the evolving social classes would itself determine how these matters were viewed, as Andy Wood summarises the situation in Europe in the eighteenth and nineteenth centuries, and in some parts of the world even today:

> It was a capitalist society, for sure, but it was a capitalism which, while hegemonic, was never monolithic—in many places, spaces had been carved out by poorer people within which they could still find a decent living. (Wood 2013, 391)

So the rigorous demands of capitalism were squeezing the poor out of the entitlements by which they had lived until this time. This was not an abstract point; there were real practical reasons why working together—in common—had made sense for pre-industrial people, just as it has done for the millions in Asia, Africa and Latin America currently protesting against the loss of their control over their local economy. As Wood points out for the English case of the use of land held by people in common:

> It was only by the spacious turn-out which it afforded that the people were enabled to keep cows and get butter and milk; it was only with the turf-firing cut on the commons that they could smoke their bacon … the very heart of the village economy was the open common. (Wood 2013, 345)

We tend in the twenty-first century to think about the agents of social control—the police—as being the guardians of the actually existing government and its laws. But there have been many cases where the people have actively policed their society against perceived threats and thereby acted to challenge government. One example from the last 50 years was the mass defiance shown towards the British state by Northern Irish 'Loyalists' from the 1970s to the 1990s. In eighteenth and nineteenth-century England, Bob Bushaway describes how villagers used the act of ringing the bells to assert customs like the right to glean, that is for those poor enough to need to do so to be able to gather grain from the farmers' fields after the main harvest has been gathered in. This was a custom that harked back to a period where landowners felt socially obliged to allow this practice, rather than putting efficient monopoly of property rights above all else, as the landowner and the law were asserting increasingly. In 1759, Oliver Goldsmith wrote:

> Custom … is kept by the people themselves, and observed with a willing obedience. The observance of it must, therefore, be a mark of freedom … but a conquered people, a nation of slaves, must pretend to none of this freedom … having, by degeneracy, lost all right to their brave forefathers' free institutions, their masters will in policy take the forfeiture; and the fixing a conquest must be done by giving laws, which may every moment serve to remind the people enslaved of their conquerors: nothing being more dangerous than to trust a late subdued people with old customs, that persistently upbraid their degeneracy, and provoke them to revolt. (Bushaway 1982, 27)

Goldsmith seems to emphasise the dynamic nature of the relationship between these two contenders—masters and men. The rulers use their control of the law to enforce their control, but by asserting their customary right, the people show their capacity to revolt. Revolts of African slaves on British and French plantations were to explode into the Haitian Revolution later that century (James 1983). In Britain, radicals like Wilkes and Priestley initially argued for more civil rights and democracy in a climate of rioting and voting to demand accountability—arguing that rulers must rule and make the law 'in the public interest'.

One English rural custom where these factors were played out was that of rogation or 'beating the bounds' of the parish a fortnight before Whitsunday (late May). By parading around the boundaries of their manor the villagers confirmed the existing land ownership patterns and were able to correct any incursions. The priest accompanied them, thus sanctioning their arrangements and customs and adding a sense of legitimacy to their resistance to enclosure and privatisation of resources held in common by the community. All should 'be content with your own, and not contentiously strive for others, to the breach of charity by any encroaching one upon another'. Bushaway notes this 'provided a very potent motivation for the crowd during the processioning of the parish'. Doubtless, parishioners remembered the invocation from the Old Testament: 'accursed be he who removes his neighbours' doles and marks' (Bushaway 1982, 82).

The higher status clergy often felt dictated to by those bell ringers and other parishioners who attended church meetings (vespers) to argue for lower tithes to be paid and higher daily wages, more 'holy days' and other festivities to be observed, and bringing food, drink and entertainment into public life wherever possible:

> Mummers and wassailers at Christmas, dolers on St Tomas' day, soulers on All Hollows Eve, and catters and clemmers on the feasts of St Catherine and St Clement. (Bushaway 1982, 87)

This older vision of community government that existed before capitalism monopolised all social relations took many forms and invoked the right to celebrate and bargain for improved terms of access to the profits accrued from their own labour by the enclosing and exploiting landowning classes, both the aristocracy and upper clergy, i.e. second and first estate.

The need to maintain control over the land was expressed very clearly by the miners of Kingswood Forest in 1727. They objected to toll gates being erected on the roads going through their communities, with no reduced rates for locals like themselves whose work was mining coal and/ or transporting it to the neighbouring city of Bristol. On 3 July they wrote 'The Colliers' Letter to the Turnpike'. They complained about proposals 'to remove furze and heath from any common lands, for road repairs, without paying for them. The concern here was for the preservation of the commons and the sustenance derived from them: furze bushes, for instance, might be useful not only for firing but also for pasturage and shelter for livestock' (Malcolmsen 1983, 96). Their complaints were ignored and on 26 July, the first day for the collection of the tolls, the local paper reported the miners 'assembled in a body and pulled down four of the turnpikes … some of which they set on Fire, and some they threw in the River' (Malcolmsen 1983, 94). Later in their campaign they marched through Bristol 'with clubs and staves in a noisy manner'. Troops arrested four miners who then threatened to march into the city and 'pull down the gaol where the prisoners were held' (Malcolmsen 94–95).

The letter to the authorities also blamed local landowners for their abuse of the roads through the use of wheeled transport—only used by the wealthy, without fulfilling their obligations for its upkeep. They stated 'by the Omission of your Duty and your Carelessness and Over sight, you have lost your Honourable Magistracy, and brought your self under the reproach of a Turnpike' (Malcolmsen 1983, 96). They had used powerful legal argument to expose the neglect of the law. According to Brewer and Styles, 'the rule of law, "the law" was used as a standard by which to judge the just exercise of authority. Authorities therefore chose to limit themselves to acquire greater effectiveness' (Brewer et al. 1983, 14). They were writing about how the English and their belief that they were entitled to interpret the law in the seventeenth and eighteenth centuries were proving to be 'an ungovernable people' to the newly emerging capitalist regime.

Of course, people's class location shaped their perception: 'one man's view of the public good was regarded by another as a flagrant instance of private interest' (Brewer et al. 1983, 16). As the rich became more centrally involved in business, profit assumed a greater place in their priorities, threatening to displace the old attitude whereby they would be judged, by themselves and the broader society, according to how justly they governed and how attentive they were to 'their people'. At the same time, the poor were also changing, evolving into a working class:

> Their work bred militancy, they were a ready-made crowd, with feelings of communal solidarity they were vulnerable to a sudden rise in prices especially when it coincided with unemployment, and they were better placed than more scattered workers to resist it. (Gilmour 1992, 232)

If those in authority were to be accountable, 'did it imply, as many plebeians clearly thought, that injured parties could take extra-legal action to
secure redress?'

> It was legitimate to show the magistrate how he ought to enforce the assize
> of bread or to demonstrate the fundamental illegality of imprisonment for
> debt by a mass breakout from gaol. (Brewer et al. 16)

Deference to their masters was clearly breaking down, especially as long-
held ideas of a community of masters and tenants with mutual respon-
sibilities declined. For these miners, it was no crime to defend their
common customs and they were prepared to take action that would be
condemned as criminal to assert their rights. We can see a clear class
consciousness evolving here, not only judged by their deeds but also their
words. Malcolmsen (1983, 97) quotes a short verse from the letter:

> Now Turnpikes are grown mutch in Fashion
> The hardest Tax in all our Nation –
> For where Wine and Women and Stock-jobbing past –
> The Turnpike must help us at last.

They believed the rich were encroaching upon the rights of the commons,
and the only way to see justice done was to resist these actions. E. P.
Thompson's term for their actions was that they were informed by a sense
of 'moral economy'. Many social historians and social scientists have
explored this idea. The editors of one collection state that 'Thompson
couched the concept of the moral economy in a dialectic tension with
the market economy' (Randall and Charlesworth 2000, 2). This correctly
emphasises the way in which popular acts of riot and protest were part of a
thought-out process of resistance. Then and now they are not committed
by a 'mindless mob' lacking appreciation of their situation. This is what is
so wrong about the starting point of so many recent analyses of the 2011
English riots which see their actions as either mindless criminality (the
Right and the government) or a product of alienation so extreme that
they are simply mimicking the desire for consumer goods that capitalist
ideology promotes as a sign of status (the Left critical realist response).

More accurate is the interpretation of Randall and Charlesworth: 'riots might be atypical events, but they advanced many of the values of a common people which in other times went unvoiced' (Randall and Charlesworth 2000, 2). The sound of the riotous crowd tells us something of the hopes, fears and dreams of those involved:

> It was the crowd which most actively resisted changes in marketing practice and the crowd which ensured that those who sought to break old market customs and culture encountered real and effective intimidation or retribution. These actions were underwritten and legitimized by the community character of protest for Thompson believed the moral economy was not the value system of the few; it was the value system of the entire plebeian society. (Randall and Charlesworth 2000, 4)

To illustrate this argument, listen to the reported sound of the crowd: 'in 1766 a mob led by William Russell marched along the turnpike … urging "come one and all to Newbury in a body to make the price of bread cheaper" '. In 1795, we hear 'the colliers from Hook (Wales) chanting "one and all, one and all" as they march along. This was echoed nearly 200 years later across the country as miners marched on strike for a year from 1984–5 when their chant was the popular refrain: "Here we go, Here we go, Here we go!" '. As this study concludes, 'mobs were held together by common purpose, not by bully boys' (Randall and Charlesworth 2000, 5, 6).

Peter Linebaugh makes a related argument about his subject, namely 'the hanged men and women whose views and actions challenged both law and their own class'. They should be neither lionised nor condemned:

> If we categorize them too quickly as social criminals taking from the rich, or criminal criminals stealing from the poor, in the process of making these judgements we cloud our attentiveness to theirs.

What do we mean by 'social criminals'? It is a phrase that was employed by some historians and criminologists in the 1970s to emphasise the way in which many acts described as crimes are in fact so labelled by those in authority who often have a vested interest in condemning them. As Andy Wood put it in his exploration *The Memory of the People*: 'the assertion of use-rights shift from custom to social crime as elite definitions of property undercut long-existent entitlements' (Wood 2013, 32–33).

Thompson goes further. He argues that these shared notions of rights and customs underlay 'almost every eighteenth century crowd action' (Thompson 1991, 188)—and since this seminal work, a whole host of historical studies have shown that this conclusion need not be limited either in space to England or in time to the eighteenth century. Take, as one example, Reddy's (1977) study of textile crowds in Rouen over two centuries. He concludes that 'the targets of these crowds glitter in the eye of history as signs of the labourers' conception of the nature of society' (p. 84). Putting all the examples together, we can abstract a more general message: the targets of crowds glitter in the eye of history as signs of the participants' conception of the nature of society.

Thompson went on to define custom not as some passive tradition, but rather as an act that affirms the people's sense of justice: 'at the interface between law and agrarian practice we find custom. Custom itself is the interface, since it may be considered both as praxis and as law' (Thompson 1991, 97).

Those Enlightenment thinkers who proposed useful schemes for social improvement had a very low opinion of those customs that they perceived as forming an obstacle to progress. For the likes of the utilitarians, Mill, Chadwick and Bentham, progress was measured by the increasing commercialisation of social relations. Therefore 'the despotism of custom is everywhere the standing hindrance to human achievement' (Mill 1972, 60). By calling 'custom' despotic he labelled it as something from the past age of feudalism which ought to go. Bentham, famous for his scientific prison designs, was similarly emphatic: 'written law was the law for civilized nations, custom was merely for brutes' (Wood 2013, 342). Such maxims became official policy as the last great wave of parliamentary acts enclosing the land took it away from the common people, despite centuries of tradition that had underpinned their running their communities 'in common'. According to the 1794 report to the Board of Agriculture it was 'irrational' for 'their memory to be the cause of grievance to the most useful part of the community' (Wood 2013, 342). The government is in no doubt as to who is the 'useful part of the community': the encloser, the improver of the land is to usurp the people. As will be explored below the centuries-long struggle to rob the common people of control of the land has been the cause of more human misery and more riot and protest than any other factor. Once they have lost control of their commons, the mass of people are truly mobile—no longer tied to the land—which in turn has led to the growth of the moral panic over mobs of people ganging together to use their strength in numbers to resist. This is what George Rudé calls 'the crowd in history'. Le Bon's demonisation of the crowd, like the scientific pronouncements of the utilitarians, reflects the establishment's fear of those they govern.

This begs the question: what is their common purpose, or alternatively, what is the point of being in a crowd as opposed to acting for yourself? Well, you can still, of course, act in your own interests; but is there any advantage to be gained by being part of a crowd acting together? The Romans clearly thought so. Their symbol of the bundle of rods, the *fasces*, tied together was a sacred symbol representing the belief that their strength as a people lay in uniting. The slogan of Alexander Dumas's three musketeers 'All for one, and one for all' was written at a time when associations of people had combined together to defeat the absolute power of the monarch: thus the people's liberty, equality and solidarity had been won. Dumas himself admired his father who was a general in Napoleon's army, 'the black count' (Reiss 2012), and celebrated the act of revolution in his novel *Taking the Bastille*. The lesson of history seemed to be that acting collectively was the key for groups of people to realise their interests. By combining together they could assert their traditional entitlements, or, in a rapidly modernising situation, they could negotiate and demand new rights and living conditions in the new world when the era of state and church regulation was breaking down.

This was not just a matter for country people seeking to preserve their 'customs in common', but also the artisans and citizens in the cities who felt their rights and liberties were being suppressed. This was highlighted by the beliefs of the radical London MP John Wilkes and his supporters:

that all Englishmen enjoyed certain rights and liberties under the law and … [their] readiness to act upon their view of the law that made them radical and threatening. (Brewer 1983, 137)

Wilkes himself was certainly pushed into action by the severity of the punishment he faced for editing a satirical newspaper. He was imprisoned in the Tower of London and only freed after winning his case in court, proving he was not legally charged. After his release from jail he was wounded by a government supporter in a duel and fled to France, returning four years later in 1768 and becoming elected MP for Westminster, despite his being returned to prison (Brewer 1983, 129). What happened next prompted a riot on the day that Parliament opened:

> Huge crowds gathered in St George's Fields, Southwark, to cheer Wilkes. The magistrates feared that the crowds watching him at his window in the King's Bench prison would try to effect a rescue, and they therefore requested military aid. In the ensuing affray … Gillam, one of the Surrey magistrates, was struck by a brickbat. Captain Murray and three guards were ordered to chase and apprehend the assailant, but they bungled the job and, contriving to shoot a young cowman, William Allen, who was almost certainly innocent of any involvement in the demonstration. Later the same afternoon Gillam was again struck by missiles hurled by the demonstrators and, on this occasion, he ordered the troops to fire on the crowd … several people were shot and killed. (Brewer 1983, 143–144)

Juries later found a soldier and 'person or persons unknown' guilty of these murders, and the memory of state-sponsored violence and injustice figured deeply in the public consciousness, making the authorities think twice about acting so brutally again. Indeed Brewer argues 'the activities of the Wilkites may, in part, explain the tardiness and prevarication of the magistracy during the Gordon riots of 1780' (Brewer 1983, 145).

These riots saw the mass of the population allied with what we would now call the liberal bourgeoisie, that is the commercially minded middle class of merchants and lawyers who had the education and opportunity to wield these legal weapons against the establishment. In Britain these were almost the last mass protests that were backed by both of these classes. As capitalism became more firmly established then the commercial classes would become the new masters and riot and protest would be directed against them. As Reg Groves explains:

> The grievances of the London crowds who rioted with the cry of 'Wilkes and Liberty' were economic; they saw, wrongly, in Wilkes their champion;

for their mistake they paid dearly ... Wilkes's actions in later years show where his interests lay. Although many old 'Wilkites' took part in the Gordon Riots—it was the 'Wilkite mob' who formed the main body of rioters—Wilkes helped to suppress them, declaring that he 'would not leave one rioter alive'. The French Revolution was denounced by Wilkes as the work of 'the bloody savages of Paris'. (Groves 1930)

So even though Wilkes advocated the use of the law, his new-found membership of the establishment by the time of the French Revolution led him to see the lawyer Robespierre and his supporters as enemies. This reactionary attitude was in evidence when Wilkes played his part in the violent suppression of the biggest and bloodiest riots that London has ever seen—so far—the Gordon Riots.

On 2 June 1780 there was a mass protest against the government bill to let Catholics run schools and own estates. This was less than a hundred years since mass demonstrations had ushered in a Glorious Revolution to prevent James II ruling as a Catholic king; the commitment to Protestantism, the reformed religion, was still very strong. From St George's Fields (again) 40,000 marched to present a monster petition to Parliament. Gatrell reports: 'it didn't take long before fiercer elements in the crowd were abusing and stoning the coaches of Members of Parliament, bishops and lords as they arrived for the debates'. A contemporary account of the scene by Horace Walpole gives us a real flavour of how ordinary people viewed their so-called masters:

There were the Lords Hillsborough, Stormont, Townshend, without their bags [wigs], and with their hair disheveled about their ears, and Lord Willoughby without his periwig, and Lord Mansfield, whose glasses had been broken, quivering on the woolsack like an aspen, Lord Ashburnham had been torn out of his chariot, the Bishop of Lincoln ill-treated [dragged from his coach, in terror he escaped through a gentleman's house and then over the rooftops] ... Alarm came that the mob had thrown down Lord Boston and were trampling him to death—which they almost did. They had diswigged Lord Bathurst on his answering them stoutly and told him he was the Pope and an old woman. (Gatrell 2013, 340)

For five days that summer the crowds ran the streets of London. Fearful of an even greater reaction if they resorted to repression, the Hanoverian state hesitated: 'for nearly a week thereafter, magistrates dared not read the Riot Act for fear of reprisals upon themselves' (Gatrell 2013, 340). And they were right; 'when on 6 June the magistrate William Hyde read the Riot Act at Palace Yard and ordered the crowd to disperse or be shot, a sailor named James Jackson hoisted a red and black flag and shouted "Hyde's house a-hoy", and the crowd trooped after him to Hyde's house in St Martin's Street and within an hour they had sacked it' (Gatrell 2013, 347).

Hardly surprisingly, besides the magistrates the crowd targeted the police—in the form of Sir John Fielding's office in Bow Street. In an action that sums up the values of twenty-first-century government, this historic location is currently being converted into a hotel for London's super-rich. Back then, it was:

> the most symbolically loaded target. It had long been the source of ever-tightening supervision and discipline, staffed by magistrates who were understood to be corrupt. And many of the lately arrested rioters had been committed to trial here. (Gatrell 2013, 349–350)

The new class formation of protest unambiguously placed the poorer classes in opposition to the rich—both the rising bourgeoisie and the flustered old aristocracy. In England the lawyers, and therefore the law, were now on the side of property, and the artisans and newly emerging working class could no longer rely on the laws of the commons to buttress their claims for social justice. As the state began to build up its instruments of social control, the association of the propertyless mass of the population with crime and as a dangerous threat to social order became more institutionalised (Rudé 1964). Therefore new methods of social control were required: Fielding's aim was to collect 'all Information of Fraud and Felony into one point [Bow Street], registering Offenders of all Kinds, quick Notice and sudden Pursuit, and keeping up a correspondence with all the active Magistrates in England' (Gatrell 2013, 352).

There is blatant hypocrisy on show here. John Fielding had succeeded at Bow Street his brother Henry, the novelist, who had no illusions about the double standards employed in judging these 'felons', as illustrated in his ditty:

Great whores in coaches gang
Smaller misses,
For the kisses,
Are in Bridewell hang'd;
While in vogue
Like the great rogue, (Walpole)
Small rogues are dozens hang'd. (Gatrell 2013, xviii)

No wonder then, when the poor rose up, Bow Street was thoroughly ransacked. Hundreds gathered to destroy this symbol of state oppression. William Elliot, a tobacconist, reported:

> a great many chairs and a good deal of furniture were thrown out and set on fire in the street in five different places. I saw Roberts throw out several chairs, and a good deal of bed linen; by this time the fires were so large that one might have seen to pick up a pin in the street. (OBSP t178000628-1)

Another famous fire was set at Langdale's Distillery. According to William Corner, at the trial of the accused, James Henry, this was a case of a delirious crowd running riot:

> I am clerk to Mr. Langdale, distiller, at Holbourn Bridge. I found the mob rushing in below and going up stairs … turning the cocks, letting the liquor run out, and the mob taking away five gallon casks and two gallon casks of liquor, besides what they could in their hats. I staid sometime in the shop; in about a quarter of an hour after they came in they began pulling down the things in the shop. (OBSP t17800628-21)

James Henry's defence was defiant but brief:

> I was not there; I am quite innocent of the charge they have laid to me; I was at Marylebone all that day. I have no witnesses here. (OBSP t17800628-21)

He was found guilty and sentenced to death.

It seems, however, that the mindless destruction of the drink-sodden rioters at the distillery was an exception to the rule during the week of rioting. One witness, Susan Burney, commented that 'the people brought a fire pump to protect neighbouring houses from fire—"a precaution which it seems has been taken in every place that these lawless Rioters have thought fit to attack"'. A French journalist made a similar point, 'The Londoner, even up in arms … concentrates his rage upon some definite object [and] draws a line of conduct beyond which, though provoked, he will not go' (Gatrell 2013, 346). Targets were selected either by general concerns for popular justice or individual acts of opportunism, the kind of looting which often arises out of situations of social disorder.

Looting was certainly an element in the riots, as people took advantage of the unusual situation to lay hands on what property they could find. According to the transcripts from the Old Bailey trials following the riots, one thief was convicted of taking 60 carnation plants, another the iron grating for a stove in Bethnal Green. Often they did a poor job in explaining their actions, with the stove thief claiming in his defence: 'I heard that Justice Wilmot's house was burnt. I was very sorry to hear it. I went and saw these things lying in the road' (OBSP t17800628-9).

This was the era of the thief takers—men who could earn significant rewards by convicting the guilty—a time when many were ripe for corruption (Paley 1989). One Richard Ingram, a witness, accused Henry Maskell of organising the riots, claiming he overheard him say 'but don't stay long in Devonshire [meaning the house of the Duke of Devonshire], but go to the Bank, there is a million of money to pay you for your pains, and at the Excise-office there are forty thousand pounds not paid in'. The accused's reply was forthright:

God forbid that I should insinuate that the reward of fifty pounds could have any influence on the evidence of any honest man, however poor, however distressed; but when infamy is united with poverty, such a sum carries with it irresistible temptation. It is to me a painful task to expose the characters of these witnesses, though they have been unfeeling enough to attack, upon false grounds, not only my character but my life. In justice therefore to my other witnesses, and to relieve you from any difficulty in determining to whom you should give credit, I ought, and doubt not to be able, to prove that the witnesses the prosecution are worth of no credit. I will shew you by the most undeniable testimony, that Ingram has been a bankrupt, that he has been discharged by an act of insolvency, that he is now insolvent, and that his word and his conduct are as exceptionable as his credit. (OBSP t17800628-10)

Several other witnesses then confirmed the untrustworthy character of Richard Ingram. The last to be called, Atkinson Bush, stated: 'When I went to school with him he was known by the same appellation by which he has now been described, that of Lying Dick' (OBSP t17800628-10). Maskell was acquitted.

The mob had gathered in massive numbers and wrought destruction on leading politicians and industrialists as they fired their houses. Although ostensibly anti-Catholic riots, class resentment was certainly also present, as in the case of a barge-builder who protested at his trial that 'no gentleman should be possessed of more than £1000 a year' (Rudé 1971, 98).

This certainly evoked a violent reaction from the government, which authorised troops to fire upon crowds burning down London's prisons, assaulting the Bank of England and destroying the tollhouses on Blackfriars Bridge. Describing events in their immediate aftermath, Lord Wraxall declared the slaughter of civilians to be in the hundreds: 'the corpses fell like rats into the river' (Hibbert 2004, 115). The descriptions of the battles between rioters and troops over the Bank of England are dramatic. They were led by a brewery drayman, who 'rode a cart horse decorated with the chains and fetters stolen from Newgate the previous night. Wave after wave of rioters rushed towards the bank to be met by the fire of Colonel Holroyd's hard-pressed militiamen. At each volley a few fell, but others re-formed and came on again' (Hibbert 2004, 113). In a later attack, the fourth in 24 hours, the Horse Guards 'lashed out so furiously with their bayonets that twenty of the rioters fell dead almost at the point of impact' (Hibbert 2004, 128).

In both England and France, then the world's two most powerful states with growing empires, the foundations of monarchy and government were being shaken by riots and revolution. In France, the absolute monarch had opposed the bourgeoisie and the poor, and been swept away as a result. In England, as we have seen, the merchants who had backed riots and protest in the 1760s were largely on the side of authority in 1780, but the scale of violence necessary to repress the riots impressed upon the government the need for a new policing system more effective than the old constables and better equipped to avoid inflaming riots than the military:

> Authority's only means of dealing with riots in England was the use of troops … it wanted to avoid bloodshed, knowing the certainty with which this inflames passions and resentment. There was an issue of pompously worded warnings … A route of escape and dispersal was always left open … These frequently failed to produce the required effect, and tended rather to expose authority's weakness, and to inspire the insults of stone throwing or shots from the mob. In one form or another incidents would occur which shattered in an instance the entire fabric of authority's pose of dignity and produced the quick reaction of sudden and undignified exhibitions of brutality and rage in the form of severe and unnecessarily excessive exercise of military force. Harsh repression could be successful but never more than temporarily … by the second decade of the nineteenth century, even the sight of troops on the occasion of a riot was the pouring of oil on flames. (Reith 1952, 52–53)

Reith's acute analysis of the shortcomings of the military approach to 'preserving social order', that is suppressing riotous mobs, was a justification for replacing troops with a regular, professional police force. The problem, as Nadine El Enany explains, was that after the Riot Act was read, justices and their servants were 'free, discharged and indemnified' for the 'killing, maiming or hurting of such Person or Persons' who resisted. 'The Riot Act was, in many senses, a law to abolish law, a kind of modified martial law against rioters, a crucial aspect of state power … What the state presents as "disorder" matters for the maintenance, and indeed expansion of its own power' (El-Enany 2014, 73–74). This dangerous tactic of outright repression risked retaliation: the government had certainly had enough warnings.

We know that in 2011 hunger was not the immediate trigger for the riots that it was in early nineteenth-century Britain. That was provided by the actions of the agencies of social control, namely the police, when shooting dead Mark Duggan. Again, this action sounds very different from earlier episodes in the history of English riots, but parallels abound. After the urban apocalypse of London's Gordon Riots there was a provincial massacre in Bristol in 1793, when troops fired upon crowds dismantling the toll booths on the city's new bridge, killing 11 (Manson 1997; Clement 2014). In the riot at Bristol Bridge, troops shot dead one John Abbot. When enraged citizens confronted him over the matter the next day, the city's mayor pronounced it a 'justifiable homicide' (Manson 1997). The difference may be found in what happened next. A further demonstration at the bridge caused mayhem when troops massacred another 11 citizens. In hindsight, this was a prelude to Peterloo, the armed incursion by troops in a crowded city square, so labelled by protestors and the press in ironic reference to Britain's much lauded military triumph at Waterloo four years earlier.

The 1819 Peterloo Massacre in Manchester was the fundamental event that demonstrated beyond doubt that a new policy was needed. The sheer size and scale of the crowds gathered in St Peter's Fields reflected the enormous wave of migration into the new industrial cities across the country. The expanding system of industrial capitalism needed their labour. Employers even called workers 'hands', signifying what was important to them was a supply of human raw material to maintain the process of production. What many of them were not prepared to consider though was their stomachs—the welfare of these new masses. In 1813–14 the government had repealed the Statute of Artificers (Rule 1992, 108), a law dating from 1563, which had regulated working conditions. All those working in trades must serve a seven-year apprenticeship, and all rates of wages for these trades were to be set by magistrates. Now state regulation was over and the Industrial Revolution ushered in a new era of free trade.

This suited the new industrial employers who were recruiting masses of workers, regardless of any restrictions or regulations concerning their age, gender, level of skill or indeed the methods to be employed and length of shift in their working day. This did not suit the workers: their 'freedom' from regulation was terrifying as all worked tirelessly for 12 or 14 hours a day in the new factories and textile mills. But this 'bleak age', as the Hammonds called the period in Britain from 1810 to 1847 when the Ten Hours Bill became law (1947, 196), also forged a shared class consciousness amongst these 'huddled masses' migrating to the workshop of the world. Like today's migrants they often had little choice but to flee their old lives and lands if they were to survive. This consciousness was shaped by a growing awareness of how your class position determined your destiny. You had a miserable shared present, but together could you secure a better future? The dream of economic reform, of living and working conditions and rewards for your labour, and political reform of parliament towards a truer democracy, were what had drawn so many to St Peter's Fields:

> The crowd numbered possibly up to 150,000, larger than any riot or uprising since the English Revolution almost two centuries earlier. In addition, many of the protestors had been carrying out practice drills for weeks in advance. With just 1,000 troops and 400 constables, the authorities would only be able to break up the protest through the use of extreme violence, and so it was. Men, women and children were stampeded by horses, sabred and whipped relentlessly through the streets of Manchester … at the end of which at least 11 were dead and about 500 injured. (Behrman 2011, 44)

Were the Tory Government so proud of this great 'victory' over their own people? The public outrage was enormous, not only in the words of Shelley's odes to revolt 'The Masque of Anarchy' and 'Men of England', but also echoing in the pronouncements of the likes of Thomas Carlyle who dramatically denounced the disastrous consequences of this state-sponsored terror. In his *Past and Present*, published in 1843, Carlyle highlights the 'Manchester Insurrection' as a sign of the times, proclaiming:

> Peterloo stands written, as in fire-characters, or smoke-characters prompt to become fire again … Some thirteen unarmed men and women cut down—the number of the slain and maimed is very countable, but the treasury of rage, burning hidden or visible in all hearts ever since … is of unknown extent. (Carlyle 1912, 16)

Peterloo is frequently cited as the definitive reason for Britain establishing a police force in 1829. They were designed to be a less violent alternative to using the troops to quell social disorder. But Carlyle's admission of a 'treasury of rage' indicates the new urban masses were not immediately reconciled to the police being a solution to this problem. Perhaps he was recalling the crowd who had demonstrated in London's Coldbath Fields in 1833. The protestors were so outraged by the brutal actions of one PC Culley that he was assaulted and killed—with the jury bringing in a verdict of 'justifiable homicide'. Clearly the Metropolitan Police did not have the degree of consent from the public for their actions that they later enjoyed. This verdict was plain evidence of how at least some of the newly forming working class viewed the 'new police', with commemorative medals and tankards made for the jurors.

The government put a brave face on their error and sought to justify their actions: 'after Peterloo, the Lord Chancellor told the Lords "that numbers constituted force, and force terror, and terror illegality"'. This attitude is still present in government today, the latest example being the attempt by the French Government to ban climate protests after the December 2015 summit using the state of emergency legislation brought in after the Paris terror attack: 'the assumption that crowds are an inherent danger underlies public order offences currently in force' (El-Enany 2014, 75). Any ambiguity over the right to 'negotiation by riot' was to be legislated against. The law was now unequivocally an instrument of the state and oppressor of the people:

> After the Peterloo Trials the offence of unlawful assembly was firmly established. This elaboration of the use of public order offences against political activity paved the way for the case law of the nineteenth century which developed the concepts of breach of the peace, obstruction and nuisance. (El-Enany 2014, 78)

Now that both defence or rural custom and protest at urban injustice in various forms have been criminalised, it is worth revisiting the concept of social crime which 'occurs when there is a conflict of laws, e.g. between an official and an unofficial system, or when acts of law-breaking have a distinct element of social protest in them, or when they are closely linked with the development of social and political unrest' (Hobsbawm 1972, 5; Lea 1999, 308).

Roger Wells later recounts the story of Sussex gang leader Stanton Collins as 'the organizer of an extensive criminal fraternity' (Wells 1992, 143). In a nearby village in 1829 'a massive fire, started in different places, consumed thirteen hay and wheat ricks, and the barn containing the offensive technology … threshing machines' (Wells 1992, 142). This was a year before the 'rural war' (Griffin 2012) of Autumn 1830 when the whole of Sussex, Hampshire and Wiltshire was engulfed in a wave of burnings, riot and protest against the use of threshing machines—the notorious Captain Swing riots of 1830.

The threshing machines were cutting jobs and undermining the value of their labour. The rioters' actions 'combined calls for an advance in wages and machine-breaking'. Karl Griffin explains how they justified their actions:

> There was a sense also of transcending the 'moral economy'. By operating threshing machines, by manipulating the Poor Laws to keep the cost of labour down, by watching their premises to ward against labourers firing their ricks, and acting as witnesses and prosecutors in the ensuing Swing Trials, large(r) farmers had clearly broken the compact. Such actions also gave labourers licence to act differently. In throwing off work and going about the parish demanding higher wages we see a coming together of ritual and proto trade unionism. (Griffin 2012, 323)

Public concern mirrored these sentiments: a correspondent to the Home Office from Gosport, near Portsmouth, wrote that 'by an illiberal, grinding economy [the farmer has] wickedly thrown his labourers on the Poor Laws … hence has followed a reckless desperation of temper among the people' (Griffin 2012, 171).

The ruling nobility and their retainers were certainly alarmed. 'A revolution is possible', 'the whole rural machine is going wrong' (Griffin 2012, 190), wrote a steward at Highclere Castle, the ancestral home of Lord Carnarvon, now infamous as the set for the TV soap, *Downton Abbey*!

They had good reason to fear. The French Revolution of the summer of 1830 had finally done away with the restored monarchy and caused much celebration in England. Griffin reports mass meetings in Horsham and Chichester in Sussex and Maidstone in Kent, where amid placards with radical slogans and a tricolor flag, speakers called for 'reform in the Commons House of Parliament. Vote by ballot or 2 years or nothing. In the City of London a royal visit had to be cancelled due to a "conspiracy to cause confusion" by cutting off the gas mains, which was seen as 'a general attack on the new police' (Griffin 2012, 199).

A number of factors appeared to be coming together to threaten the existing social order. The increasing use of technology in the countryside was threatening to replace substantial sections of the agricultural workforce in the 1820s. The previous decade had seen a similar process occurring in textile districts as manufacturers replaced weaving at home with the economies of scale to be gained from building new mills to house more advanced mechanised looms. Workers had formed secret societies, meeting on the moors of Nottingham and Derby, and planning a series of dramatic attacks on the new mills. Troops were called in and magistrates across the counties organized to try and repress these protests and force the workers into accepting the inevitable, sacrificing their independence and becoming a more disciplined and controlled workforce.

The workers declared their intention not to give in and sent threatening letters in the name of the mythical General Ludd. Their defeat encouraged the pace of technological change to quicken, as even those employers reluctant to change began to realise that they would have no choice if they wanted to match the prices of their competitors and thus maintain or increase their share of the market. Also, the new technology required less 'hands', as the workers were called by their bosses. How would the newly unemployed survive?

It is important to remember that the relative harmony in previous relations between masters and men had been built on a pattern of social relations of deference and authority that had evolved over long centuries. These arrangements added up to the 'customs' which all parties agreed should be a guide as to how society should run. Despite the riots and protest that occurred from time to time, this more stable pattern of civilisation had shaped the consensus views and traditional ways of thinking and acting that had constituted everyday life up until the Industrial Revolution. Now this was all changed. As Marx described it, 'all that is solid melts into air. All that was Holy is profane'. The rulers' neglect of their subjects' welfare in the name of efficiency looked like an abuse of their obligations, and workers felt they had little choice but to resist.

The 'Rural War' began with the changes in outdoor relief that meant that the unemployed were now set to work in order to receive benefits, much of which was barbaric and degrading, such as men being put in the shafts to carry rubble to the roads in the place of horses. The idea of the workhouse was extended, whose inhabitants were sometimes chained to the walls, as was the case in Selborne, Hampshire in 1830, leading to the riots there which consisted of attacks on the house of the workhouse chief. Quite reasonably, the farm labourers and farmers agreed that if only the tithes—taxes taken by the church—were cut back then the farmers could afford to pay a better wage. They called meetings in local churches and through weight of numbers put pressure on the church authorities to agree. In a variation of the traditional custom of 'beating the bounds' or rogation, they marched in substantial numbers to the estates of the great landowners demanding money. It was a classic case where the protestors saw themselves as upholding the spirit of the law and custom, believing that a demonstration of the justice of their cause by these symbolic actions could lead their betters to recognise their neglect of their duties. But now it was not 1730, but 1830, and capitalism—as Marx described it 'red in tooth and claw'—was now so driven by the imperative to maximise profits that Britain's rulers saw no room for the compromises of the previous century. This had been the line of the Conservatives through the 1820s, and even though a new Liberal of Whig government had just taken over in late 1830, there was no change of direction.

The Duke of Wellington was very clear in his instructions. He had been prime minister for the last few years and was also a major landowner in Hampshire, at the epicentre of the 'Captain Swing' revolt of the agricultural labourers. As the lord lieutenant of the county, his directions recall the glories of his military past, vanquishing the dangerous revolutionary aspirations not of Napoleon but of Hampshire's farmworkers:

I induced the magistrates to put themselves on horseback, each at the head of his own servants, retainers, grooms, hunters, gamekeepers armed with horse whips, pistols, fowling pieces, and what they could get, and to attack in concert, if necessary, or singly, those mobs, disperse them and take and put in confinement those who could not escape. This was done in a spirited manner in many instances, and it is astonishing how soon the country was tranquillised … by the activity and spirit of gentlemen. (Kent and Townsend 2002, 126)

Maybe Dickens was thinking of this brand of authoritarian hypocrisy in Martin Chuzzlewit when he denounced the notion of 'duty': 'Oh late-remembered, much-forgotten, mouthing, braggart duty, always owed, and seldom paid in any other coin than punishment and wrath'. The greater crime, surely, is the neglect of the powerful of their duties:

Oh ermined Judge whose duty to society is now to doom the ragged criminal to punishment and death, hast thou never, Man, a duty to discharge in barring up the hundred open gates that wooed him to the felon's dock … had you no duty to society, before the ricks were blazing and the mob were mad? (Dickens 2004, 471–472)

In the Special Commission where the labourers were put on trial, the court heard from Abraham Childs, aged 48, of Alresford Hampshire, that he had protested 'for our lawful rights, to break machines and get higher wages'. He was arrested along with 45 others by the 3rd Dragoons at Stoneham (Eastleigh) (Griffin 2012, 113). However, for the labourers, their undoing came when they started to attack the property of the Baring family, major landowners and leading members of the judiciary. When 700 gathered in Micheldever in Hampshire, a member of the prominent family of bankers, Bingham Baring, demanded to speak to their representative:

Baring cornered spokesman John Silcock prompting someone to shout out 'Go to work!' Henry Cook stepped forward, demanding to Baring: 'God damn you, get out of my way' before raising his sledgehammer and striking the rim of Baring's hat and his shoulder. Baring collapsed … bloodied and bruised, but Cook suffered his life on the Winchester scaffold for his 'impetuosity'. (Griffin 2012, 104)

As David Kent argues, 'the landed gentry were troubled by riot and destruction but more worrying was the prospect that the labouring poor might learn political lessons from their successful protest. Richard Pollen was particularly alarmed by the labourers' "mode of combining" which he had thought was limited to 'the Manufacturing Classes'. The agricultural poor, it was also argued, had now discovered the 'power of forcing concession' which would 'become so congenial' that, in time, they would exercise it 'towards the climax of absolute domination'. Magistrates recommended the 'insurgents' had to be assaulted 'with unwonted terror and severity' (Kent 1997, 15).

Summary justice for the nineteenth-century poor is the equivalent of 2011's 'exemplary sentences', where the Department of Justice sentencing guidelines were purposely torn up as minor crimes became major offences. Months in jail for stealing an ice cream or a bottle of water, and the infamous four-year term handed out to two young men convicted of organising a riot in Warrington, Cheshire, by setting up a Facebook page: a riot which never took place.

For example, according to Baron Vaughan, the chief Judge at the Hampshire Special Commission that tried the 1830 Swing rioters, one of those on trial, James Annells of Barton Stacey, like others also charged, was 'acting under some delusion … instigated by the suggestions of evil designing persons', by which he meant the Mason brothers who had stimulated others 'to tumult and riot' (HC 3.1.1831). The Special Commission ended in mass transportation to Australia, with Baron Vaughan pronouncing: 'you will leave this country … never to return'. Wives, sisters, mothers, children, beset the gates of Winchester gaol with displays of grief which *The Times* correspondent found to be 'truly heart breaking' (Kent and Townsend 2002, 133). Executions were to set an example: 'many of the prisoners assembled to watch the executions wept uncontrollably, at least one fainted and all were angered by the barbarous injustice they witnessed. When they left the yard an epitaph was discovered chalked on a door—"Murder for Murder—Blood for Blood"' (Kent and Townsend 2002, 140).

Neil Davidson concludes his survey of Scottish riots, noting 'there were major structural limitations on the independence and capacity for self-activity of pre-industrial crowds during the transition to capitalism' (Davidson 2015, 116). In other words, however justified their cause, the protesting crowd—labelled the 'mob' by their masters—were not in a position to overthrow the conditions that so oppressed them. The Irish revolutionary James Connolly, himself executed following the Dublin Easter rising of 1916, made much the same point:

> There was a time, stretching for more than a thousand years, when the mob was without power or influence, when the entire power of the governments of the world was concentrated in the hands of the kings, the nobles and the hierarchy. That was the blackest period in human history. It was the period during which human life was not regarded as being of as much value as the lives of hares and deer; it was the period when freedom of speech was unknown, when trial by jury was suppressed, when men and women were tortured to make them confess crimes before they were found guilty, when persons obnoxious to the ruling powers were arrested and kept in prison (often for a lifetime) without trial; and it was the period during which a vindictive legal code inflicted the death penalty for more than one hundred and fifty offences—when a boy was hung for stealing an apple, a farmer for killing a hare on the roadside. (Connolly 1910)

This is a key lesson from history as to why revolts, even when successful, led to incorporation of opposition elements within the process of civilisation by which feudalism was evolving into capitalism—between 1550 and 1800 in the British case. However, if the capacity of the mobile population to resist was limited by the structure of feudalism, Connolly now believed 'at last, with the development of manufacturing, came the gathering together of the mob, and consequent knowledge of its numbers and power, and with the gathering together also came the possibility of acquiring education':

> Then the mob started upon its upward march to power—a power only to be realised in the Socialist Republic. In the course of that upward march the mob has transformed and humanised the world. It has abolished religious persecution and imposed toleration upon the bigots of all creeds; it has established the value of human life, softened the horrors of war as a preliminary to abolishing it, compelled trial by jury, abolished the death penalty for all offences save one, and in some countries abolished it for all; and to-day it is fighting to keep the children from the factory and mine, and put them to school. The mob, 'the most blind and ruthless tyrant of

all', with one sweep of its grimy, toil-worn hand, swept the stocks, the thumbscrew, the wheel, the boots of burning oil, the torturer's vice and the stake into the oblivion of history. (Connolly 1910)

Connolly was here following Marx and Engels, who had famously labelled the mobile population flooding into the new cities the industrial proletariat, what we would today call the global working class. The members of this class were to be the 'gravediggers of capitalism' because the way in which capitalism organised them so as to exploit their labour also created the conditions for the type of organised class consciousness and action that could put the collective interests of humanity and its needs above the selfish profiteering of the tiny minority of rulers. Connolly calls this 'civilising, humanising work' and concludes: 'all hail, then, to the mob, the incarnation of progress!' (Connolly 1910).

So for all the savagery with which the Tories put down the monster demonstration in Manchester, the events of 'Peterloo' told the rulers of the world's most advanced capitalist power that the new world had placed a new weapon in the hands of this newly organised working class. Combination, association and union became its catchwords as they struggled to form organisations and carry out the actions that would signal that the mob now had the power to reform their living conditions by concentrating their efforts into controlling the use of their labour power by 'pulling the plug' and organising strike action in the new factories that William Blake famously labelled 'England's dark satanic mills'.

All the effort of this new working-class movement became increasingly channelled into reforming and regulating industrial society. Factory hours were restricted to a maximum of ten per day in 1847, trade unions were now legal, a rudimentary standard of universal education was introduced in 1870 and various campaigns saw a gradual widening of the right to vote into the upper echelons of the (male) working class. The industrial riots or strikes in Newport in 1839 and especially in the great industrial metropolis of Manchester in 1842 had helped propel these changes; and there was actually a reduction in street riots and demonstrations through the latter part of the nineteenth century until the 1887 Trafalgar Square episode. Radicals and socialists had helped to build this demonstration of around 100,000 in the heart of the capital, but faced a

Metropolitan Police force determined to preserve order. In a manner that has become all too familiar ever since, their use of violence with the aim of intimidating protestors into refraining from such action had a contradictory effect as an innocent person, in this case entirely unconnected with the demonstration, was struck down and killed by mounted police. The outrage expressed at this injustice was well expressed by Annie Besant when speaking to the crowd of 120,000, gathered for the funeral of the unfortunate Alfred Linnell:

> Many a public funeral has been given to statesmen and to generals, but London has not seen in our generation a public funeral given to a poor man killed by the violence of the police. And the lesson of this funeral to each who sees it will be that Alfred Linnell's fate may be his or her own, unless the police terror is put an end to … he was merely a harmless, indifferent, curious spectator, and he has been slain by the new tyranny. The lesson will not be lost by the thousands who will read it on Sunday next. (Creighton 2015, 22)

The political ripples extended a long way from these events. William Morris—artist and socialist—composed a 'Death Song' denouncing the actions 'of the ruling class making this great town of London nothing more than a prison'. The Battersea and South London parliaments—local assemblies in working-class districts—argued for 'a municipal government for London' and deplored 'the disgrace of poverty in the city' (Creighton 2015, 22, 26). They argued for the right of local authorities to control the police, and that the council should be allowed to employ its workforce directly at trade union rates for the job and equal pay for women instead of using private contractors. In 1888 the London County Council was formed, and the following year the unskilled workers of East London struck successfully for higher wages and trade union membership went through the roof. These themes of local democracy and building unions to gain the rate for the job echoed through the twentieth century and indeed right up to today.

In Britain, ever since 1889, until the defeat of the miners' strike of 1984–85, strikes were generally seen as a more effective form of protest than riots. Workers bound together in organised form through their unions and/or workplace assemblies are likely to be a more coherent collective body than those rioting on the streets. Especially important is the fact that strikes are directed at challenging the power of the company to exploit their workforce in order to make their profits. Perhaps it is significant that twentieth-century British riots have tended to feature the unemployed—for example during the 1930s depression in Liverpool and Bristol, or the post-war return of the riots in 1981, which will be discussed in the next chapter. However, strikes—despite sometimes being highly organised, bureaucratically controlled and legal—often attract the sort of vilification from modern politicians that used to be reserved for riots. For example, the infamous 1977 Ridley Plan—the document that outlined Conservative plans to destroy the power of the trade unions—referred to the need for 'a large, mobile squad of police who are equipped and prepared to uphold the law against the likes of the Saltley Coke-works mob'. Once again it is the crowd, the mob, who are, in Thatcher's words, 'the enemy within': the crowd of pickets who forced the police to order the gates closed at a coal distribution depot during the 1972 miners' strike, thus demonstrating the power the working class had to control production when they acted together (Bennett 2009; Clement 2015).

This is not a book about strikes, but these crowd actions are often labelled as riots by their opponents, and when they generalise across workplaces they are often accompanied by the sort of mass demonstrations which challenge the right of governments to rule. They sharpen class consciousness and point to the most powerful way of achieving social goals. As one US commentator put it: 'at best, strikes are also moments of education and even transformation of workers … strikes open new vistas for workers, thereby clearing the way for higher forms of organisation and consciousness' (Winslow 2010, 8), giving the example of a 1965 wildcat strike of truck drivers:

> Hundreds of striking teamsters milled around City Hall, in defiance of a judge who threatened them with jail … the truck drivers patrolled Philadelphia's streets and stopped all trucking … They blocked highways with overturned trailers and fought pitched battles with police in a guerrilla-type war that continued for several days. (Winslow 2010, 8–9)

No wonder that a leading Marxist, Tony Cliff, argued for the superiority of the strike weapon in the midst of the 1981 British riots, stating that 'we must teach [the kids] to take the bakery, not just the bread' (Birchall 2011, 452).

References

Behrman, S. (2011). Police killings and the law. *International Socialism, 129,* 39–67.

Bennett, A. (2009). *When the lights went out: Britain in the 70s.* London: Faber and Faber.

Birchall, I. (2011). *Tony Cliff: A Marxist for his time.* London: Bookmarks.

Bloom, C. (2010). *Restless revolutionaries: A history of Britain's fight for a republic.* Stroud: History Press.

Bonger, W. (1969). *Criminality and economic conditions.* Bloomington: Indiana University Press.

Brewer, J. (1983). The Wilkites and the law, 1763–74. In J. Brewer & J. Styles (Eds.), *An ungovernable people: The English and their law in the 17th and 18th centuries.* London: Hutchinson.

Brewer, J., & Styles, J. (1983). Introduction. In J. Brewer & J. Styles (Eds.), *An ungovernable people: The English and their law in the 17th and 18th centuries.* London: Hutchinson.

Bushaway, B. (1982). *By Rite: Custom, ceremony and community 1700–1880.* London: Junction Books.

Bushaway, R. (1992). Rite, legitimation and community in southern England, 1700–1850: The ideology of custom. In B. Stapleton (Ed.), *Conflict and community in southern England* (pp. 110–135). Stroud: Alan Sutton.

Carlyle, T. (1889). *The French revolution.* London: Chapman and Hall.

Carlyle, T. (1912) [1843]. *Past and present.* London: Dent.

Clement, M. (2014). Mobs versus markets. In D. Pritchard & F. Pakes (Eds.), *Riot, unrest and protest on the global stage.* Basingstoke: Palgrave Macmillan.

Clement, M. (2015). Thatcher's civilising offensive: The Ridley Plan to decivilise the working class. *Human Figurations, 4*(1). http://hdl.handle.net/2027/spo.11217607.0004.106

Connolly, J. (1910). Labour religion and nationality. https://www.marxists.org/archive/connolly/1910/lnr/index.htm

Creighton, S. (2015). From revolution to new unionism: The impact of "bloody sunday" on the development of John Burn's politics. In K. Flett (Ed.), *A history of riots.* Newcastle: Cambridge Scholars Press.

Davidson, N. (2015). The Scottish pre-industrial urban crowd and the riots against the treaty of union 1705–1707. In K. Flett (Ed.), *A History of Riots*. Newcastle: Cambridge Scholars Press.

Dickens, C. (2004) [1844]. *Martin Chuzzlewit*. London: Penguin.

El-Enany, N. (2014). Innocence charged with guilt, the criminalisation of protest from Peterloo to Millbank. In D. Pritchard & F. Pakes (Eds.), *Riot, unrest and protest on the global stage*. Basingstoke: Palgrave Macmillan.

Gatrell, V. (2013). *The First Bohemians*. London: Allen Lane.

Gilmour, I. (1992). *Riot, risings and revolution*. London: Pimlico.

Griffin, K. (2012). *The rural war*. Manchester: Manchester University Press.

Groves, R. G. (1930, September). Wilkes and liberty, *Labour Monthly*, pp. 509–511. Available at https://www.marxists.org/history/etol/writers/groves/1930/09/wilkes.htm

Hammond, J., & Hammond, B. (1947). *The bleak age*. Harmondsworth: Penguin.

Hibbert, C. (2004). *King mob*. Stroud: Sutton.

Hobsbawm, E. (1972). Social criminality: Distinctions between socio-political and other forms of crime. *Bulletin of the Society for the Study of Labour History, 25*, 5–6.

James, C. L. R. (1983). *The Black Jacobins*. London: Allison and Busby.

Kent, D. (1997). *Popular radicalism and the Swing riots in central Hampshire*. Winchester: Hampshire County Council.

Kent, D., & Townsend, N. (2002). *The convicts of the Eleanor*. London: Merlin.

Lea, J. (1999). Social crime revisited. *Theoretical Criminology, 3*(3), 307–325.

Lefebvre, G. (1973). *The great fear of 1789*. New York: Pantheon.

Malcolmsen, R. (1983). "A set of ungovernable people": The Kingswood colliers in the eighteenth century. In J. Brewer & J. Styles (Eds.), *An ungovernable people: The English and their law in the 17th and 18th centuries*. London: Hutchinson.

Manson, M. (1997). *'Riot!': The Bristol Bridge massacre of 1793*. Bristol: Past & Present Press.

Marx, K., & Engels, F. (1975). *Collected works volume 1 1835–43*. London: Lawrence and Wishart.

Mill, J. S. (1972). *On liberty*. Harmondsworth: Penguin.

OBSP. Old Bailey State papers 1780. http://www.oldbaileyonline.org

Paley, R. (1989). Thief-takers in London in the age of the McDaniel gang *c.* 1745–1754. In D. Hay & F. Snyder (Eds.), *Policing & prosecution in Britain 1750–1850*. Oxford: Clarendon.

Randall, A., & Charlesworth, A. (Eds.). (2000). *The moral economy and popular protest: Riots markets and social conflict.* Basingstoke: Macmillan.

Reddy, W. M. (1977). 'The textile trade and the language of the crowd at Rouen, 1752–1871'. *Past and Present, 74*, 62–89.

Reiss, T. (2012). *The black count: Glory, revolution, betrayal, and the real count of Mont Cristo.* London: Harvill Secker.

Reith, C. (1952). *The blind eye of history.* London: Faber & Faber.

Rudé, G. (1964). *The crowd in history.* Oxford: Oxford University Press.

Rudé, G. (1971). *Hanoverian London 1714–1808.* London: Secker and Warburg.

Rule, J. (1992). Labour consciousness and industrial conflict. In B. Stapleton (Ed.), *Conflict and community in southern England* (pp. 92–110). Stroud: Alan Sutton.

Wells, R. (1992). Popular protest and social crime. In B. Stapleton (Ed.), *Conflict and community in southern England* (pp. 135–182). Stroud: Alan Sutton.

Winslow, C. (2010). Rebellion from below. In A. Brenner, R. Brenner, & C. Winslow (Eds.), *Rebel rank and file: Labour militancy and revolt from below in the long 1970s.* London: Verso.

Wood, A. (2013). *The memory of the people.* Cambridge: Cambridge University Press.

6

1968: Protest and the Growth of a Critical Criminology

Matt Clement and Vincenzo Scalia

This study is framed by the ideas of critical criminology. The perspective was outlined over 40 years ago in *The New Criminology*:

> One of the central purposes of this critique has been to assert the possibility—not only of a fully social theory—but also of a society in which men [*sic*] are able to assert themselves in a fully social fashion. With Marx, we have been concerned with the social arrangements that have obstructed, and the social contradictions that enhance—a state of freedom from material necessity … a set of social arrangements, therefore, in which there would be no politically, economically, and socially-induced need to criminalize deviance. (Taylor et al. 1973, 27)

Here critical criminology echoed the critical view that Marx himself took of the world, in works such as *A Critique of Political Economy*, stressing that it is both possible and necessary to change fundamentally social relations in order that people can live free from the kind of exploitation and oppression that damages their lives. Without recognising this reality, and acting upon it, any analysis is superficial and pointless. Perhaps this view is most succinctly summarised by Marx as 'philosophers have interpreted the world, the point is to change it' (Molyneux 2012). It is this 'central

© The Editor(s) (if applicable) and The Author(s) 2016
M. Clement, *A People's History of Riots, Protest and the Law*,
DOI 10.1057/978-1-137-52751-6_6

purpose' that the new criminologists tended to downplay in later years, and in doing so they moved away from the classical Marxist tradition that I believe is still crucial for developing an appreciative account of how crime figures in capitalist society and what is to be done about the question of law and order.

In order to achieve a more balanced reaction to this phenomenon, we should start by thinking about who are the perpetrators of crime and violence today. Marx agrees that crime is deviance and believes that humanity can create the conditions where criminal tendencies will lessen, that is, a non-exploitative society. This is the 'realm of freedom' for Marx—where a woman or a man realises that freedom is to be obtained 'through the positive power to assert his free individuality':

> If man is unfree in the materialistic sense—that is, free not through the negative capacity to avoid this or that, but through the positive power to assert his free individuality—crime must not be punished in the individual but the anti-social sources of crime must be destroyed to give everyone social scope for the essential assertion of this vitality. If man is formed by circumstances, then his circumstances must be made human. (Marx 1971 [1844], 32–33)

It is interesting to speculate about Marx's meaning here. Particularly striking is the strength of his assertion that 'crime must not be punished in the individual'. This is blunt and to the point: blaming, and therefore punishing, people for criminal actions addresses the symptoms rather than the causes. Marx here is not excusing crimes or seeking to paint their impact as minimal, neither is he suggesting that there is some principled reason for every criminal act. But he is telling those who advocate punishing criminals that their action is pointless: punishment cannot prevent crimes as long as the society in which the act occurred is based upon the kind of exploitation, oppression, racism and sexism which twists human relations—these are 'the anti-social sources of crime'.

The point that should be taken by those of us studying crime and deviance is that the very norms of society—whether ancient, feudal or capitalist in its pattern of relations—are themselves deviant. They function within a hierarchy whose control is based on their ability to monopolise the means of violence sufficiently to prevent the mass of the population choosing the truly social option of controlling society for themselves collectively through democratic systems of their own devising. Furthermore, of course, that physical control is buttressed by the ideological control, summarised in Marx's famous phrase, 'the ruling ideas in society are the ideas of the ruling class', so that these—what would in other circumstances be 'common sense'—ideas of popular democracy are demonised by those in power and their mouthpieces in the media, education and the political mainstream; they are characterised as the dreaded 'rule of the mob'. For Marx, such a society, whose ruling institutions are tyrannical because they prevent human freedom, is itself deviant and in many ways is essentially criminal and therefore 'must be destroyed'.

This is why crime cannot be explained or reformed without addressing the central question of political power, the state and its methods of social control. Of course not all states or governments are the same, but nowhere can they be ignored. Marxist ideas of this nature were applied quite extensively within criminology in America, Britain and Europe in the late 1960s and 1970s, and many important insights into the issues emerged during this period. Marxists believe people's ideas evolve in relation to their material conditions and, crucially, the social relations between the exploited and oppressed and their rulers. A recent discussion of critical criminology quotes Marx and Engels's definition in *The German Ideology*: 'if power is taken as the basis of right, as Hobbes etc. do then right, law, etc. are merely the symptom, the expression of other relations upon which state power rests' (Ugwudike 2015, 213). Therefore:

> Crime is the expression of the struggle of the isolated individual against the prevailing conditions, whilst also being a struggle conditioned by those prevailing conditions: A dialectical tension is apparent between man [or woman] as a determining actor (exercising free will) and man as an actor whose 'will' is a product of his times. (Ugwudike 2015, 215)

So it is logical to explain how the rising tide of struggle against war, oppression and economic exploitation undermined the hold of those rulers' ideas—what the Italian Marxist Antonio Gramsci called their hegemony. From the mid-1960s to the mid-1970s in much of Europe and the USA, there was an increase in the belief of the usefulness of protest and struggle as a vehicle to realise social change, caused partly by the increased visibility of such events, but also by the way in which the act of protest itself seemed to change people's consciousnesses of the possibilities of changing society more generally.

Many years of working alongside people from working-class backgrounds who have found themselves excluded from labour markets and educational institutions through no fault of their own has provided the authors with that 'insider's outlook' which actively resists the labelling process that marks people out as 'outsiders' and somehow as deviating from a set of 'norms'. David Matza believed that this appreciative outlook was essential for a true contextualisation of the situation of that part of society which is often termed deviant, marginal or even precarious. After all, even a zero hours contract looks like a valid employment solution from the point of view of the employer—whereas for the worker a much richer, truer and more three-dimensional appreciation of the impact of such an arrangement is evident.

This is an approach that sociologists of deviance such as David Matza, Howard Becker and Jock Young explored and appreciated in the early 1960s: do not condemn the deviant, examine the label, appreciate the context and imagine the feelings of any one of us in that situation in order to treat people with the empathy that helps explain the 'deviant phenomenon' in question. Matza spends a lengthy part of his *Becoming Deviant* analysing in depth all the implications held within Becker's article, 'Becoming a Marijuana User'. He believed it was understanding the process itself, that is learning to smoke, and learning to appreciate the effects of smoking within a shared experience typical of the Jazz musician lifestyle of his subjects, that was crucial to developing an appreciative outlook:

> He is open to a consideration of the problem from inside it … he first discovers that the deviation is an experience with its own features and problems … inside the phenomenon, actually doing the thing and possibly being with others who also do it, the subject becomes so situated as to sense the meaning of affinity. He builds its meaning. (Matza 1969, 117–118)

Jock Young extended this notion into the expanding drug-taking figuration of the late 1960s in both his contribution to 'Images of Deviance' and (Young 1971a) *The Drugtakers* (Young 1971b). His findings proved that social stigma and establishment paranoia about such behaviour was actually creating amplification spirals within so-called deviant lifestyles—as cannabis and heroin users found themselves ghettoised together and a counter-cultural habitus emerged in reaction against the 'establishment view'. Young's solutions were based upon counselling, self-help and encouraging society to see drug use as a 'normal' illness to be treated, rather than a moral vacuum to be condemned. Not only have his predictions been thoroughly vindicated, that recreational drug use would explode unless society learned to condemn a little less and understand a little more, but his prescribed solutions are now the norm in clinical practice—whereas they looked outlandishly progressive and dangerous to the authorities at the time.

Mentioning the establishment points to another sociologist who looked at these problems in the 1960s. Norbert Elias and John Scotson's *The Established and the Outsiders* was written in 1965 and also reinforces the idea that it is only possible to research the world of the outsider within the context of the establishment that places them there. The established are very keen to discuss the shortcomings of the outsiders, but what about themselves? The authors write that:

> The self-enhancing quality of a high power ratio flatters the collective self-love which is also the reward for submission to group-specific norms, to patterns of affect restraint characteristic of that group and believed to be lacking in less powerful 'inferior' groups, outsiders and outcasts. (Elias et al. 2008, 30)

I contend that an appreciative account that sees the world from the point of view of those labelled as outsiders can provide a truer picture of the situation than the stigmatising discourse so prevalent today that places so-called 'working families' at the epicentre of its norms and roundly condemns all others. Critical criminologists insist that it is impossible to understand fully a social phenomenon such as that labelled 'criminal' in a rounded and balanced way without appreciating its context. And 'appreciation of deviant phenomenon requires a consideration of the sub-ject's viewpoint' (Matza 1969, 18). This perspective was for a while so well-established as to be in the mainstream of criminological thinking, but over the last 30 years these views have been extensively criticised as 'left idealist' and the sociology of the process of 'becoming deviant' has been sidelined. This study of riot, protest and the law marks an attempt to return it to the centre of the criminological imagination.

Why is this important? Recent studies of riots, in the UK in particular, have tended to focus on this phenomenon as symptomatic of people who are in some way damaged and/or blinkered: even commentators who are critical of capitalism tend to regard riots as dysfunctional alienated acts of flawed consumers (Bauman 2011) or as an inarticulate politics (Winlow and Hall 2012). This theorising runs the risk of both alienating the rioters themselves and those who are supportive of their acts of protest. Matza remarked that 'intimate knowledge of deviant worlds tends to subvert the correctional conception of pathology' (Matza 1969, 25). Obviously, if people are not rioting and protesting because there is something wrong with them, then the emphasis fall back upon the 'anti-social sources' of the deviant act: how can the rioters' circumstances be humanised? If this means achieving 'a state of freedom from material necessity' then stu-dents of riot and protest need to appreciate how the act of resistance can be a step towards achieving it. 'Those who do not move do not notice their chains', declared the Polish/German communist Rosa Luxemburg. By acting for themselves, the activist/protestor/rioter embarks upon the process of losing their illusions about the world around them and of start-ing to believe that there is an alternative to blindly accepting their subor-dinate status in the social order:

> For Marxist criminologists, deviance is not objectively immoral and illegal, but a socially constructed label that the state and its agents attach to acts of rebellion against oppression; crime, then, is a political act … individuals who react against exploitative economic conditions, unequal wealth distribution and class conflict in capitalist societies are criminalised to protect the powerful. Therefore, the best strategy for eradicating crime is to transform society and restore equality. (Ugwudike 2015, 87)

Those people subject to the institutionalised discrimination of states and their agents of social control often find themselves labelled as deviant on the basis of ethnicity or membership of an undesirable group as defined by those in power. Resistance to such an arbitrary and unjust approach is surely inevitable in most circumstances. As Patel and Tyrer comment, 'black and minority ethnic victims of such a racist discipline do not passively accept their marginalised position. Rather, at different points and to varying degrees a form of resistance often takes place'. They are also clear as to its purpose:

> This resistance … seeks to free its victims from a system that is dominated by agents of a state whose aim is to maintain white power, regulation, control and authority over the black and minority ethnic body. (Patel and Tyrer 2011, 13)

Of course, this resistance is not always expressed in an overt way. A sense of powerlessness can ensure it remains real but hidden:

> The greater the duplicity in power between dominant and subordinate and the more arbitrarily it is exercised, the more the public transcript of subordinates will take on a stereotyped, ritualistic cast. In other words, the more menacing the power, the thicker the mask. (Scott 1990, 3)

The thickness of the mask of consent has often fooled observers—even those sympathetic to revolt—into believing that people are unwilling to express their opposition or are actually incapable of resistance—despite the many objective structural features of inequality, injustice, exploitation and violence that bear down on the vast majority of the world's peoples. Paul Willis believes this to be false, declaring 'structuralist theories of reproduction present the dominant ideology under which culture is subsumed as impenetrable. Everything fits too neatly. There are no cracks in the billiard ball of process' (Willis 1977, 175). For Scott, this is proven by 'the persistent existence of resistance':

> Even in the relatively stable industrial democracies to which the theories of hegemony were meant to apply, their strongest formulation simply does not allow for the degree of social conflict and process that actually occurs. (Scott 1990, 78)

He identifies 'hidden transcripts' of resistance and subversion which to him prove that the oppressed mass of society feel and resent their oppression constantly. Their decision to act upon it in open rebellion is tactical rather than a product of ignorance or blindness to social reality: 'tactical prudence ensures that subordinate groups rarely blurt out their hidden transcript directly' (Scott 1990, 15). Collective action is often the means by which this hidden resentment bursts out into overt acts of riot and protest. What happens within a crowd, a significant grouping, that changes people's sense of what is possible? According to John Berger:

> A mass demonstration distinguishes itself from other mass crowds because it congregates in public to create its function, instead of forming in response to one … It is an assembly which challenges what is given by the mere fact of its coming together. (Berger 1968)

By drawing upon examples of resistance from the past as well as the present, one idea this study aims to endorse is that groups of people involved in social movements and human figurations are more than capable of making a better world. Scott's description of 'the arts of resistance' is pertinent here in answering those criminologists who believe that resistance is useless:

> The obstacles to resistance, which are many, are simply not attributable to the inability of subordinate groups to imagine a counterfactual social order. They do imagine both the reversal and negation of their domination, and, most important, they have acted on these values in desperation and on those rare occasions when the circumstances allowed. (Scott 1990, 81)

Writing in May 1968, in the midst of the mass strikes and demonstrations across France, Berger saw crowd action as central to the growth of a revolutionary consciousness:

> The truth is that mass demonstrations are rehearsals for revolution: not strategic or even tactical ones, but rehearsals of revolutionary awareness … The importance of the numbers involved is to be found in the direct experience of those taking part in or sympathetically witnessing the demonstration. For them the numbers cease to be numbers and become the evidence

of their senses, the conclusions of their imagination. The larger the demonstration, the more powerful and immediate (visible, audible, tangible) a metaphor it becomes for their total collective strength. (Berger 1968)

Berger's radical perspective was shaped by his times. Another prominent '68er, Chris Harman, founder member of the London School of Economics Socialist Society and the Vietnam Solidarity Campaign, and a life-long revolutionary, wrote:

> There are millions of people throughout the world who still feel their lives were changed decisively by what happened in those 12 months … the year that the peasant guerrillas of one of the world's smaller nations stood up to the mightiest power in human history. It was the year the black ghettos of the US rose in revolt to protest at the murder of the leader of non-violence, Martin Luther King … the year the Mexican government massacred more than a hundred demonstrators … above all, the year that the biggest general strike ever paralysed France and caused its government to panic. (Harman 1988, 7)

He maintained 'the shock waves broke the fetters on the minds of many people' (Harman 1988, viii). They were free to think differently, hence the slogan 'All power to the imagination' that celebrated humans' ability to change their living conditions far more fundamentally—to move beyond ideas of the free market and the status quo, beyond individual dreams of achieving better opportunities within this life, to collective visions of how the world can be controlled democratically, embodying social justice and equality. Again it is useful to consider the impact from the perspective of the participants themselves. Twenty-five years earlier France was occupied by the Nazis. Being part of a movement of resistance at that time was a patriotic duty as well as a practical necessity to avoid their brutal oppression. It was led by the same de Gaulle who had now become an authoritarian president himself. Moreover France's withdrawal from Vietnam and Algeria, following *their* widespread resistance to imperial occupation, had been accompanied by violence on the streets of Paris:

> The calculated use of state violence against the Algerian community in Paris planned and executed by the Parisien préfect de police Maurice

Papon—whose qualifications for office included the persecution of the Jews of Bordeaux under Vichy and the ruthless colonial repression in Morocco and Algeria—culminated in the hunt and murder of over 200 demonstrators by the police in Paris a year later on 17 October 1961. (Caygill 2013, 1)

Once again, as so often in this study, the violence of police repression was a major factor in detonating '*l'explosion*' of Paris in May 1968: 'whereas in Britain, West Germany or Scandinavia, the use of the police was rarely a feature of industrial disputes in the 1960s, in France they played a central role' (Harman 1988, 92). The other factor was the 'austerity' whereby the government of General de Gaulle more than doubled the number of students from 200,000 in 1960 to 550,000 in 1968 without spending the extra money required. Faculties were massively understaffed and over-crowded and 60% of students dropped out. When students protested about issues such as being unable to access the language labs or the university banning male students from visiting female students' residences, the government reacted harshly: the police were sent in to enforce the authorities' decision to close down the university. Harman describes the scene on 10–11 May:

> Then, around 10 o'clock, the demonstrators found the police had barred their way across the bridges of the Seine. The police aim was to bottle up the protest in the streets around the Boulevard Saint Michel. The students turned the police's tactics inside out, creating a 'liberated', police-free area by throwing up barricades in all the adjoining streets—to the traffic signs, grilles and cobblestones were added scores of overturned cars, material from nearby building sites … They were joined on the barricades, from which red and black flags flew, by large numbers of young workers. (Harman 1988, 84)

The students were defending themselves, and inspiring the workers through their acts of riot and protest. Therefore, when the police 'cracked down', they fought back:

> Again and again the police charged the barricades, shooting tear gas and percussion grenades, beating up anyone—student, worker or simply passer-by—who fell into their hands. The demonstrators threw everything

at hand at the police—cobblestones ripped up from the street, tear gas canisters and grenades that had not exploded ... the police were forced to halt their offensive. It took them four hours to regain control of the area. (Harman 1988, 85)

The unions called for a one-day general strike on Monday, 13 May, which was the largest since the city was liberated from Nazi control in 1944, with hundreds of thousands united under the banner 'Students, teachers, workers, solidarity'. The atmosphere was euphoric and liberating, not least because the government had backed down—they let students occupy the university that night and the police maintained a low profile. The problem was that the protestors had learnt from their success. As one union leader described it:

First of all ... action pays ... No one thought 'the old man' [de Gaulle] would be beaten in the streets. 'The old man' didn't say anything ... People had never imagined themselves so strong. All the barriers the government had erected against strikes had been broken ... The government was incapable of making people respect its laws ... The result was workers discovered it was possible to fight, and that when you fight well, not only is there the chance of winning, but the risks involved are quite small ... From that to action to resolve old problems was only a small step. (Harman 1988, 97–98)

At this time the month of May in France became a festival of the oppressed as workers in their millions took action, occupying their workplaces in acts of 'contestation' that challenged the established authority. This went far wider than just revolting students or manual workers. Architects, planners, medical students, artists, film-makers, footballers and small farmers all protested and occupied their workplaces. Even the dancers from the Folies-Bergère struck for higher wages. Revolution seemed a possibility as de Gaulle fled the country. Significant wage rises were granted as France's rulers retreated in the face of this massive crowd action. Tragically, the willingness of the largest political voice in the working-class movement, the French Communist Party, to go along with de Gaulle's call for fresh elections and in the meantime call for a return to work, led to a return to 'normality'.

Criminalisation Through Force: How Social Demand Turned into Terrorism

Post-war Italy provides a fertile field to analyse social and political riots, their development and the response of repressive state apparatuses. Firstly, Italy is a singular case, as it combines aspects of an industrialised country with elements of backwardness, being what Immanuel Wallerstein (1974) would call a 'semi-central' area of the world economy. Despite the fact that Italy was, in the 1970s, the tenth most industrialised country in the world, massive emigration to northern Europe, Canada and Australia still occurred, and internal migration was a matter of fact, if we consider that 5,000,000 Southerners and Islanders moved to the northern industrialised areas between 1951 and 1971 (www.istat.it2015).

The abrupt industrialisation led to the breakout of social and political conflicts, such us the mass workers struggle for better wages and work conditions (Panzieri 1962), which was carried out by the more precariously employed ranks of southern Italians recruited to the factories of Turin and Milan. Their character was different from the 'traditional' workers' struggles carried out by the skilled northern workers. This period also witnessed the women's liberation movement's fight to get rid of the clerical-fascist legacy, which kept Italian women oppressed, and the student revolts against the Christian Democrat-hegemonised patronage model of government (Moroni and Balestrini 1997). Other struggles, such as for the improvement of prison conditions and the abolition of asylums (Crainz 2004; NAP 1973; Basaglia 1977), developed after all this social and political unrest, which broke out quite spontaneously and overran the traditional left-wing context, dominated by the Italian Confederation of Labour CGIL trade unions and the Italian Communist Party (PCI).

Secondly, the Italian riots occurred within quite a contradictory political framework. Despite the fact that Italy had been a democratic state since 1946, becoming a republic and adopting an advanced constitution, many laws dating back to fascism, such as those which enforced the rights of employers or which restricted the rights to strike, were never repealed. Moreover, the state apparatuses were still teeming with fascist personnel: judges, police officers, bureaucrats and schoolmasters appointed by the previous regime were never removed, and among them prevailed the same attitude to law and order. The consequence was a typically authoritarian reaction to acts of social and political protest (Ginsborg 1991). Since 1967, when the University of Pisa student Soriano Ceccanti was paralysed by a bullet fired by a police officer attending a demonstration, violent state repression became a regular aspect of the Italian riots, culminating in the Legge Reale (Real Act) of 1975, which gave police forces the licence to kill.

Finally, Italy was, between 1946 and 1991, a 'borderline country' because it was not only adjacent to the iron curtain, but also had the strongest communist party in Western Europe, whose peak was between 1975 and 1976, when the communists gained control of the local councils in most of the main cities. Rome, Milan, Naples, Turin, Genoa, Bologna, Florence and Venice, as well as many other minor cities, elected either a communist or a communist-backed mayor. In the 1976 general election, the PCI gained 34.4% of votes, forcing the Christian Democrats into the 'national solidarity' government proposed three years before by the communist leader Enrico Berlinguer. The authorities then manufactured a full-scale moral panic about the country collapsing into political extremism. The 'red scare' was fought both by legal means, such as the mobilisation of traditional Catholic forces, as in the case of anti-divorce and anti-abortion movements, and through the tolerance by the government of neo-fascist organisations, such as Avanguardia Nazionale and Ordine Nuovo. Neo-fascists were actively involved in the so-called 'strategy of tension', which cruelly manifested itself in the several *stragi di stato* (state slaughters), or the explosion of bombs in public places: Milan (1969), Brescia (1974), San Benedetto Val di Sambro (1974) and Bologna (1980) (Ferraresi 1993). Moreover, two coup attempts in 1964 and 1970, named Piano Solo and Golpe Borghese, occurred. It is a common assumption in social science that 1945–75 were decades of consensus in Western Europe, but events in France and Italy show otherwise. De Gaulle had effectively suspended democracy and ruled a 'presidential republic' from 1958 to 1968: the attempted coups in Italy occurred in the context of military dictatorships holding power in Portugal and Spain until the mid-1970s, and seizing control in Greece in the same period. The lesson of history is that the violence of the rulers triggers a reaction from the repressed—just as in England in 1688—'that the violent compression of so powerful and elastic a spring would be followed by as violent a recoil' (Macaulay 1989, 350).

The point we aim to make in this chapter is that the repression of riots in Italy is the consequence of the deviance amplification strategy (Cohen 1973), enacted by the Italian governments. In the first stage, Christian-Democrat governments chose outright repression, both through public demonstration and through state slaughter. In this stage, the strategy was not very successful both because the state slaughters mobilised anti-fascist and democratic public opinion to create a mass reaction, and because the struggles for better working and living conditions bridged the gap between the old and the new left-wing forces. In this stage of mass struggle, so-called terrorist organisations like the Red Brigades were a marginal force; though part of the resistance movement they were not yet committed to the tactic of armed struggle.

It was in the second stage, when repression through *isolation* was enacted, that riots deteriorated into terrorism. This occurred because the old left, namely the PCI, changed their attitudes. The communist leader, Enrico Berlinguer, implemented from 1973, following the Chilean coup, the *historic compromise* strategy. He argued for the evolution of the PCI into a democratic, governmental party to prevent any authoritarian degeneration of the fragile Italian republic. In Berlinguer's view, the PCI should have been the 'democratic dam' of Italian politics (Valentini 1993). For this purpose, an alliance with the Democratic Catholics (DC) was necessary in order to stimulate the democratic forces of the ruling Catholic Party and to isolate the right-wing forces. The first stage of historical compromise was a 'national solidarity' government, which the communists first backed from outside, then as an organic part of the parliamentary majority. Austerity—necessitating mass dismissals and public expenditure cuts—was the main plank of the policy of the national solidarity government. The communist CGIL union backed the government's programmes in the so-called '*svolta dell'EUR*' (EUR turn) of 1977, in a congress where the idea that dismissals could benefit the economy and create new jobs in the long term gained the support of the majority of trade union delegates (Scalzone 2001). National solidarity was set against a context of hard economic recession, which broke out after the 1973 oil crisis. Mass unemployment spread not only among the working class, but also among the middle class, whose expectation of upward mobility through education were disappointed. A new 'youth proletariat', urban, educated and politicised, spread across the country, criticising the historical compromise, which in turn unleashed the reaction of the PCI, who labelled these protestors as 'new squads', recalling the origins of fascism. As in France in 1968, the Left was demobilising those elements who were trying to maintain the struggle for better conditions.

The police repression of social movements in 1977 dug a gap between the old and the new Left, making room for the rise of the Red Brigades, as well as of new armed groups such as Prima Linea (Front Line), Formazioni Comuniste Combattenti (Fighting Communist Groups) and Comitati Comunisti Rivoluzionari (Revolutionary Communist Committees). All these groups theorised and practised what they called an armed uprising against the party-state, which was later to result in a defeat both of their project and of the whole social movement, paving the way for the *riflusso* (roll-back), out of which the new neo-liberal Right arose. The thesis of this chapter is that widespread social movements deteriorated into terrorism because of repression and, in particular, of isolation. All the special laws against social movements were passed with the active support of the PCI, which prevented any contamination between the old and the new Left and made armed struggle the only possible form of social and political opposition. There were left organisations who looked to maintain the mass struggle but they were derailed by events and the shortcomings of their own political strategies (Harman 1979).

In order to demonstrate this, we will focus on a case study of the riots and political fights occurring in Milan in the 1970s. We chose Milan not only because it is the main economic centre of Italy, but also because the Lombard metropolis contains all the contradictions and transformation Italy underwent in the post-war period. We will differentiate between *union* riots, or the movement for better work conditions, wage rises and better schooling, and *social* riots, carried out by the new youth proletariat. The former occurred between 1969 and 1975, and still faced a common ground between the old and the new Left. The latter occurred between 1975, when the Legge Reale was approved, and 1979, which saw the rift between the two lefts resulting in a violent clash embittered by such events as the Moro Affair and the 7 Aprile case, when 62,000 extra-parliamentary left-wing members were reported by the judge and special prisons were created for political opponents. The Legge Reale was a watershed, as its outspokenly repressive aims spread across the movements the idea that it was necessary to reply with violence to state violence, as summarised by the slogan *mai più senza fucile* (no more without a gun). This strategy proved to be wrong, not only because the balance of forces between the state apparatus and relatively unorganised students was uneven, but also because its outcome was an escalation of violence which caused both the criminalisation of social movements and the triggering of harsh repressive measures, ranging from special laws to special prisons.

The Moon Behind Your Door: Milan and the Rise of Social Movements

From 1951 to 1971, the population of Milan grew from 1,300,000 to 1,750,000. The growth was even more significant in the province, whose population rose from 2,200,000 to 4,000,000 (www.istat2015.it). This massive increase turned this area of the Po Valley from agricultural land into the heart of Greater Milan, a metropolitan area of more than 8,000,000 people. The new Milanese inhabitants came from every corner of Italy, though most of them were of southern origin, mainly Apulians (Montaldi and Alasia 1998, II ed.). The backbone of immigration consisted of the so-called 'mass workers', that is former peasants who were employed as unskilled workers in the factories operating in Milan. Intellectual migration was also important, as well as a peculiar group of former prostitutes from the areas of Veneto and Ferrara who settled in the metropolis as owners of laundries. Milan became the centre of Italy's economic boom in the 1960s, consolidating its reputation as the 'moral capital' of the country, against the decaying, bureaucratic and parasitic Rome. International successes, such as that of the two football teams, AC Milan and Inter Milan, who won the Champions League four times between 1963 and 1969, boosted the presentation of Milan as a modern, dynamic and rich city.

Behind this glamourous veil, social and political unrest was growing in Milan. Firstly, the traditional capital/labour conflict was taking a new shape. The new working class, mostly southern Italian, was unskilled, working on assembly lines, devoid of any political awareness, class identity or historical memory at all (Balestrini 1969; Fofi 1961). They were usually hired after bringing the bosses a letter from their village priests and police constables, which ensured the employers they were not about to hire 'subversive' people. Mass immigration caused a worsening of the conditions of the Milanese working class, both in terms of wages and professional identity. The *crumiri terroni* (southern scabs) were blamed for destroying the labourers' unity and were kept out of such institutions as the trade unions and the left-wing parties.

Secondly, the improvement of material conditions and the elevation of compulsory education from five to eight years in 1963 (Rossanda 1992) resulted in a massive growth of secondary education and university students. Studying was regarded more and more as a means of upward social mobility; an attitude that met the labour market requirement. Unfortunately, assembly line work was spreading also among aspiring white-collar workers (Panzieri cit.; Tronti 1970), disappointing the hopes of those who thought of getting a well-paid, skilled jobs through higher education.

Thirdly, the abrupt industrialisation and urbanisation brought about new challenges to lifestyles. Women became more and more involved in public life, both as workers and as students. Claims for women's emancipation were even sharper in a country whose laws, at that time, stated that women had to obey their husband and could be sentenced for adultery if they ever had a child from a married man. Those who believed Catholic morality was too backward and unfit in a modern society, such as the hippy magazine *Re Nudo* (*Naked King*), campaigned for more liberal lifestyles also.

For Italy, 1968 and 1969 were years of intense social and political mobilisation; some authors (Scalzone 1992) call them the second 'red years' (*biennio rosso*) after the one in 1918–19. Mass workers, mass students, women and libertarians coalesced into a radical social movement, which challenged the existing social, economic and political pattern. Following the anti-war protests and the Paris riots, students occupied the two main universities of Milan—Statale and Cattolica—from early 1968, taking politicians and police forces aback. Their protest, though, would have remained isolated without a connection with the workers' struggles. Many students paid for their studies by working part-time in factories. Others went to the gates of factories to distribute leaflets advertising their political activities, as the myth of the *terroni crumiri* was quite popular also among students. The new working class was about to take by surprise Italian public opinion. *Gatto selvaggio* (wild cat) style strikes broke out across the industrial areas of Northern Italy. It was a peculiarly striking technique (Revelli 1993), as the strikers stopped production out of the blue and started demonstrating across the factory by drumming, singing and dancing, after the fashion of Southern Italian popular feasts, inviting the other workers to join them. The outcome of the strike was the occupation and picketing of factories, which were directed by spontaneous committees, independent of either the left-wing parties or the trade unions. Students and people outside the factory, as well as the workers of other factories, were also admitted into committees, the most famous of which was the Comitato Unitario di Base (CUB, Rank and File Unitarian Committee), founded in the Bicocca Pirelli factory, out of which the Red Brigades were born, though only from a small fraction of it.

The consequence of these two years of political turmoil was a massive reshuffling of the Italian left's political spectrum. The PCI gained the reputation of being an old-fashioned, Stalinist, conservative party, particularly after 1969 when a group of Central Committee members, who had founded the magazine, later a newspaper, *Il Manifesto*, were expelled for criticising the Soviet invasion of Czechoslovakia during the party congress, forcing the Soviet delegation to leave the room (Rossanda 2005). *Il Manifesto* was the first extra-parliamentary group founded in those years. They mainly focused on moving the PCI leftward, by linking the working class with the new social groups which had emerged among the social movements (Edited Book 1973). Lotta Continua (LC, Continuous Struggle) was founded in Turin in 1969, combining mass workers with students. They argued for a wide-ranging struggle, embracing such libertarian issues as the legalisation of drugs and the emancipation of women, and, in particular, the need to side with the dispossessed, the under-proletariat, that is the Southern Italian lower classes.

Potere Operaio (PO, Workers' Power), founded in Venice in 1969, later to become Autonomia Operaia (Workers' Autonomy) (Caminiti 2008), argued that capitalist hegemony reached far beyond the factory gates. It was then necessary to boycott the capitalist way of production, both by engaging in actions of Luddism inside the factory, and by practising mass illegality in the city, as well as creating a relational productive network not based on capitalist hegemony. Avanguardia Operaia (Working Class Vanguard) theorised the need for a new Leninist vanguard to be created among mass workers to lead the revolutionary process. Finally, the last important organised group was the Movimento dei Lavoratori e degli Studenti (MLS, Workers and Students Movement), whose militants were mainly students of Statale University, and who enacted a Stalinist strategy of hegemonising the extra-parliamentary groups through their protection squad, dubbed Katanghesi (Katangans), who used motorcycle helmets and wrenches to club down other groups' militants. Given the youth of many of these activists and the cultural climate, it was as if the subcultures of deviance seen on the streets of Britain and America were represented in the workplaces in Italy. Even though all of these organisations had their own private protection squads, which later on evolved into paramilitary groups (Della Porta 1997), the Katanghesi were known for their outright brutality. LC was the most popular movement across the country, whereas PO and *Il Manifesto* gained a reputation for their refined Marxist analysis, as they could rely on such key thinkers as Toni Negri, Valentino Parlato and Rossana Rossanda and involved in their discussions such internationally renowned thinkers as Louis Althusser (Manifesto 1978). Also for this reason, the *Il Manifesto* militants rarely engaged in riot initiatives, so that the others dubbed them 'the professors'.

Riots in Milan began in 1968 through an initiative of the MLS leader, Mario Capanna (Capanna 1988), who organized a demonstration against the premier of the Theatre Alla Scala in Milan, an event in which the Milanese bourgeoisie invites the most outstanding international VIPs. Workers and students awaited for the attendants, and, as Capanna started a speech about class differences and hardships, some of the demonstrators threw rotten eggs at the furs of the upper-class ladies. Demonstrators rejected the order to stop, issued by the Milan Chief of Police, who ordered his men to clamp down on the rioter. Capanna kept speaking, but, at this point, he addressed the police forces, reminding them they were from the same southern, lower-class background as most of the demonstrators, and that they shared the same economic hardships, yet that night they had to protect those people who forced them to lead a hard life. Some policemen started crying on hearing this speech, and the police chief himself ordered his forces back just so as to cordon the theatre off from the demonstrators. This episode gained both the MLS and the Katanghesi a couple of years of hegemony among the Milanese social movements, which reached its peak in December 1970, when the police fired tear gas against the demonstrators commemorating the Piazza Fontana slaughter. The Katanghesi member Saverio Saltarelli died from a tear gas bullet blasted into the middle of his chest.

After 1970, as the other groups gained more followers and started an increased active campaign on the territory, the MLS idea of a homogeneous movement through the paramilitary support of the Katanghesi changed the balance between the groups. They remained restricted to the Statale, tried to establish connections with factory workers, and accused other groups of being rooted in the petty bourgeoisie, though their Stalinist approach was ruled out, partly because the social movements erupted in a plurality of directions and performed different actions:

(1) Sabotage, occupation and picketing of factories to improve work conditions. Lotta Continua (LC), Potere Operaie (PO) and Avanguardia Operaia (AO) took the lead in these initiatives, which rapidly gained the consent of those section of the working class, that is, mass workers, who were reluctant to accept the discipline and mediation-oriented policies proposed both by the PCI and by the CGIL.

(2) *Spesa proletaria* (proletarian shopping), mostly organized by LC and AO. This consisted of entering supermarkets, taking the goods and paying for them below their price, or, sometimes, stealing them. The *spesa proletaria* raised discussion about the goods to be targeted; whereas LC claimed the need to buy the primary good and to pay for them at a low price, PO were more keen on stealing goods, including such luxury goods as champagne, claiming 'the right to luxury' of proletarians.

(3) *Autoriduzioni* (self-discount), organized and practised by all the groups, consisted of paying for concerts, the cinema, shows and bus tickets at half or a quarter of the prices, as a means to attend public events or using public transport for students and workers.

(4) *Mercati rossi* (red markets), organized by LC, wherein food and clothes to meet basic needs were sold at cheap prices.

(5) *Antifascismo militante* (militant antifascism), consisted of beating fascist militants, assaulting the headquarters of fascist organizations and parties, and robbing and vandalising shops belonging to alleged fascist shopkeepers. All the groups were actively engaged in *antifascismo militante*. There were tragicomic episodes, such as what happened in Milan in 1971, when an American tourist raised his hands to call a cab and two Katanghesi, thinking he was making the fascist salute, beat him. Or the tragic episodes such as the beating and killing of the 17-year-old fascist student Sergio Ramelli by a few AO members.

(6) *Campagna delle fabbriche* (factory campaign). This was a typical initiative by the Red Brigades. It consisted of scaring either the line managers (*capetti*) or the fascist trade unionists by damaging their belongings (mainly their cars), abducting them, shaming them publicly by tying them to a pole with a board stating such things as 'I am a fascist pig' or 'I suck the workers' blood.

(7) Facing the police forces in demonstrations. All the groups usually reached a certain degree of unity in these cases, as they met the day before and divided their task. As Italy has two police forces, that is the police, active in the main cities, and the *carabinieri*, a military body policing the national territory, they planned how to dodge the clamp downs, for example by deciding that a part of the demonstrators should face the PS and another group would face the CC. All the groups had their paramilitary squads *(servizio d'ordine)*, who directed their own militants and provided them with such weapons as stones, cobblestones, iron and glass balls, bolts and nuts, which were to be thrown against the police forces.

(8) School and university occupations.

(9) Occupation of council flats for the homeless, mostly led by LC and PO.

(10) Armed robberies to support the group financially. These were typical of PO and usually took place outside Milan so they would not be recognised (Pozzi 1977).

Besides these riot-oriented initiatives, there were other political activities: the creation of clandestine hospitals to help access to abortion, which
involved the activity of 'comrade' doctors and nurses (abortion was only
legalised in 1978); the creation of alternative kindergartens, nursing centres and school assistance for the children of workers; the setting up of
committees to support the jailed comrades, also involving lawyers, journalists and such artists as Dario Fo; the creation of the so-called *circoli del
proletariato giovanile* (young workers' circles), meeting places which were
subsequently to evolve into alternative, libertarian places. One of these
was the Macondo, founded by the LC, and where hashish and marijuana
were sold freely, which was later to be closed by the police because it had,
indeed, turned into a haven for drug pushers and junkies. As Jock Young
theorised, the stigma visited upon drug use by mainstream society ghettoised the users into an introverted counter-culture which tended to separate them off, reinforcing society's idea of their 'deviance' (Young 1971a).

Political actions were usually decided by the *collettivi di quartiere* (district committees), in which all the groups took part, despite the fact some
prevailed over others. Moreover, some of the *collettivi* decided to develop
their own structure and political activity apart from other groups, and
evolved into independent structures. Such was the case of the Banda
Bellini (Bellini Gang) (Philopat 2002), founded by the Bellini brothers,
sons of the famous Milanese partisan, based in the working-class district
of Casoretto. Their rejection of unity brought about some conflicts with
other groups, but mostly gained them a positive reputation among the
militants for their openly facing and fighting the Stalinist attitude of the
Katanghesi. Another *collettivo* who sought its own way, which we will discuss shortly, was the one located in Porta Vittoria, a mixed-class district
in east Milan.

Riots were a widespread practice, partly spontaneous—to the extent
they did not emanate from a decision made by bureaucratic structures—
partly organised—as the *collettivi* had, to a certain extent, a permanent
structure, though there was no formal leadership and everyone was able
to participate at meetings and no regular commitment was required. The
extra-parliamentary Left had gained, at this point, a political and military
hegemony over the territory, which made them able to confront police
forces in their repressive actions. This situation ended up alarming both

the conservative forces and the PCI. The second half of the 1970s led to a change of this situation, ending in the decline of riots and in their repression after the abduction of Aldo Moro by the Red Brigades.

Mai più senza fucile: The Armed Degeneration of Riots

The economic crisis, which broke out in 1973, plunged Italy into a ten-year recession, with inflation rates soaring to 22% in 1980, giving legitimacy to the policy of industrial restructuring which gained the consent of trade unions in 1977. Moreover, the Chilean coup of 1973 made the PCI secretary, Enrico Berlinguer, argue for the impossibility of a left-wing government, making him search for an alliance with the 'democratic catholics', that is the DC, the outcome of which was the national solidarity governments of 1976–79. These two events broke the thin red thread that had kept the old and the new Left together under the shield of anti-fascism, giving force to the workers' request for better wages and conditions.

The PCI boosted its 'democratic' transformation, interpreting the 1975 victory in local elections as a request for moderation and responsibility, that is, as an approval of an historical compromise. The extra-parliamentary Left entered a deep crisis, because the rising unemployment attracted in its ranks wide layers of both skilled and unskilled labour whose expectations for a positive change had been frustrated. The LC ended in 1976, the PO in 1973 and the AO and MLS in 1975. The narrowing of political spaces made all of them think that armed struggle was the only way to achieve revolution. Moreover, the 1976 Festival of the Youth Proletariat held in Milan, at Parco Lambro, ended up a massive failure, demonstrating how heroin use was spreading among youth and putting to the fore the necessity to fight the pushers, most of which bought the drug from such fascist dealers as Rudy Crovace, killed in 1983 (Colaprico 2008). Militant anti-fascism turned into anti-pusher actions, with such tragic episodes as the still mysterious killing, in 1978, of Fausto Tinelli and 'Iaio' Iannucci, two comrades who had set up a file containing the names of the fascists involved in drug dealing, which was later to disappear.

Former members of the LC protection squads founded with some ex-PO militants the journal *Senza Tregua* (*Without Truce*, named after the book of the former partisan commander Giovanni Pesce), which proposed the necessity of a 'Front Line' (Prima Linea, PL), whose military organisation would have supported the social and political struggles. That was the beginning of the PL, whose first action was the killing of the neo-fascist MSI Alderman Enrico Pedenovi, in 1976. Other members of the PO, together with some former members of other groups, founded the journal *Rosso* (*Red*), whose positions were similar, except for the importance the latter gave to the struggles of women and movements against homophobia, as well as issues like the legalisation of drugs and prison reform. It was among the members of *Rosso* that the Formazioni Comuniste Combattenti (FCC, Fighting Rank and File Communists) were founded (De Lorenzis et al. 2008). This was the beginning of Autonomia Operaia (AUTOP, Workers' Autonomy), a cluster of structures that were '*di movimento*' (movement-oriented), including the radio station Radio Popolare (People's Radio), and lots of small *collettivi* which marched side by side with other armed groups and micro-groups which campaigned feminist, ecologist or homosexual issues. They were pulled together only by a common ideological root, that of Toni Negri and his ideas of 'mass illegality' which were put forward in several books (Negri 1997). Mass illegality consisted of a multiplication of clashes, ransacking of luxury, record and book shops, and vandalising of the city centre. Any *collettivo* could start an action, claiming workers' discontent as a justification, without any political direction or project. The killings of Claudio Varalli by a fascist in 1975, followed by the death of Giannino Zibecchi, who was run over by a police jeep during the protests that followed the killing of Varalli, embittered the mood of the extreme Left.

New assaults on police and *carabinieri* barracks, followed by militant anti-fascism-inspired action, provoked the reaction of the parties. The ruling DC passed a bill, voted for by the PCI and the PSI, which was called Legge Reale (Reale Act), after the minister who drafted it. It allowed the police forces to adopt harsh repressive measures against the demonstrators, such as the possibility of shooting point blank to scare rioters away. The consequences of such a law were soon to come, causing a gulf between the PCI, the traditional working-class movement and the rioters, giving way to a vicious circle of challenges and counter-attack whose out-come was the isolation of the *untorelli* (poisoners) of the extreme Left and the disruption of the Italian Left. On 17 February 1977, in order to quench the protest of students, workers and unemployed masses, the PCI member and general secretary of the CGIL trade union, Luciano Lama, decided to give a talk at the occupied La Sapienza University, in Rome, that is, the biggest Italian higher education institution. As Lama feared dissent, he encouraged PCI and CGIL members to arrange a protec-tion squad for him during the speech. The tension inevitably soared as the 'creative' wing of AUTOP, or the *indiani metropolitani* (metropolitan redskins), booed and teased Lama, provoking the reaction of his pro-tection squad. Clubs hit the demonstrators, who were also armed, and who promptly reacted. For the first time in republican Italian history, the PCI and CGIL faced an open, violent and bitter dissent from other left-wing militants, and were forced to rush away from the university's main square. The chasing of Lama turned critics and polemics between old and new left into an open clash, and the reaction of the PCI, in its symbolic 'capital city', were soon to be seen.

On 11 March 1977, in Bologna, the police (*carabinieri*) tried to repress a demonstration against integralist catholics. Pier Francesco Lorusso, a 25-year-old medical student, was shot dead in the back by a *carabiniere*. Three days of urban guerrilla uprising rattled Bologna, the so-called 'lab-oratory' of the democratic PCI, forcing the then Ministry of Interior, Francesco Cossiga, a future president of the republic, to send the tanks to repress the uprising at the request of the PCI mayor of Bologna, Renato Zangheri. A national rally was called in Rome on the following day, with new episodes of urban guerrilla action in the capital. The Milan groups decided not to participate in the national rally, claiming the secret ser-vices were trying to influence the outcome. Regardless, they decided to organise their own rally. Unlike a few years before, the *collettivi* also chose to go their own way, so the *collettivo* of Porta Vittoria, a lower-middle-class district of Milan, detached themselves from the main group of dem-onstrators. A few shots were fired against the building of Assolombarda, the Lombard Industrial Entrepreneurs Association, with a Winchester rifle, while other members engaged in armed clashes to keep the police forces busy.

The repression that followed this episode was bound to draw heat, as two months later, on 12 May, in Rome, a group of women gathered to celebrate the victory of the referendum that had kept divorce legal in Italy, violating the decree issued by Cossiga after the March events, forbidding public political rallies. Some police agents were present, disguised as demonstrators, as the pictures published by the newspaper *La Repubblica* were later to prove. One of them shot point blank, killing the 21-year-old Giorgiana Masi, who, ironically, was not a communist, but a member of the liberal-oriented Partito Radicale. A new wave of riots spread across the country, particularly in Milan. As in March, some groups did not accept the discipline of shared and agreed decisions of common action. Some members of the Proletari Armati per il Comunismo (PAC, Armed Proletarians for Communism) decided to face the police with guns and balaclavas. They justified their actions by claiming that Milan on that day was being patrolled by the Celere (Quick Squad), a police squad created in 1948 by the DC Minister Mario Scelba for the purpose of repressing demonstrations. The Celere had killed more than 150 people since its inception. Two PAC members, Giuseppe Memeo and Marco Ferrandi, faced the police and fired against them, killing the Celere member Antonio Custra. This episode was the peak of Italian riots, as the reaction of the government, coupled by the stigmatisation of the rioters by the PCI, resulted in a fierce repression that fragmented the radical movements. Some members withdrew from political activism, whereas others were to become heroin addicts, swelling the ranks of drug deaths, which reached 800 per year throughout the 1980s. Some others converted themselves to new age ideologies, whereas a few of them decided that the only solution was a face to face armed struggle against the state. It was after 1977 that the Red Brigades (BR) reached their peak and gave birth to the so-called '*anni di piombo*' (years of lead), whose most famous episode had to be the abduction and killing of former Prime Minister Aldo Moro.

The Italian riots failed for many reasons: the first was the extreme fragmentation of social movements, which became contagious in the second half of the 1970s. The reasons for it were neither the economic crisis nor the birth of new political sensitiveness to issues such as that of gay liberation and feminism, but, sometimes, the narcissistic leadership and its impact on some of the militants of the *collettivi* and other groups. Any movement from below should be the property of the crowd that creates and supports it. The second, very important, reason was the institutional choice of the PCI to participate in putting down the riots, as well as the repressive governmental attitude, which, coupled with the economic crisis, turned the possibility of radical political changes into a desperate rebellion. Thirdly, rioters rarely considered the international context, failing to find other alliances or common cause with the other post-68 movements of the revolutionary Left. In any case their short-lived experience tells us how a mixture of spontaneity and organisation, under a common political perspective, can bring riots close to a positive political outcome.

SUBCULTURES OF RESISTANCE

University students were at the heart of many of these changes and the social sciences reflected upon all these new questions and challenges to established ways of thinking. Many criminologists who were sympathetic to this new environment called themselves 'sociologists of deviance' to emphasise that thinking about crime should start with the situation—the state of society, physically and mentally—in order to put crime and deviance in context. The fact that in Britain many 'crimes' such as abortion and homosexuality were decriminalised in 1967 reinforced the point that crimes are officially acts that are labelled as crimes and that their status can change. Using phrases like the 'new criminology' and 'critical criminology' in the years following 1968, this radical and Marxist-influenced way of thinking mushroomed. We will explore in the next chapter how criminology was radicalised on the university campus in America in the early 1970s, and how the state reacted.

Another key element in the development of a critical criminology, influenced by Marxism and an anti-capitalist outlook, was the work headed up by the Jamaican academic, Stuart Hall, at the Centre for Contemporary Cultural Studies (CCCS) based at Birmingham University in the 1970s, which especially built upon Stan and Phil Cohen and Jock Young's insights into the evolution of youth subcultures. In order to understand them better they thought it was key to understand the sociology of the mainstream society that was labelling them, thus unpacking and critiquing any notion that being a 'deviant' was the choice or responsibility of the people so labelled. They were exploring the state of mind—the consciousness of this group—this configuration of people adopting shared values and behaviours in a reaction that Hall et al. called a 'double articulation', that could be best analysed and understood in the context of this opposition to the dominant culture.

The shorthand for this process was the title of their 1976 collection *Resistance through Rituals*. Its introductory essay, 'Subcultures, Cultures and Class', looked right across society and begins by quoting some key arguments from Marx himself about how people make their own history 'under circumstances directly encountered, given and transmitted from the past' and how the ruling classes 'among other things rule also as thinkers, as producers of ideas, and regulate the production and distribution of the ideas of their age: thus their ideas are the ruling ideas of the epoch' (Clarke et al. 1976, 11–12). These quotes from Marx's *The 18th Brumaire of Louis Napoleon* and *The German Ideology* respectively place their explanation firmly in the Marxist tradition. They were discussing the question of how ideas become dominant in society and make some incisive comments about notions like 'affluence' that were commonly believed to have changed the position of the working class to its rulers in Britain to one of 'consensus'. They argued 'the real element in "affluence"—cannot be questioned. The years 1951–64 saw … a steadier and much faster increase than at any other time this century' (Clarke et al. 1976, 22). But did it lead to consensus? Rather, they concluded:

> The overwhelming emphasis in the ideology of affluence on money and consumption may well have had the unintended effect of stimulating an awareness of 'relative deprivation' and thereby contributed to the 'wage militancy' of the 1960s and 70s. The affluent workers in engineering and the motor firms pioneered the shift to work-place power … These, too, were responses to 'affluence' which its ideologues neither did nor could foresee. (Clarke et al. 38)

So history had shown that 'affluence' had not transformed relations between social classes into a consensus. Indeed it was the scale of strikes, protest movements and mass demonstrations—often labelled as riots by the police or those in authority—that had made this Marxist-influenced understanding of society relatively prominent. Despite these successes for the working class and resistance movements in Europe and the USA during this period, in the 1970s the ruling class were still in control.

But their degree of control varied over time: 'the 1950s seem to us to be a period of true "hegemonic domination"'. In later decades:

> Society has polarised, conflict has reappeared on many levels. The dominant classes retain power, but their 'repertoire' of control is progressively challenged, weakened, exhausted. One of the most striking features of this later period is the shift in the exercise of control from the mechanisms of consent to those of coercion (e.g. the use of the law, the courts, the police and the army, of legal repression, conspiracy charges and of force to contain an escalating threat to the state and to 'law and order'). This marks a crisis in the hegemony of the ruling class. (Clarke et al. 1976, 40)

Stuart Hall and his colleagues also analysed how the government, the police and the media constructed the image of young black men as 'folk devils'—who they held responsible for a 'general social crisis and "rising crime" first, a particular kind of robbery occurring, in British streets second, and later' (Hall et al. 1978, 23). Thus the 'crime' of mugging—the name itself is a social construction—was inflated beyond the limits of the criminal act of street robbery per se into a symbol of a societal crime-wave occurring within a general crisis of law and order. They believed that the sheer scale of the moral panic inflated around black criminality allowed this group to become stigmatised with a pervasive label that criminalised their very existence on a far wider scale than merely the particular crime of 'mugging'. Hall et al. (1978) expanded their analysis that had begun by deconstructing the mugging moral panic into a perceptive overview of how the state were 'policing the crisis'. This historical view of British riots will help us to appreciate the context of the more recent outbreak in 2011 (see below).

Hall was himself a member of the British Communist Party (CP), unlike most of his colleagues whose political affiliations were less determined. The CP had played an important role in the class struggles of the late 1960s and 1970s and Hall was later to be at the forefront of the British interpretation of European communist ideas taking place as the much larger communist parties of Italy and France sought to explain the changing patterns of conflict that had anticipated a growing popularity for communism from 1968 onwards, but was in many ways advocating compromise and retreat by the end of the 1970s. Hall's initial reaction, however, was a radical one, as Alex Callinicos summarised in his 2014 obituary:

> Stuart Hall's development of Gramsci's conception of ideology … is most fully on display in 'Policing the Crisis', a collective Centre for Contemporary Cultural Studies' work published in 1978 that uses the case of a moral panic over mugging under the Heath government in the early 1960s to unravel the different dimensions of crisis—economic, political, ideological—affecting British capitalism and to trace the moves preparing for the distinctive mix of economic liberalism and traditional Tory invocations of family, nation and state that was to characterise Thatcherism … 'The Politics of Mugging' … contains the closest he came to a discussion of revolutionary strategy, exploring the then current idea that wageless black youth could act as a political vanguard. (Callinicos 2014, 145)

The moral panic describes a process where the police, politicians and the media conspire to create a distorted racialised image of the 'black mugger'. The CCCS Mugging Group quoted Mr Justice Caulfield's statement in Leicester Crown Court—'the newspapers have made it known that sentences for attacks on the open highway will no longer be light'—to illustrate how all the parties involved are complicit in inflating the moral panic (CCCS 1976, 76). Highly dubious statistics allege this folk devil to be the new public enemy, manufacturing an unjustified fear of crime. Such distortions fuelled the growth of racism, and openly racist organisations like the British National Front capitalised on the greater traction this institutionally racist offensive created amongst sections of the majority white population. In both the UK and the USA this resistance has led to many protest actions and demonstrations, from the 'Rock against Racism' and 'Anti-Nazi League' campaigns of the 1970s to 'Black Lives Matter' in the 2010s, in reaction to racist organisations and police practices towards black people; namely aggressive stop and search and the use of lethal force.

In May 1975, the *Daily Mail* reported the summing up of Judge Gwynn Morris as he sentenced five black youths to five years in jail, describing two south London inner-city areas Clapham and Brixton thus:

> Within memory these areas were peaceful, safe and agreeable to live in. But the immigrant resettlement which has occurred over the past twenty-five years has radically transformed that environment. Those concerned with the maintenance of law and order are confronted with immense difficulties. This case has highlighted and underlined the perils which confront honest, innocent and hardworking, unaccompanied women who are in the street after nightfall. I notice not a single West Indian woman was attacked. (Hall et al. 1978, 333)

For the judge, these once 'peaceful, safe and agreeable' areas had been tarnished by the presence of black people who he alleges are making life difficult for the police and white women. This is a classic example of the institutionalised racism present within the criminal justice system which unjustly persecutes those it stigmatises. Later that year the National Front (NF) organised a march against what they called 'black muggings', whilst in the same month Judge Morris claimed to have received 'hundreds of letters' from 'petrified' women and suggested perhaps 'some form or other of vigilante corps … would become necessary' (Hall et al. 1978, 333, 337). A new spectre was thus thrown up—the folk devil of the 'black mugger'. As Hall put it, 'the three themes subtly intertwined in the earlier treatment of "mugging" were now fused into a single theme: crime, race and the ghetto' (Hall et al. 1978, 329). The message was clear, 'the coupling of "social control" and "social-problem" perspectives appears to be flowing from highly contradictory forces within the urban race problem, as it is intensified and pressured by the crisis' (Hall et al. 1978, 333).

This explains how the rebellion initiated by black youth was a reaction to these stigmatising processes:

> It is in the modality of race that those whom the structures systematically exploit, exclude and subordinate discover themselves as an exploited, excluded and subordinated class. Thus it is primarily in and through the modality of race that resistance, opposition and rebellion first expresses itself. (Hall et al. 1978, 347)

This moral panic was not unchallenged. Another of Hall's colleagues, Paul Gilroy, chronicled how the anti-racist struggle imaginatively countered the NF through the mobilisation and propaganda of 'Rock against Racism' and the 'Anti-Nazi League'. In his book, whose title was borrowed from the NF slogan, 'There Ain't no Black in the Union Jack', he had also written about the anti-police and anti-racist riots of 1980–81 and the process of militaristic entrenchment carried out by the police and government, with media endorsement in 1982s 'The Empire Strikes Back'. The strength of 'Policing the Crisis' stems initially from the detailed explanation of how this moral panic is inflated—leading into a powerful analysis of why these institutions used their levers of social control to uphold their power through a racist strategy of divide and rule. If sections of the working class could be educated to fear part of itself—a racially demonised 'other', then its resistance to austerity and the imperatives of the market that hamstrung the Heath Government could be undermined.

In order for this to happen, it was important that the Labour Government of 1974–79 bought into this racist myth construction by adhering to the idea that a heightened 'fear of crime' was a legitimate anxiety which it was their job to feed. Such a situation demanded that a Marxist analysis engaged with the economic and political crisis that was driving the social democratic government to abandon its commitment to reform and defending working-class living standards. A minority of revolutionary Marxists were attempting this task (Cliff and Gluckstein 1988), but leading communists such as the historian Eric Hobsbawm (1978) were falling into line with a form of realism that argued that resistance would no longer be effective in preventing capitalism lurching in a more authoritarian direction.

From a Glorious Summer to the Winter of Discontent

The late 1970s certainly felt full of the atmosphere of protest and rebellion. Punk, new wave and ska music were all subversive and revolting youth subcultures, many with overtly political and protest-focused themes that reflected the atmosphere of crisis in creative and inspiring ways. The trade union movement had started the decade resisting government legislation, marching, striking and picketing their way to a momentous wave of victories over the Conservative Government of 1970–74. The dockers marched and freed their strikers, the 'Pentonville Five' from jail (Darlington and Lyddon 2001). Miners struck, with a momentous display of their organisation and the level of solidarity they could win from other workers, when they closed a coke depot at Saltley in Birmingham. Their control threatened the power supply which kept industry going. These both took place in 1972 and caused complete panic in the government. One Treasury adviser described the mood:

> The lights went out and everybody said the country would disintegrate in a week. All the civil servants rushed round saying, 'Perhaps we ought to activate the nuclear underground shelters and the centres of regional government, because there'll be no electricity and there'll be riots on the streets'. The result of this was the government had to give way and pay the miners. (Whitehead 1985, 76)

The Tories were so fragmented and defeated by these events that they were later to plan a drastic solution to the problem. In 1977, Nicholas Ridley wrote a notorious secret document where he argued 'we must be prepared to deal with the problem of violent picketing' and arrange for 'a large, mobile squad of police who are equipped and prepared to uphold the law against the likes of the Saltley Coke-works mob'. The mention of Saltley reminded his readers that mass picketing by miners, supported by thousands of engineers, had defeated the law—in the sense that police resistance was broken—and the chief constable of Birmingham, Sir Derrick Capper, was forced to order the Gas Board to 'close the gates' (CRD 1977, 25). Tory Home Secretary Reginald Maudling explained in his memoirs that at the time (that phrase again!) there was no alternative:

> I am sure the decision he took was a wise one, because the number of strikers involved was so great, and feelings were running so high, that any attempt by the relatively small body of police who could be assembled to keep the depot open by force could have led to very grave consequences. Some of my colleagues asked me afterwards, why I had not sent in troops in support of the police, and I remember asking them one single question:

'If they had been sent in, should they have gone in with their rifles loaded or unloaded?' Either course could have been disastrous. (Callinicos and Simons 1985, 29)

The phrase 'the Saltley Coke-works mob' closes Ridley's report, reminding the reader of how governments have for centuries felt most frustrated and liable to use force when they feel unbearably restrained by the power of the people, the mobile proletariat. The power of the working class when it united together and withdrew its labour was demonstrably enormous. The tragedy was that the majority of those involved felt the best way to secure their gains was through the election of a Labour Government. The triumph of the workers and their unions was institutionalised in 1974 when Prime Minister Heath called an election demanding an answer to his question 'Who runs the country—the government or the unions?'. 'Not you' came the answer as the Labour Party won.

However, the new government's commitment to economic orthodoxy meant they had no plans to control and regulate capitalism and, despite their verbal commitment to maintaining working-class living standards, they had no answer to currency devaluations caused by the financial markets, and so they accepted the moral necessity of austerity—damaging the very people whose militancy had pushed them into government (Beckett 2009; Clement 2014). This could only lead to demoralisation, and eventually reaction. In the winter of 1978–79 many public sector workers went on strike against pay freezes that had impoverished them as inflation shrank the real value of their wages. Lorry drivers joined them and in some cities, like Hull, the strikes left rubbish piled up, fuel shortages and important services neglected. The sense of crisis deepened. Whereas the early 1970s' strikes had been anti-Tory and led to important gains for those taking part, now workers were acting against the government which was supposed to represent their interests. Instead of the elation of victory, many sensed the foreboding of defeat. In Italy the communists had sought a historic compromise with the right-wing Christian Democrats; in Britain the urge for compromise with the forces of capitalism had neutered the Labour Government and so, demoralised, the workers found themselves believing there was no alternative. This defeatist self-fulfilling prophecy ushered in Thatcher's historic election victory.

The campaign effectively hoisted Labour by its own flag. A billboard image of a dole queue created for the Thatcher campaign by Tim Bell of the Saatchi and Saatchi advertising agency 'invented the famous "Labour Isn't Working" slogan (itself a deception that used Hendon Conservatives to "play" at being unemployed)' (Bloom 2015, 34). A sufficient number of Britain's then 13 million trade union members agreed with the slogan and were profoundly disillusioned with a government that claimed to speak for them but had refused to listen. In May 1979, by a combination of disillusion with Labour, apathy and Tory protest-voting, Thatcher was elected, and the Left in Britain found itself believing that the Right had won the battle of ideas.

In reality the class struggle was far from over. Initially, the battle against racism intensified. In the summer of 1979 an anti-racist activist, school teacher Blair Peach, was killed by a police blow to the head on an Anti-Nazi League protest march against the fascist National Front in Southall, West London. No one was convicted. 'Policing the Crisis, Mugging, the State and Law and Order' proved to be one of the most influential criminological texts of the decade; especially because it came to be seen as correctly predicting the British inner city riots of the 1980s. The riots were led by black youth, with many white inner-city residents joining in. They were a cry of anger and resistance to their unjust treatment, especially by the police, but it was far broader than this, as Stuart Hall says:

> The 1970s was a period of profound alienation, when young black folk could not think of themselves as British … The dream of assimilation was buried. We are not going to stay on the terms of becoming just like you. (Hall 2013)

These riots began in St Paul's, Bristol, in April 1980 (Clement 2007), but really took off when 13 cities rioted the following summer. The largest and longest was probably that which began in Brixton, the subject of Lord Scarman's subsequent public inquiry (Scarman 1982). Although it contains many important observations, Scarman's defence of the police left many frustrated at this apparent inability to recognise their culpability and institutional racism, although perhaps the strength of the tone of his denial hints at a subconscious acceptance of the charge. He pronounced:

> The direction and policies of the Metropolitan Police are not racist. I totally and unequivocally reject the attack made upon the integrity and impartiality of the senior direction of the force. (Scarman 1982, 105)

It was not until the MacPherson report in 1999 that institutional racism was finally recognised, and it is evident that successive government's failure to admit its existence ensured that resentment and resistance to racist policing practices has remained prominent amongst multicultural communities. Indeed the very term multiculturalism embodies the unity of interests forged amongst inner city residents in resisting the National Front and racist policing through marches, demonstration, festivals and carnivals from Lewisham in 1977 to Welling in 1993. Resistance and riots have shaped our multicultural present (Richardson 2013).

However, in the 1980s some criminologists were becoming reluctant to show a partisan appreciation for the cause of those involved in the riots. Hall developed concepts like 'Thatcherism' and 'authoritarian populism' which claimed that the Right had gained hegemony over popular thinking and therefore the Left had to change their way of thinking about the modern world. As Bloom puts it:

> Older-style Marxists were also to suffer from left-positioned Continental Marxism, a post-modern and post-humanist way of looking at politics which was suspicious of all positions and produced powerful critiques of both sides ... not only was power culturally based but it was an ephemeral production of language formations, which created narratives of power rather than actual power. (Bloom 2015, 102)

Whilst Stuart Hall was rewriting Marxism for what he called 'new times', there were other related developments amongst critical criminologists. In their analysis of the 1981 riots, two 'prominent radical criminologists', John Lea and Jock Young (Rock 2012, 60), sought to critique both the

Conservative thesis that saw black people as 'others' and the source of the disorder, *and* what they called Liberal thinking, by which they meant those who were on the side of the rioters:

> Precisely because part of the cultural mix in Britain today is a counter-culture of discontent, co-existence is precarious … Street culture can be competitive, disorganized, anti-social as much as the reverse. (Lea and Young 1982, 8)

This statement sounds like common sense: we know that street gangs can be involved in crime—as exemplified by Mike Davis's classic definition 'gangs … mint power for the otherwise powerless through their control of small urban spaces' (Davis 2008, xi). But by naming it a 'counter-culture' Lea and Young don't simply mean a culture countering authority and the racist establishment, but also appear to imply that the interests of those involved in the riots are opposed to others in their community—indeed they threaten it with their 'anti-social' actions. They argued: 'according to police estimates the vast majority of "footpad robbery" (mugging, bag snatching, etc.) in Lambeth was committed by black males aged between 12 and 17' (Lea and Young 1982, 9).

They go on to quantify this vast majority at 80%, citing the Scarman report as their evidence. Whereas in the 1970s Stuart Hall and his colleagues had shown how the very category of 'mugging' was invented and magnified by spurious use of police statistics and media magnification, now left-wing criminologists were describing it as a real and measurable crime which was damaging its victims in working-class communities. In an earlier book introduced by Jock Young and Stanley Cohen in 1973, they had written how 'the stereotype carried of deviants by the media is a way of simplifying reality … a translation of reality into stereotypes' (Cohen and Young 1981, 18). Now Lea and Young were reproducing an argument that placed some of the onus of their explanation for the riots on 'black criminality'. An appreciative account of riots does not seek to *blame* the criminal, or simply condemn the criminal act. In *The New Criminology* Young and his colleagues cited Marx to define crime as 'the struggle of the isolated individual against the prevailing conditions'

(Taylor et al. 1973, 215) and went on to discuss the importance of appreciating deviance:

> 'Appreciating' as distinct from romanticizing a deviant phenomenon involves most importantly the understanding (and faithful representation) of the deviant actor ... [who is] guided in action by purposes and motives, keenly felt and experienced, and that to ignore or underplay these purposes and motives in one's descriptive and explanatory account is an act of bad faith and a faulty portrayal of the world as it is. (Taylor et al. 1973, 233)

The Police: Shock Troops of the Civilising Offensive

Although Lea and Young do see police racist practice as the root of the problem, describing the notorious 'Swamp 81' mass stop and search of black people as 'a tailor-made example of how to antagonise the greatest possible number of people' (1982, 11), they show little appreciative understanding of the keenly felt purposes and motives of the rioters, instead claiming:

> Events assume the status of a vicious circle of cumulative causation ... the tendency of the community to dry up as an information source and the general alienation further undermines the basis of consensus policing, leaving military style action as the only viable strategy for the police. (Lea and Young 1982, 12)

Surely an appreciative account would never justify acts of state brutality and violence as viable? Because they have underplayed the motives of the rioters they have ended up justifying military style policing. This rightward shift in criminological thinking in the early 1980s would evolve into what became known as left realism over the next few years. 'Realism' was deemed preferable to the alleged 'idealism' of other Marxist criminologists such as Phil Scraton (1987) and Dario Melossi (1979). Jock Young was even prepared to acknowledge his own idealist past, stating 'the left idealist position is not a million miles away from the work of the new criminologists whether they be Taylor, Walton and Young, Richard

Quinney or Carol Smart; or ... Michel Foucault' (Young 1979, 19). Downes and Rock summarised this journey:

> Its genesis as the 'new criminology' was later to be termed 'left idealism' by one of its authors, Jock Young, who in the 1980s revised the approach to become the more social democratic 'left realism'. (Downes and Rock 2011, 285)

Ironically, the book which epitomised the new left realism, Lea and Young's *What is to be Done about Law and Order?* came out in 1984, at the same time as the year-long miners' strike exposed the militarised British Police Force as the greatest threat to the livelihood of the working class, treating them as 'the enemy within' (Milne 2014; Green 1990). Fortunately for the government, the riots of 1981 had justified the militarisation of the police's equipment, and in a way their mentality: they were now ready to forsake their *Dixon of Dock Green* image of policing by consent for a more continental model of riot squads—climaxing with the full-scale police riot against the miners picketing at another coke-works: Orgreave, South Yorkshire in June 1984—in hindsight the decisive battle in the civilising offensive to humiliate the British trade union movement. Police historian Clive Emsley describes the scene:

> Police tactics were also new. Lines of men carrying long shields took the brunt of any missiles hurled at the police; the lines then parted to release either squads of men carrying small round shields and batons, or mounted police—the former, according to the new Manual were to 'disperse and/or incapacitate' demonstrators, the latter 'to create fear'. (Emsley 1996, 184)

The media coverage of these events notoriously adjusted the audience view of events so it appeared as if the miners had charged the police—causing their civilised reaction to reimpose order—when in fact later enquiries proved the police culpability for the violence that day. This was just the most notorious episode in the controversial militaristic policing of the strike which involved the occupation of mining villages, arresting 11,312 people of which 5,653 were put on trial (Percy-Smith and Hilyard 1985).

Just as the Labour Party and trade union leadership refused to back the miners in the name of a spurious 'new realism' that declared militancy outdated and irrelevant, so the left realists argued for a retreat from seeing social control as the fount of crime and criminalisation:

> Left Realism was to follow the earlier radical criminologists' injunction to act, but action was now as much in the service of more effective and practical policing and crime reduction strategies as in the cause of radical social change (if not more so) … it was at times difficult to distinguish between the programmes of the Home Office or other state criminal justice ministries, on the one hand, and of Left Realism, on the other. (Rock 2012, 61–62)

In part this dilemma is unavoidable for criminology. Common sense decrees that 'effective and practical policing' is one of its policy goals, but the police's role as agents of social control and servants of the government will frequently put the force at odds with sections of its own population. Those being arrested and punished will not feel like they are being 'protected and served'. But surely it points to the importance of a Marxist perspective on crime and deviance that recognises the role of the state and champions popular democratic action from below to achieve social justice?

Over 30 years later, sadly, some of the pioneering sociologists of deviance such as Jock Young, Stuart Hall, Stan Cohen, Geoff Pearson and Julia Schwendinger are no longer with us. There are still some 'left realists' such as Roger Matthews taking to task critical views that do not advocate practical policy changes, and criticising the likes of Stan Cohen and Loic Wacquant who he believes 'have been overly critical of state policies and institutions' (Matthews 2014, 20). As I explore below, given the state's role in contemporary polity, it is hardly possible to be *overly* critical. Earlier, Matthews cited Jock Young's statement from 1975, when he criticised Stuart Hall and the CCCS Mugging Group, claiming: 'it is unrealistic to suggest that problems of crimes like mugging is merely the problem of miscategorization and concomitant moral panics … We have to argue, therefore, strategically, for the exercise of social control' (Matthews 2014, 7).

By 2013 however, Young seemed to have revised this provocative stance that had led from critical criminology to left realism. Today's equivalent folk devil to the 1970s 'black mugger' is surely the urban street gang—of which Young says in a book review: 'the "gang" has become a magical word to explain away crime, riots, sexual assault, drug dealing and almost every manifestation of violence in our society' (Hallsworth 2013). Exercising social control is clearly seen as the problem here not the solution, in a statement more in line with Stuart Hall's exploration of *Mugging, the State and Law and Order*. Lea meanwhile has consistently argued for a Marxist position in many publications over the decades (Lea 2002, 2013), despite still seeing some value in the left realist viewpoint (Lea 2014).

References

Bauman, Z. (2011). Interview: Zygmunt Bauman on the UK riots. *Social Europe Journal.* http://www.social-europe.eu/2011/08/interview-zygmunt-bauman-on-the-ukriots/. Accessed 15 Aug 2011.

Beckett, A. (2009). When the lights went out: Britain in the Seventies London: Faber and Faber.

Berger, J. (1968, May 23). The nature of mass demonstrations. *New Society.* Available at https://www.marxists.org/history/etol/newspape/isj/1968/no034/berger.htm

Bloom, C. (2015). *Thatcher's secret war: Subversion, coercion, secrecy and government, 1974–90).* Stroud: History Press.

Callinicos, A. (2014). Stuart hall in perspective. *International Socialism, 142*, 139–148.

Callinicos, A., & Simons, M. (1985). *The great strike.* London: Bookmarks.

Caygill, H. (2013). *On resistance: A philosophy of defiance.* London: Bloomsbury.

CCCS Mugging Group. (1976). Some notes on the relationship between the societal control culture and the news media: The construction of a law and order campaign. In S. Hall & T. Jefferson (Eds.), *Resistance through rituals: Youth subcultures in post-war Britain.* London: Hutchinson.

Clarke, J., Hall, S., Jefferson, T., & Roberts, B. (1976). Subcultures, cultures and class: A theoretical overview. In S. Hall & T. Jefferson (Eds.), *Resistance through rituals: Youth subcultures in post-war Britain.* London: Hutchinson.

Clement, M. (2007). Bristol: Civilising the inner city. *Race and Class, 48*(4), 97–110

Clement, M. (2014). Mobs versus markets. In D. Pritchard & F. Pakes (Eds.), *Riot, unrest and protest on the global stage.* Basingstoke: Palgrave Macmillan.

Cliff, T., & Gluckstein, D. (1988). *The labour party: A marxist history*. London: Bookmarks.

Cohen, S., & Young, J. (1981) [1973]. *The manufacture of news: Social problems, deviance and the mass media*. London: Constable.

Conservative Party Research Department (CRD). (1977). *Nationalised Industries Policy Group Report (PG/10/77/38)*.

Darlington, R., & Lyddon, D. (2001). *Glorious summer: Class struggle in Britain 1972*. London: Bookmarks.

Davis, M. (2008). *A world of gangs: Armed young men and gangsta culture [Preface to Hagedorn, J.]*. Minneapolis: University of Minnesota.

Della Porta, D. (1997). Le Brigate Rosse. In *Annali della Storia d'Italia*, XVII, 617–665. Turin: Einaudi.

Downes, D., & Rock, P. (2011). *Understanding deviance* (6th ed.). Oxford: Oxford University Press.

Elias, N., & Scotson, J. (2008). *The established and ousiders*. Dublin: University College Dublin Press.

Emsley, C. (1996). *The English police: A social and political history*. Harlow: Longmans.

Green, P. (1990). *Enemy without: Policing and class consciousness in the miners' strike*. Buckingham: Open University Press.

Hall, S. (2013). *The Stuart Hall project*. London: Director: John Akomfrah.

Hall, S., Critcher, C., Jefferson, T., Clarke, J., & Roberts, B. (1978). *Policing the crisis: Mugging, the state and law and order*. Basingstoke: Macmillan.

Hallsworth, S. (2013). *The gang and beyond: Interpreting violent street worlds*. Basingstoke: Palgrave Macmillan.

Harman, C. (1979). Crisis of the European revolutionary left. *International Socialism*, *2*(4). https://www.marxists.org/archive/harman/1979/xx/eurev-left.html.

Harman, C. (1988). *The fire last time*. London: Bookmarks.

Hobsbawm, E. (1978). The Forward March of Labour Halted? In Jacques, M. and Mulhern, F. (Eds.), *The Forward March of Labour Halted*. London: Verso

Lea, J. (2002). *Crime and modernity*. London: Sage.

Lea, J. (2013). From denizen to citizen and back: Governing the Precariat through crime. *Criminal Justice Matters, 93*, 4–5.

Lea, J. (2014). New deviancy, Marxism and the politics of left realism: Reflections on Jock Young's early writings. *Theoretical Criminology, 18*(4), 432–440.

Lea, J., & Young, J. (1982). The riots in Britain in 1981: Urban violence and political marginilisation. In D. Cowell et al. (Eds.), *Policing the riots* (pp. 5–20). London: Junction Books.

Negri, A. (1997). *I libri del rogo*. Rome: Deriveapprodi.

Macaulay, T. (1889). *History of England volume 1*. London: Longmans.

Marx, K. (1844). The holy family. In D. McLellan (1971) *The thought of Karl Marx*. London: Macmillan.

Matthews, R. (2014). *Realist criminology*. Basingstoke: Palgrave Macmillan.

Matza, D. (1969). *Becoming deviant*. New York: Prentice-Hall.

Maudling, R. (1978). *Memoirs* cited in Callinicos et al. (1985) p. 29.

Melossi, D. (1979). Institutions of social control and capitalist organization of work. In B. Fine, R. Kinsey, J. Lea, S. Picciotto, & J. Young (Eds.), *Capitalism and the rule of law* (pp. 90–100). London: Hutchinson.

Milne, S. (2014). *The enemy within: The secret war against the miners*. London: Verso.

Molyneux, J. (2012). *The point is to change it: An introduction to political economy*. London: Bookmarks.

NAP. (1973). *Lotta dura abbiam gridato*. Rome: Savelli.

Panzieri, R. (1962). *Le lotte operaie nello sviluppo capitalistico*. Turin: Einaudi.

Patel, T., & Tyrer, D. (2011). *Race, crime and resistance*. London: Sage.

Percy-Smith, J., & Hilyard, P. (1985). Miners in the arms of the law: A statistical analysis. *Journal of Law and Society, 12*(3), 345–354.

Richardson, B. (Ed.). (2013). *Say it loud! Marxism and the fight against racism*. London: Book Marks.

Rock, P. (2012). Sociological theories of crime. In Maguire, M. Morgan, R. and Reiner R. (eds.) *The Oxford handbook of criminology* (5th ed., pp. 39–80). Oxford: Oxford University Press.

Scarman, Lord J. (1982). *The Scarman report: The Brixton disorders 10–12 April 1981*. Harmondsworth: Penguin.

Scott, J. (1990). *Domination and the arts of resistance: Hidden transcripts*. New Haven: Yale.

Scraton, P. (1987). *Law, order and the authoritarian state*. Buckingham: Open University Press.

Taylor, I., Walton, P., & Young, J. (1973). *The new criminology: For a social theory of deviance*. New York: Harper and Row.

Ugwudike, P. (2015). *An introduction to critical criminology*. Bristol: Policy Press.

Whitehead, P. (1985). *The writing on the wall*. London: Michael Joseph.

Willis, P. (1977). *Learning to labour: How working class kids get working class jobs*. Farnborough: Saxon House.

Winlow, S., & Hall, S. (2012). Gone shopping. In Briggs, D. (Eds.), *The English Riots of 2011: A summer of discontent*, Hampshire: Waters.

Young, J. (1971a). The role of the police as amplifiers of deviance. In S. Cohen (Ed.), *Images of deviance* (pp. 27–62). Harmondsworth: Penguin.

Young, J. (1971b). *The Drugtakers: The social meaning of drug use.* London: Paladin.

Young, J. (1979). Left idealism, reformism and beyond. In B. Fine, R. Kinsey, J. Lea, S. Picciotto, & J. Young (Eds.), *Capitalism and the rule of law* (pp. 11–28). London: Hutchinson.

Italy Section

Balestrini, N. (1969). *Vogliamo tutto.* Milan: Bompiani.

Basaglia, F. (1977). *La maggioranza deviante.* Turin: Einaudi.

Caminiti, L. (2008). *Gli autonomi.* Rome: DeriveApprodi.

Capanna, M. (1988). *Formidabili quegli anni.* Milano: Rizzoli.

Colaprico, P. (2008). *Milano calibro 39.* Milan: Garzanti.

Cohen, S. (1973). *Folk devils and moral panics: The creation of the Mods and Rockers.* London: Routledge.

Crainz, G. (2004). *Il paese mancato.* Rome: Donzelli.

De Lorenzis, T., Guizzardi, V., & Mita, M. (2008). *Avete Pagato caro, non avete pagato tutto.* Rome: DeriveApprodi.

Della Porta, D., & Reiter, H. (2004). *Polizia e protesta.* Bologna: Il Mulino.

Edited Book. (1973). *La sinistra rivoluzionaria in Italia.* Rome: Savelli.

Ferraresi, F. (1993). *Minacce alla democrazia.* Milan: Feltrinelli.

Fofi, G. (1961). *L'immigrazione meridionale a Torino.* Turin: Einaudi.

Ginsborg, P. (1991). *Storia d'Italia, 1943–1991.* Turin: Einaudi.

Il Manifesto. (1978). *Il marxismo e lo stato.* Milano: Feltrinelli.

Montaldi, D., & Alasia, G. (1998). *Milano Corea.* Milan: Bruno Mondadori.

Moroni, P., & Balestrini, N. (1997). *L'orda d'oro.* Milan: Feltrinelli.

Philopat, M. (2002). *La banda Bellini.* Turin: Einaudi.

Pozzi, P. (2007). *Insurrezione. 1977.* Rome: DeriveApprodi.

Revelli, M. (1993). *Lavorare in FIAT.* Milan: Garzanti.

Rossanda, R. (1992, December 27). *Per chi voglia dirsi comunista nel 2000, Il Manifesto.*

Rossanda, R. (2005). *La ragazza del secolo scorso.* Turin: Einaudi.

Scalzone, O. (1992) *Il secondo biennio rosso.* Milan: Sugarco.

Scalzone, O. (2001). *Il nemico incoffesabile.* Rome: Odradek.

Tronti, M. (1970). *Operai e capitale.* Turin: Einaudi.

Valentini, C. (1993). *Enrico Berlinguer.* Milan: Mondadori.

Wallerstein, I. (1974). *L'economia mondo.* Bologna: Il Mulino.

7

The 2010s: A Decade of Riot and Protest

The scale of protest expressed in mass actions has accelerated since 2010. In what follows I have only included a selection from a limited number of countries. Other measures such as the Global Peace Index have borne out this trend, however.

- 2010—UK—thousands of students demonstrate in central London against the trebling of their tuition fees. Besides acts of street theatre and charges at police lines, they also broke into Conservative Party headquarters causing extensive damage. In Greece a student is killed on an anti-cuts protest which ignites the mass movement against austerity that rages for the next five years.
- 2011—A momentous 'year of dreaming dangerously' according to Žižek (2012). The Arab Spring opens with the Tunisian and Egyptian revolutions overthrowing their governments. Waves of struggle threaten to overpower governments in Yemen, Syria and Dubai. Europe sees the birth of the Spanish Indignados movement of the squares, denouncing the established political parties and bringing hundreds of thousands onto the streets. Greek protests continue with general strikes and mass demonstrations.

© The Editor(s) (if applicable) and The Author(s) 2016   **179**
M. Clement, *A People's History of Riots, Protest and the Law*,
DOI 10.1057/978-1-137-52751-6_7

In the USA the Occupy Wall Street social movement combines waves of public protest with a new lexicon labelling the richest 1% as the problem and the 99% as the solution if they mobilise resistance. City squares are occupied across the USA with associated movements springing up in Europe and the UK. The revival of the British labour movement produces the largest ever union demonstration in April and the biggest strike action since 1926 in November. Riots spread across 13 cities in August, with significant areas of London subject to widespread looting and destruction (Briggs 2012).

- 2012—Greek strikes and protest continue. Spanish miners' strike refuels the movement of the squares. Alain Badiou's book proclaims the *Rebirth of History: A Time of Riots and Uprisings*. The Marikana Massacre of miners by South African police ends all ambiguities about the so-called progressive nature of the post-apartheid regime. The strike continued and the workers won many of their demands (Alexander et al. 2013).

- 2013—Riots and repression in Istanbul, Turkey. Several cities engulfed in mass protests over rising transport costs, whilst millions were squandered constructing World Cup venues in Brazil. Sweden, once hailed as Europe's most equal and inclusive society, saw riots in one run-down Stockholm suburb which then spread to 23 others. In Bangladesh, the capital city saw strikes and riots on its streets in the wake of the collapse of a newly built textile factory complex that killed hundreds. Official data confirmed this view when the Institute for Economics and Peace produced the Global Peace Index 2013, stating 'the likelihood of violent demonstrations was one of three indicators that reached the greatest level of deterioration over the period 2008–2013. This was in large part due to the events of the Arab Spring, and demonstrations in Europe surrounding the sovereign debt crisis and austerity measures' (Pritchard 2014, 199).

- 2014—A nationalist uprising in Ukraine deposes the president and starts a war with Russia. Israel's suppression and occupation of Palestine's Gaza Strip fails to prevent a minimal armed response which is met with the wholesale destruction of the area's schools, hospitals and housing, leading in turn to militant protests in European cities like Paris and London in solidarity with the Palestinians. In Hong Kong, protestors revive the 'Occupy' slogan as massive crowds demonstrate their opposition to any limiting of their democracy. This 'umbrella movement' of students and their supporters camped out for days and resisted police tear gas and baton attacks. The police's relentless onslaught on black communities in the USA provokes rioting in Ferguson, Missouri and a mass demonstration in New York.

- 2015—Whilst the Paris police had driven the 2014 pro-Palestine demonstration off the streets, and the media accused the organisers of anti-Semitism, the police and the government were central to organising a January mass demonstration against the shooting of journalists working for the satirical magazine *Charlie Hebdo* which was attended by upwards of three million citizens. The bizarre spectacle of the entire gang of world leaders, Merkel, Obama, Hollande, Cameron and many others, *leading* a mass protest raises important questions about the relation of this 'social movement' to authority. At the same time, this collective of presidents and prime ministers must have felt somewhat uneasy to be amongst such an enormous crowd carrying giant pencils with the slogan 'Not Afraid'! General strikes returned to Greece's streets in the new situation where Syriza, an apparently hard-left government had come to power (Ovenden 2015). Meanwhile, the momentum of the American new civil rights movement accelerated with riots following another police killing in Baltimore whilst Ferguson and many other US cities protest, merging with the inspiring campaign for fast food workers' rights which had shut down many stores, marched on McDonalds HQ in their tens of thousands and won their demand for a near doubling of their poverty wages to $15 an hour in several states.

The year 2015 also saw the phenomenon of 'people on the move' which exploded as population shifts followed the semi-collapse of states in parts of North Africa and the Arab world. These refugees then faced prejudice and blocked borders across Europe, causing them to protest and demand human rights and safe passage when they found themselves caged in or interned in totally inadequate facilities. The principal news story in the UK was about the 'crime' of illegal immigration. Hundreds of migrants apparently 'stormed'—the word is well-chosen for maximum shock value—the entrance to the cross-channel tunnel at Calais, France, in a desperate attempt to stow away on vehicles travelling to the UK, the one country where many believed they had the best chance of economic survival in the summer of 2015. This action could be termed a riot—it is certainly an act of protest at the inhumane conditions in which the migrants are forced to exist. Most are fleeing from states whose regimes have broken down in terms of offering their citizens any form of human rights or means to make a living; many have themselves been imprisoned and tortured in Eritrean camps or been bombed and made homeless in Syrian cities. The mass protests in Hungary and Slovenia for the right to cross the border have not only radicalised the refugees, but also unleashed a wave of empathy from many Europeans for their plight.

Their only crime is to want to enter a state whose government declares them unwelcome, David Cameron even labelling them as a 'swarm', whilst alleging that to allow them to enter would place a burden upon British residents. Is there any justice in this rationale for criminalising thousands of desperate men, women and children? The Italian eighteenth-century criminologist Cesare Beccaria made an observation about the crime of robbery which seems to sum up the problem:

> But this crime, alas! Is commonly the effect of misery and despair; the crime of that unhappy part of mankind, to whom the right of exclusive property (a terrible and perhaps unnecessary right) has left but a bare existence. (Beccaria [1804], cited in Taylor et al. 1973, 5)

So, for Beccaria, the 'right of exclusive property' leaves the robber with little option but to steal; in this instance the right of exclusive citizenship forces the migrant into the deviant act of entering forbidden territory. Applying only the conventional morality of classical criminology we are left with an insoluble dilemma, as British Prime Minister Cameron proves by his lame solution of arranging for these people to be deported to West Africa, which will patently solve nothing. As was explained in *The New Criminology*, 'classicism is exhausted: For if there is a clear reason for theft—the "right of exclusive property"—then crime cannot be seen as irrational' and 'deviance … must concomitantly be understood more sympathetically' (Taylor et al. 1973, 6). This is the kind of understanding that this book aims to uphold, namely explaining and appreciating the context in which riots and protest take place, as opposed to the common sense nonsense of constantly demonising and deliberately misunderstanding acts of protest by labelling them criminal and anti-social.

How are we to understand such events, and what significance should we attribute to them? The Marxist concept, developed by Trotsky, of 'combined and uneven development' (Smith 1984), was used to describe how economies and their political super-structures do not always advance gradually—evolving from one state to another in a steady advance—rather, a more 'backward' economy can be propelled forward as its late development allows it to utilise technology and scale to leap ahead of its more advanced competitors. What Trotsky said about how this explained the modernisation of Russia's economy in the early twentieth century could be applied to the progress made by China in the early twenty-first (Trotsky 1969). In an age of global communication we can apply this concept to help us understand how social movements cannot be understood as developing in isolation. Just as the protests that exploded into a national revolt in Tunisia inspired the uprising in neighbouring Egypt, combining with insurgent waves that rocked dictatorships in Syria, Yemen and Bahrain to create 'the Arab Spring', so other protests in Europe and the USA, which were admittedly more localised and much further away from actually challenging state power, were doubtless triggered and facilitated by this uneven upsurge in contention or class struggle.

Given this climate of global protest it is impossible to explain and analyse their significance in a more isolated national context, even if there are 'local' policies and actions that triggered the movement concerned. Unfortunately, the manner in which the British press chose to represent the outbreak of the riots that followed the police killing of Mark Duggan was symptomatic of the demonisation of the crowd and the resurrection of the 'mob' folk-devil so evident throughout this study, as a short summary of news headlines will demonstrate:

FLAMING MORONS—Thugs & thieves terrorise Britain's streets. (*Daily Express*)
THE ANARCHY SPREADS—To blame the cuts is immoral and cynical. This is criminality pure & simple. (*Daily Mail*)
RULE OF THE MOB (*Daily Telegraph*)
MOB RULE (*Independent*)
ANARCHY IN THE UK (*Daily Star*)
YOB RULE (*Daily Mirror*) (Molyneux 2011, 2)

The events and issues surrounding the UK's 'five days in August' 2011 riots are best explained by beginning with the general situation before coming to the specific events. What factors then will contextualise an appreciative account?

- *Advanced marginality.* This term was coined by Loic Wacquant (2008) in his important account of the situation of those he terms urban outcasts (Squires and Lea 2012). He compares the treatment of these groups in the USA, France and the UK—pulling out similarities and contrasts regarding ghettoisation, levels of precarious employment, criminalisation and incarceration.
- *The state of the working class* is obviously a linked concern. For those sociologists and criminologists who believe the degree of change that has occurred within the working class is so great that it no longer can act with any cohesion, the events of the August riots 'proved' their prognosis as they attributed the rioters' actions to values such as greed, commercialism and an implicit rejection of the possibility of political change. For those of us who disagree—believing that the working class are still with us, in a changed form from the industrial or 'Fordist' model of the 1930s to the 1980s, but still representing the mass of society who need to sell their ability to work to the highest bidder— the riots have to be seen in the context of the rest of the lives of those involved. Working-class life in twenty-first-century UK is much more multicultural than the old model and educational changes are raising the expectations and aspirations of all, especially for future generations; but this is occurring in the context of rising inequalities that make more and more people aware that they cannot afford to be comfortable about other people being filthy rich—especially in London, where the rich's wealth threatens others' 'right to the city' (Harvey 2013; Dorling 2014).
- *Austerity and resistance.* Specifically, several youth centres in the borough of Tottenham were closed down in the months before the UK riots began. These are just one local aspect of the global austerity engendered by the 2008 bank crash. The sheer scale of the cuts in the public sector had already led to the largest ever trade union demonstration in Britain in April 2011, as well as the wave of anti-austerity

movements in Europe and America, and the Arab Spring which had so dramatically legitimised rising up against a failed regime.

- *Looting or Shopping?* One of the key reactions to the riots relayed through both the mainstream media and social media networks expressed outrage at the targets selected by the rioters. Unsurprisingly the government, and those shopkeepers affected, believed that smashing shop windows and taking goods was unworthy of being dignified with any other label than 'criminality pure and simple': the actions of a 'feral underclass'—a label so offensive it implies little better could be expected from 'these types of people'. But were these actions really examples of people whose rage against the system had been converted into a frenzy of anti-social consumerism—taking trainers and TVs as the 'shoplifters of the world unite'? This was the title of Žižek's article published the week after the riots, calling them 'a blind acting out … a meaningless outburst' (Žižek 2011). Undoubtedly they took the goods, but does that signify they are 'flawed consumers' unable to purchase 'the objects of desire, whose absence is most violently resented'? Bauman argues that 'looting shops and setting them on fire derive from … the wrath, humiliation, spite and grudge aroused by NOT having them' (Bauman 2011). Or are the likes of John Lea and Simon Hallsworth correct to assert 'there is nothing about violent shopping … that is not political' (Hallsworth 2015, 1). After all, what could be more challenging to the capitalist mentality than the idea that the poor are entitled to something for free?
- *Fight for your right to party.* The likes of Slater, Lea and Hallsworth are nearer the mark when they emphasise the historical continuities in this riot, which are comparable to the many thousands of similar events that have occurred over the centuries when the poor symbolically and actually challenge the dominance of their masters for a limited period. This is not a blind or post-political act, it's a celebration. It's a special time 'when the rules went down', that is when the normal hierarchies are suspended or even inverted (Hallsworth 2015). It can be compared to events like carnivals in Europe from the 1400s to the 1700s: a time when maybe peasants would play the king, or nobles play the role of servants to those who traditionally serve them. We should remember that anti-racist rioting in post-war Britain began in 1976 at Notting

Hill carnival: 'carnival was their day,' said one Metropolitan police officer at the time. 'For the rest of the year, police would be stopping them
in ones and twos in the street, where they would be in a minority. But
for one weekend they were in the majority and they took over the
streets' (Younge 2002). These events inspired The Clash's *White Riot: I
Wanna Riot of My Own*—a homage to these inspiring actors. In a riot,
the rule of money and property is suspended as those at the bottom of
the pile demonstrate their one true power—their numbers—in an act
of 'rage against the market' such as the Bristol Tesco Riot of Easter
2011 (Clement 2012a). The words of one Birmingham rioter from
August 2011 captured this sense of a special occasion:

> It's not like any other day today is it … not just some normal, routine shit
> day, same-old-same-old. I mean it's mental innit, it's just crazy, you can
> come out, get what you can, it's like everyone is on one, it's just like a party
> today, you got to join in! (Treadwell et al. 2013, 9)

- *Controlling society*. At Notting Hill, the police were ill-equipped in
  1976. Defending themselves with dustbin lids and milk crates, they
  were also outmanoeuvred. 'That whole experience made the police
  very sore,' reported one officer. 'They had taken a beating and were
  determined that it would not happen again, so when the next one
  came about, there was some desire for revenge' (Younge 2002). The
  day-to-day exercise of maintaining social order remains largely the job
  of the police. But ironically, despite the fact that the British police
  were formed in 1829 to create a more reliable way of containing outbreaks of riot and social disorder than the use of armed troops, the use
  of extreme violence by the police has been the trigger for riots in the
  USA, France and the UK for generations now. A key section of the
  1829 Police Act upholds the constable's duty 'to apprehend all loose,
  idle and disorderly people'. Combine this with the institutional racism
  of which the police have now acknowledged they are guilty and you
  have the basis of stop and search and armed policing operations targeting black people living within multicultural communities. The shooting of Mark Duggan was just such an occurrence. Institutionally racist
  practices associated with the anti-drugs Operation Trident led to

armed police shooting Duggan dead, maintaining throughout that he was a member of a notorious street gang and had threatened the officer who shot him with a gun.

- *A shift in consciousness.* Mark Duggan's death became a 'socially medi-ated tragedy' (Baker 2012) as pictures of his body at the crime scene were broadcast over the next few days on Facebook and BlackBerry Messenger. The Metropolitan Police followed up this tragedy with a number of critical mistakes, claiming Duggan was armed and had shot at an officer; neglecting to inform the family of his death; the non-arrival of a senior officer as promised the following Saturday, when friends and family demonstrated outside Tottenham Green Police Station; and the final straw—an officer assaulting one of the protestors who was venting her rage at their situation. Footage from the scene relays one person crying out: 'It's a girl, leave her alone it's a fucking girl!' (Reel News 2011). The words of Macaulay about a past reaction to state repression—'the violent compression of so powerful and elastic a spring would be followed by as violent a recoil' (Macaulay 1889, 350)—seem to describe the powerful reaction ema-nating from the Tottenham crowd that Saturday night. Two police cars, a bus and several shops were then attacked and looted as hun-dreds and eventually thousands of people took to the streets. Witnesses describe a festive atmosphere, and members of North London's Hassidic Jewish Community came down with food for the protestors. Another witness recalled how some rioters, having seized a case of wine from a supermarket, couldn't decide whether to throw the bottles at the police or drink them! Hallsworth lists the 'disor-derly conduct' as attacking the police, taking goods, violating prop-erty rights and behaving 'more generally in ways that violate … what it is to be "normal" … (swarming, shouting, running, wilding, refus-ing to take orders, fighting, attacking passers-by and so on) … attack, subvert and invert every convention around which it is established' (Hallsworth 2015, 7–8).

The great wave of social movements occurring in that momentous year of 2011 should have been seen as a vindication of the Marxist arguments; stressing the need for struggle to overthrow a global system being exposed as tyrannical, austere and ripe for destruction. But tragically, all too many didn't see it that way. As Neil Smith explained:

> The stunning thing is that, for generations of North American and European socialists, feminists, and anti-globalization activists—the people opposed to capitalism in the 1990s and into the twenty-first century—the option of revolution was not on the table. Revolutions are a fact of life, a fact of history, but for decades they've been understood as unrealistic. This orientation had a lot to do with the response to the upheaval of the 1960s, and to the events of 1968 in particular. Despite its problems, 1968 galvanized a massive number of people around the globe and across a range of struggles. (Smith 2011)

Dario Melossi recently charted the post-68 retreat in criminology, stating: 'particularly negative and specific to the Sociology of deviance, was the removal of sensibilities linked with the so-called labelling approach, the radical consequences of which had culminated in David Matza's *Becoming Deviant*' and, in 1976, 'most symbolic (for criminologists), the closing of the Berkeley School of Criminology' (Melossi 2015, x).

This is shorthand for the fact that the political reaction to the failure of left-wing forces to break through the crisis of capitalism in the 1970s had bred a new climate of neo-liberalism whose destructive impact had worn down the organisations, the ideals and the imagination of the working-class movement. In a tragic version of Robert Merton's self-fulfilling prophecy, much of the Left in Europe and America believed their masters' power was unchallengeable, that there was no alternative to the market. In Britain this phrase is associated with Margaret Thatcher, but the case for the 'moral necessity of austerity' began under the previous Labour Government in 1976 (Whitehead 1985; Clement 2014).

A recent book, *Riots and Political Protest*, draws some rather different conclusion to those advanced here. Its subtitle is 'Notes from the Post-Political Present' which signals the authors' intent to understand contemporary society as one where the old political values no longer apply. Some observations about the English 2011 riots contain truisms such as:

> Weren't the riots essentially a desperate cry, issued in the hope that it might encourage the social mainstream to turn and acknowledge the continued presence of the forgotten and ignored? (Winlow et al. 2015, 139)

Yes, riots are always what Martin Luther King called 'the voice of the unheard'. But many of their assertions appear determined to deny any specific agency or even content to the sound of this crowd. They note 'the total absence of articulate political opposition … The rioters did not demand social justice' (Winlow et al. 136). They claim 'those who took to the streets in Birmingham and Manchester had never heard of Mark Duggan' (Winlow et al. 135). This seems unlikely given the history of stop and search and deaths in police custody which has affected these cities as well as London. They took place two and three days after the initial riots when the media coverage of all these events was at saturation levels.

In order to justify their categorisation of the riots as symptomatic of a 'post-political present' the authors assert:

> The rioters were simply not equipped with an intellectual means of identifying the root cause of their frustration … they hope only to improve their circumstances within the existing capitalist system. (Winlow et al. 139)

To expect that protestors are all fully conscious Marxists or anarchists with an incisive grasp of not only the problem causing their actions but also the solution is surely asking too much of any group of strikers, demonstrators or protestors in history. Moreover, the case made by three hooded young people interviewed by Sky News in the week of the riots, points to elements of class consciousness and political awareness which challenge the post-political assumptions. One began by saying: 'Everything's expensive … we have a free opportunity. We can take whatever we want.' At first this could be read as an apolitical statement—manifesting the rioters' ensnarement within an iron cage of addiction to the goals of a consumer society. Yet he goes on to make a more explicitly political announcement: 'The government, they don't care for us. They just leave us on the block—to do whatever we do.' This leads the first rioter to specify the root of his concerns in what could be described as unmistakably class-conscious terms: 'The government, they're not thinking about us. They're thinking about that pocket'—he gestures across the river to the towers of Canary Wharf—'one pocket that's up there' (Sky News 2011; Clement 2012b, 119).

This comment inspires his 'colleague' to launch into an outburst that is little short of a political manifesto, noteworthy because it stresses how these young men identify with the aspirations of their more 'included' peers and clearly relate to how current austerity measures are contributing to their sense of alienation:

> They should put back on EMA. Help all those single mothers that are struggling. Uni, cuts, everythin'—we're not doin' this for the fun of it. We're doing it for money—to survive in this world. But until we get that, or a little bit of support from the government, then it's not gonna stop. That's what I think innit. (Sky News 2011; Clement 2012b, 120)

EMA stands for the 'educational maintenance allowance', a £30 a week payment for attending further education (FE) college for 16–18 year olds. It was brought in by the last Labour Government and the prediction that it would be axed by the 2010 coalition government had brought FE students to join in with the 10 November 2010 student protests against university tuition fees being trebled to £9000 a year. This added to the size and militancy of these protests which began with clashes between large groups battling the police and ended with a riotous march that occupied Millbank, the Tory Party HQ. Many of the 50,000 students hadn't even known that the building was the property of the party of government, but on the suggestion of a militant minority they responded enthusiastically, thoroughly trashing their offices (Callinicos and Jones 2011). There were surreal moments of protest. The son of a famous rock star was jailed for climbing up the war memorial in Whitehall, as was an FE college student for throwing a fire extinguisher off a roof—no one was hurt. Prince Charles and the Duchess of Cornwall were surrounded by rioters whilst stranded in their limousine in the West End. These student protests were the swallow before the summer of riot and revolution to come in the next year. Besides the August riots, there were Easter riots in Bristol, and Britain's biggest ever trade union demonstration of over 500,000 which gave the lie to the notion of a supine working class. Add in the mass public sector one-day strikes that bookended the August riots in June and November and it is easy to see these events as vindicating a Marxist account of the 'rebirth of history': 'since it is commonly held that

Marxism consists in assigning a determinant role to the economy and the social contradictions which derive from it, who isn't "Marxist" today?' (Badiou 2012, 7–8).

These riots and the people who took part in them were political (Akram 2014; Clement 2012a; Platts-Fowler 2013; Sutterluty 2014, Slater 2015). This is evident from the above statements, although 'the casting of the 2011 riots as non-political was initially ubiquitous' (Harvie and Milburn 2013, 561); since then the voices claiming a political continuity between these events and others elsewhere or in history have grown stronger. Even if the rioters didn't all see their actions as political, their context made them so; 'elites are attempting to impose austerity as the "new normal" ... populations are contesting this imposition, defending what they believe they are entitled to. The society that emerges from this period of crisis will, to a large extent, depend on the outcome of these struggles' (Harvie and Milburn 2013, 586).

Another voice from the riots echoes these political sentiments:

Why you gonna raise tuition fees, ... for put more people on the streets, that's not right. How many protests have we had, this country had, and nothing's gone away? ... 'And then we turn to violence.' What else we meant to turn to—are we meant to chill there, and speak quietly and say yeah—say you know what. Fuck this. We'll do it our own way. (BBC 2012)

There is a sense of purpose in these statements which contrasts sharply with comments in *Riots and Political Protest*, such as 'the riot is driven forward by an incoherent rabble of pissed off individuals' (Winlow et al. 2015, 203). It is fundamentally wrong to argue, as these authors do in an earlier paper, that:

This former class in itself, once potentially also a class for itself, has, languishing under the dominant forces of mass-mediated consumer culture and post-politics, disintegrated into an atomized and alienated milieu of competitive individuals. (Treadwell et al. 2013, 15)

This phrasing about the nature of the class of people rioting and protesting, 'a class for itself', refers to Marx's definition where he explained how the working class under capitalism had gained a consciousness that would allow it to act in its own interests and overthrow its oppressors. Writing at the same time as Marx, Thomas Carlyle also saw the new working class as a threat that could overturn society, and feared that so-called riots—in reality mass working-class demonstrations—prophesied a future revolution:

> Peterloo stands written, as in fire-characters, or smoke-characters prompt to become fire again ... the treasury of rage, burning hidden or visible in all hearts ever since ... is of unknown extent. (Carlyle 1912, 16)

The equivalent of these 'fire characters' in 2011 were the burning shops and warehouses in Tottenham, Enfield, Clapham, Ealing and Croydon. These rioters were not languishing under the dominant forces of mass-mediated consumer culture, they were actively engaging in resistance that is celebratory, political and points to a rejection, not an embrace, of capitalism and consumerism's values. As Gary Younge wrote at the time:

> They were looting, not shop-lifting, and challenging the police for control of the streets not stealing coppers' hubcaps. When a group of people join forces to flout both law and social convention, they are acting politically. (Younge 2011)

Far from social media trivialising the action, it augmented it: the source of the 'treasury of rage' was the image of the victim of police violence, Mark Duggan, lying dead in the street—sent across London via BlackBberry Messenger and Facebook in the days preceding the outbreak of rioting:

> These mediums engendered a sense of social cohesion by connecting actors from disparate geographies into a common symbolic space ... a common feature of the 2011 protests was that these forms of 'mediated crowd' membership largely emerged in response to a perceived 'social tragedy', wherein the interactive online relationships enabled by social media connected aggrieved users into intense relationships that transpired offline. (Baker 2012, 175)

In areas like Clapham and Ealing in London, the middle classes and the poor live in close proximity, with the former stridently denouncing the actions of the latter when their actions impinged upon 'their' community—leading to the much-publicised 'clean-up', where the memory of the riots was actually and symbolically swept away by the self-appointed guardians of the community (Baker 2012). In Eltham, south-east London, where Stephen Lawrence was murdered, supporters of the English Defence League gathered in a mob declaring their intent to protect 'their community' from the rioters. Racism and class privilege appeared to be the motives governing these crowds. Language, such as that of the then Justice Minister, Kenneth Clarke's term of 'the feral underclass', was employed to emphasise the moral superiority of the propertied over their social inferiors. Public policy was little more than name-calling allied to exemplary punishments for those arrested. Thomas Carlyle's warning about 'fire characters' and the likelihood of harvesting 'a treasury of rage' were part of the raging 'condition of England' in the 1830s and 1840s, when the Industrial Revolution was accompanied by massive economic inequality, riot, reform and revolution, as we have seen. Since the last UK riots, these inequalities have become greater still, especially in London where the riots spread further than ever before—well beyond the traditional inner cities. The new 'zones in transition', to use Ernest Burgess's typology, are spreading out across the metropolis as sustainable living in the capital threatens to become the privilege of a favoured minority. Rather than attempting to protect the most vulnerable, government policy seems to be one of austerity, a dangerous policy which can have unexpected political consequences, as we have already seen in the eurozone (Clement 2013).

We need to bring the state back to our consideration of how and why deviant behaviour such as riots and protest occurs. People do not have to become principled opponents of the policing system, or the government that controls it, in order to find themselves protesting. Is this something that mainstream criminological thinking is prepared to recognise? Matza (1969, pp. 143–4) remarked that:

> Among their most notable accomplishments, the criminological positivists succeeded in what would seem the impossible. They separated the study of crime from the workings and theory of the state … Scientists of various

persuasions thereafter wandered aimfully, leaving just a few possibilities uncovered, considering how deviation was produced. Throughout, a main producer remained obscure, off-stage … The role of the sovereign, and by extension, instituted authority was hardly considered in the study of deviant behaviour.

If criminology ignores the state's role in repression it ends up seeing urban uprisings such as occurred in the UK in 2011 and in the USA since the summer of 2014, as about something other than politics and resistance to racialised state violence. As illustrated above, this viewpoint is evident among some contemporary criminologists writing about the UK 2011 riots. Even left-wing critics, whilst correctly criticising 'the sheer theoretical narrowness and superficiality of the politically truncated Weberian and liberal-modernist sociology that has been dominant since the 1980s' (Hall and Winlow 2014, 107), believe that in the events of August 2011, which were sparked off by the police shooting of Mark Duggan, 'the initial protest against injustice seemed to disappear into the background':

> The most common motivation for participation in the riots and their brief, limited but nonetheless spectacular diffusion was that those looking on became envious of others who had taken the early initiative to loot desirable designer goods … and on the spur of the moment decided to join in. (Hall and Winlow 2014, 108)

This is a classic example of explaining how people are 'becoming deviant' by focusing on their (alleged) state of mind as a primary explanation for their actions. It overlooks the fact that the state and their agents of social control—the police—were central to the creation of the rioting crowds that assembled so rapidly in cities across England in that 'summer of discontent' (Briggs 2012). Surely this is a political act—a social movement reacting against state violence and racism which proves that we are *not* living in some 'post-political' era? John Lea observes that 'the rioters may have understood more about the crisis of liberal democracy than Winlow and Hall (or Briggs) give them credit for':

> Why march on Parliament when real power now lies with the banks and the markets? What better place to demonstrate this than through its

theatrical re-enactment on the high street? If neoliberalism celebrates the identity of politics and consumption then 'shopping' and 'taking stuff' could be a very practical political critique of neoliberalism! (Lea 2013, 418)

Not according to these authors, and colleagues, in the conclusion to their latest discussion of *Riots and Political Protest*:

> No progressive politics exists within the frame of the riot, and there is no seductive image of an ideological alternative for people to rally around. Instead, the riot is driven forward by an incoherent rabble of pissed-off individuals incapable of joining together to form a genuine political community. In the context of the post-political present, the riot is more a depressive acting out of deep, objectless frustration and anger than a concerted proto-political intervention demanding change. (Winlow et al. 2015, 202)

Whilst I would agree that emotions like frustration and anger do occur in riots, and that they are often spontaneous acts without a worked-out political strategy, this does not make them necessarily incoherent, post-political or individualist. Indeed the US actions of 2014–15 are plainly a political response to state violence as Steve Hall has acknowledged: 'the Ferguson events indicate the degree of brutality the state is willing to dish out to restore order. If these incoherent protests against unjust treatment ever get political in any coherent and purposeful way, the brutality will increase to "shock and awe" proportions'.[1] The emergence of the Black Lives Matter campaign, alongside movements for economic justice such as that of the US fast food workers, demonstrate a new and growing political consciousness within capitalism's most powerful territory.

The UK police's stop and search process of public humiliation, and institutionalised enactment of powerlessness in the face of unjust authority, has been proven to be racially discriminatory so often and so comprehensively that its continuance rankles those affected to still greater depths of outrage that such a practice continues. Britain's recognition of institutionalised racism is one obvious example of a process where the

---

[1] Personal communication with the author, August 2014.

links between injustice and infraction are undeniable. Almost every riot since World War II has broken out in reaction to acts of police violence.

In the USA the story is the same—albeit on a much greater scale. Howard Becker began his *Outsiders* by writing: 'the person who is thus labeled an outsider … may not regard those who judge him as either competent or legitimately entitled to do so … the rule-breaker may feel his judges are outsiders' (Becker 1963, 1–2). We can see how this whole process is reactionary. People refusing to understand or appreciate the motivation behind actions nevertheless condemn them as anti-social, causing further alienation. Black people in countries diverse enough to be defined as multicultural are disproportionately criminalised by the legal system operated by their respective machineries of state. This group, or figuration, is a reluctant consumer of justice—its members are often rightly enraged by the many acts of policing and crime control in which they are singled out. What David Matza wrote about juvenile delinquents is also true of this group: 'since he is a major consumer of justice, his standards are quite high. Justice must not only proceed fairly and with great care, it must not be too petty' (Matza 1964, 87).

During the first US civil rights movement, whites ganged together to enforce discrimination upon blacks. Citizens' organisations, state institutions and racist associations like the Ku Klux Klan took the lead. More often than not, they were backed up by the police. Such blatant racist repression, on top of the segregation and ghettoisation of which the Jim Crow laws in the south were the most powerful example, bred resistance, which itself strengthened and deepened the movement. Its direction of travel was radical—because the more people campaigned for civil rights, the greater the violence of the reaction. More liberal and peaceful methods of opposing this racist violence were both unsuccessful and unsatisfactory. As Manning Marable argues in explaining the impact of the 'Nation of Islam':

> Part of the Nation's newfound appeal had to do with the black reaction to southern whites 'massive resistance' to desegregation beginning in 1955. The growth of white 'Citizens' Councils across the South and the slayings of local NAACP and civil rights workers in the late fifties convinced a minority of African Americans that the Nation of Islam (NOI) was right. Whites would never grant full equality to blacks. (Marable 2011, 123)

Sixty years on, this prophecy remains true. The fact that the 2014 social movement, launched in the wake of the Ferguson shooting, needed to be called 'Black Lives Matter' epitomises this lack of equality. American capitalism remains racist in its economic division of labour, its civic allocation of housing and especially in its methods of enforcing social control through the agency of both police and prison. This 'deadly symbiosis' between the ghetto and the jail remains crucial to understanding US society (Wacquant 2001).

The campaigner who epitomised this rising militancy above all others was surely one of the NOI's leaders, Malcolm X. Like any good sociologist, he took a long-term view of the phenomenon under discussion, preaching in a 1955 sermon that 'you have been fighting for civil rights ever since the enemy brought you to Jamestown, Virginia, in the year of 1555' (Marable 2011, 117). No one articulated the problem with greater clarity. Firstly, on the problem of advocating only non-violent resistance:

If the leaders of the nonviolent movement can go into the white community and teach nonviolence, good, I'd go along with that. But as long as I see them teaching nonviolence only in the black community … we throw ourselves off guard. In fact, we disarm ourselves. (Breitman 1966, 139)

He believed that this approach is not only a recipe for failure, but also frustration and anomie. Greater satisfaction is generated in the act of fighting back:

You'll get your freedom by letting your enemy know that you'll do anything to get your freedom. It's the only way you'll get it. When you get that kind of attitude, they'll label you as a 'crazy negro' … they'll call you an extremist or a subversive, or seditious, or a red or a radical. But when you stay radical long enough, and get enough people to be like you, you'll get your freedom. (Breitman 1966, 145)

This was advice to African Americans in the northern cities as well as the racist south. Black Panther leader Bobby Seale explained: 'we kept getting one overwhelming response from almost every question that began with "What do you want?" Almost to a person, he said, their response was related to the police and how they behaved toward and treated Black people in their own communities' (Forbes 2000, 236). This echoes the famous slogan which achieved global prominence in the 1992 LA riots, and has accompanied every campaign ever since against police violence going unpunished—'No justice, no peace'.

Writing at the time of the first civil rights movement, Matza describes how:

> A sense of injustice … provides a simmering resentment—a setting of antagonism and antipathy … Antagonism takes the form of a jaundiced view of officials, a view which holds that their primary function is not the administration of justice, but the perpetuation of injustice. (Matza 1964, 101–102)

In Europe and the USA today, we hear a great deal about the government's need to monitor and police 'extremists'. The thought police experiment whereby peoples' communications are subject to surveillance and key words are flagged as 'evidence' of the need for further monitoring is now well-established in the USA and the UK. Some of the words highlighted by the US Department of Homeland Security include (Table 7.1):

Table 7.1 Domestic security keywords

Assassination	Emergency management	Gangs
Attack	Emergency response	National security
Domestic security	First responder	State of emergency
Drill	Homeland security	Security
Exercise	Maritime domain awareness (MDA)	Breach
Cops	National Preparedness initiative	Threat
Law enforcement	Militia	Standoff
Authorities	Shooting	SWAT
Disaster assistance	Shots fired	Screening
Disaster management	Evacuation	Bomb (squad or threat)
DNDO (Domestic Nuclear Detection Office)	Deaths	Crash
Mitigation	Hostage	Looting
Prevention (Greenburg 2013, 139)	Explosion (explosive)	Riot

Therefore someone using any these words on their phone or Facebook may not only be monitored, but runs the risk of being labelled an extremist, even a terrorist, with all the consequent loss of civil rights this implies. Such labelling was rampant in the original Civil Rights campaign. In a 1962 article in *Nation* Loren Miller explained: 'The Negro is outraged at being an extremist. Since he takes the position that the Constitution confers complete equality on all citizens, he must rest his case on the proposition that there is only one side, his side' (Clark 1965, 233).

So while protest is criminalised, the law itself appears the root of injustice. The startling statistic bearing out the deadly urgency of this state of affairs is supplied by the US website 'Killed By Police' (2015) which lists 1159 deaths at police hands between 1 January and 20 December 2015. In this deadly climate, the struggle for civil rights—a matter of basic equality—tends to evolve into something more. The struggle for freedom is presumably a larger goal, and leads Malcolm X on to discuss achieving peace, justice and even power: 'actually, you can't separate peace from freedom because no one can be at peace unless he has his freedom'.

> Power in defense of freedom is greater than power in defense of tyranny and oppression, because power, real power, comes from conviction which produces action, uncompromising action. It also produces insurrection against oppression. (Breitman 1966, 148, 150)

He is pointing out how a powerful urge to live in peace is aggravated by its blatant violation. When a person just like yourself is shot dead by a paranoid citizen who believes the 'stand your ground' legislation entitles him to kill, as happened to 17-year-old Trayvon Martin in 2012, and then the killer is acquitted—the injustice becomes unbearable: it must seek an outlet in an act of defiance, sanctioned and justified by this sense of 'no justice, no peace'. In Malcolm's opinion, the 1964 Harlem riot 'all started when a little boy was shot by a policeman, and he was turned loose, the same as the sheriff was turned loose in Mississippi when he killed the civil-rights workers' (Breitman 1966, 154).

An unjustified death at the hands of the police has been the spark for virtually every British riot since the 1980s. Despite a higher media profile, the number of black deaths in UK custody in controversial circumstances continues to rise (IRR 2015). In Paris, the 2005 wave of suburban riots began when a police chase led to two boys dying whilst hiding from them. But America's trail of police killings and beatings is so long and unbroken it stretches back to the days of African American slavery, through the period of lynchings and pogroms of the nineteenth and twentieth centuries and the era of assassination of civil rights leaders like Malcolm X in 1965 and Martin Luther King in 1968 (Campbell 2013). It was outrage at the acquittal of the officers who assaulted Rodney King that sparked the 1992 LA riots—the biggest to date.

What is different in the 2010s is that we are in the age of Obama, the first black president, who yet appears powerless to prevent the continuation of this trend. If Obama's election, certainly aided by a wave of enthusiasm from the black community who had up until then proven too disheartened by the quality of available candidates and parties to exercise their right to vote, was meant to signal their inclusion in American society, then the reality of police oppression and state-sanctioned violence and extortion has only made 'the American Dilemma' greater still.

This phrase, from the study by Swedish sociologist Gunnar Myrdal in 1948, referred to the way US society is so racist it locks black people out of the promise of a better future that is supposed to be its rationale. Malcolm said 'I'm not an American. I'm one of the 22 million black people who are the victims of Americanism … I don't see any American dream; I see an American nightmare' (Breitman 1966, 26). Another African American Harlem activist from this period, Professor of Psychology Kenneth Clark, expanded upon this theme:

> The discrepancy between the reality and the dream burns into their consciousness. The oppressed can never be sure whether their failures reflect personal inferiority or the fact of color. This persistent and agonizing conflict dominates their lives. (Clark 1965, 12)

The wave of riots that began in Harlem in 1964 spread to Watts, a suburb of LA in 1965, Newark, New York and Detroit in 1967 and many more riots and protests ensued, especially in the wake of Martin Luther King's 1968 assassination. Manning Marable outlines the scale of revolt: 'the number of Black urban uprisings increased from 9 in 1965, 38 in 1966, 128 in 1967, and 131 in the first six months of 1968'

(Marable 2000, 208). The growth of the Black Panther Party accompanied these events, and their militancy, alongside this rising tide of struggle, terrified elements of American society into a brutal and murderous reaction. Jesse Jackson, a direct witness to King's assassination, told the *New York Times* how 'an informal coalition of white racist vigilantes, the police and government officials were conspiring to kill Blacks' (Marable 2000, 233). This continued into the next decade with the into the next decade with the Panthers' murder and incarceration, but was present in many cities such as Atlanta, Georgia, where 'in 1973 and 1974 23 Blacks were gunned down by police; 12 were under 14' (Marable 2000, 235). In the 1980s, when he wrote *How Capitalism underdeveloped Black America*, Marable concluded that 'the use of physical coercion and terrorism against Blacks' is not inevitable. It results from "the absence of a powerful, democratic and progressive movement by Blacks which challenges racism in the streets as well as in the courts"' (Marable 2000, 242). The fact that so much changed in American society over the next half century, but black people are still subject to the *same* brutal violence from the police and racist vigilantes in 2015, explains the rebirth of the US civil rights movement.

In Ferguson, a suburb of St Louis, Missouri, it is estimated that an overwhelmingly white police force was subjecting a majority black population to fines and court fees totalling $2.6 million, or $321 per household per annum. There were also cases of asset seizures without sufficient proof (*Webb* 2014). Ferguson is 'a 67% black community in a regional economy badly hit by the recession. Yet its police force is 95% white ... 86% of stops, 92% of searches and 93% of arrests were of black people ... racial injustice ... remains the great enduring national wound' (*The Guardian* 2014). After Michael Brown, an 18-year-old youth, was shot dead by white policeman Darren Wilson in August 2014 there were mass protests as hundreds paraded on the streets, arms aloft, calling out to the police 'Hands Up, Don't Shoot'. Their actions and motivation appear to be in exactly the same spirit as those 1964 Harlem rioters so perceptively described by Clark as engaged in 'social defiance' and 'deliberate mockery':

> Even those Negroes who threw bottles and bricks from the roofs were not in the grip of a wild abandon, but seemed deliberately to be prodding the police to behave openly as the barbarians that the Negroes felt they actually were. (Clark 1965, 16)

So far, what began at Ferguson in August 2014 spread to Staten Island, New York, where 100000 marched after the grand jury decision not to indict the officer who killed Eric Garner (Trudell 2015), followed by LA, Ohio, Wisconsin and Baltimore. One difference between then and now has been the technological scale of the police reaction. A large amount of military equipment no longer needed for US troops operating abroad has been recycled back to domestic police forces. These included 'bomb suits, night-vision goggles, drones, shock-cuffs … Armoured Patrol Carriers … and personal protective armour' (ACLU 2014, 5, 11). As a result in Ferguson we saw the fire power of the state—armoured vehicles and guns, gas grenades and tear gas, even a no-fly zone being imposed as once again 'the war comes home'. The police killing in Baltimore, a larger city that also rioted in 1968, sparked greater reaction still.

Freddie Gray, a 25-year-old black man, died of spinal injuries a week after being arrested by Baltimore police on 12 April. He was cuffed on his hands and ankles but did not have a seatbelt on. Bundled into a police van, during the 45-minute drive to local police headquarters, Gray was subject to 'a highly controversial police practice called the "rough ride", in which an officer drives erratically to toss his handcuffed prisoner around the vehicle as a form of punishment':

> By the time he emerged, after four stops, including one where he was placed in leg shackles for 'irate' behaviour, Mr Gray was reported to be in 'serious medical distress' … the practice is not new to Baltimore. In 2004 the city paid a settlement of $39 million to Jeffrey Alston, who was paralysed. A year later, another man received $7.4 million. (*Spence* 2015)

Freddie had a spinal cord injury and a crushed larynx. He lapsed into a coma and died after a week. Protests continued daily. More than 200 people were arrested in the disturbances. Police bail for people arrested during the disturbance was set at levels many could not hope to pay, such as £330,200. The habeas corpus law in the state of Maryland says that no one can be detained without charge for more than 24 hours. But Republican Governor Larry Hogan effectively suspended this. Hogan also brought in 1500 National Guard troops and a nightly 10 p.m. curfew for a week.

As more than 1000 protesters marched through the city on the follow-ing Wednesday, municipal employees came out of their offices to show support. One of them told journalists, 'to see this unity … it portrays to the world that what you see on TV is not what Baltimore is about'. Protesters cheered when they heard that the six police officers who arrested Freddie Gray in Baltimore were being charged over his death. Thousands of people had protested and rioted for nearly a week over Freddie's death. When the charges were announced crowds celebrated on the streets, the curfew was lifted and the National Guard withdrawn. The officers face a number of charges including 'involuntary manslaughter'. But it is a long way from officers being charged to anyone getting convicted over the kill-ing. Institutional racism is key to the case, though, in this majority black city, three of the six police officers charged are black. Campaigner Safi Edwards explained: 'we are used to being underdogs,' she said. 'Even our football team are underdogs. We're used to people viewing us in a certain way. This has been happening for our whole history and they've been get-ting away with it. They wonder why the kids are broken.' But she added that hope came out of the protests:

> For the first time in my life I've seen the whole community come together, there were gang members with their faces covered. We felt safe right next to them for the first time. I was talking to one of the little guys last night with his black hoodie on. He's been through it. We just stood there and talked and hugged. I said, 'What's your name?' He said, 'I don't tell nobody my real name', but he told me. (Olende 2015)

All of these ingredients appear to add up to the birth and growth of a new social movement. There are three other important parallels between the first and the present civil rights movements: the fight against economic injustice, the targets of the white backlash, and the growth of political con-sciousness. In the early 1960s, New York black civil rights leaders set up a 'Working Committee of Unity for Action'. One of its key demands was a minimum wage of $1.50 an hour (Marable 2011, 193). In 2014–15 the fast food workers campaign for a $15 an hour minimum wage has spread right across the country and won its demands in several states. On 21 May 2015, 3000 employees and union activists marched on McDonald's headquarters near Chicago where they were holding their Annual General Meeting. They handed in a petition of 1.4 million signatures backing their demands. Chanting 'We work, we sweat, put $15 in our cheque'. Placards and banners proclaimed 'Mcdonald's: $15 and union rights, not food stamps' and 'McShame McDonald's' (Neate 2015).

One powerful act symbolising the white backlash over the last 60 years has been the terror attacks on black churches. Perhaps the most notorious was the bombing of the 16th Street Baptist Church in Birmingham, Alabama, on 15 September 1963, which killed four young black girls, Carole Robertson, Cynthia Wesley, Addie Mae-Collins—all 14—and 11-year-old Denise McNair. They were childhood acquaintances of another key civil rights fighter, Angela Davis, who was brought up in an area of Birmingham called 'Dynamite Hill' because of frequent acts of racist terror by the Ku Klux Klan (Davis 1998, 2). She was haunted by the horror of these events, later joining the Black Panther Party and the US Communist Party. A wave of church burnings swept the nation, again in the 1990s, prompting the then President Bill Clinton to sign the Church Arson Prevention Act. This is the context for another bloody parallel—the mass murder of blacks attending a bible class at Emmanuel AME Church in Charleston in 2015 by a white supremacist youth. This act shocked the nation and led to calls for the Confederate flag no longer to be flown in the state capital. But that was not the end of the affair. Also in South Carolina is the Glover Grove Baptist Church in Warrensville. This was one of at least six black church burnings in the South, all of which took place in the week and a half since nine people were killed in Emanuel AME Church. President of the Southern Poverty Law Centre, Richard Cohen, said, 'it's not unreasonable to suspect that what we're seeing [now] is a backlash to the taking down of the Confederate flag, the determination of our country to face its racial problems' (NPR 2015).

Whilst today's movement has not yet radicalised to the same degree as was achieved in the late 1960s, it has sustained itself for well over a year now, spreading the wave of protest across America in a number of innovative actions. The first anniversary of the Ferguson uprising led to another mass demonstration. The police shot dead another youth, although this time he was apparently armed himself. The contrast between his immediate execution and the police's tolerance of the white, armed group calling themselves the 'Oathtakers', who patrolled the streets alongside the police carrying automatic weapons and machine guns with impunity, will only have served to radicalise the protestors still further. The protestors themselves recognise the parallels with the past and comment on them in their actions. In 2015 some wore T-shirts with the slogan 'This ain't your momma's civil rights movement': others carried an American flag deliberately reversed.

Below I will explore what the barriers are to its success, and whether criminology can help us to understand this phenomenon. Clearly, the implementation of the law is central to all of these concerns. What are the obstacles preventing due legal process trying and convicting these criminals in uniform? To answer these questions we need to look at the problem from all sides, in Becker's words relating to the LA riots in the 1960s: 'we must grasp the perspective of the resident of Watts and of the Los Angeles policeman if we are to understand what went on in that outbreak' (Becker 1967, 244). Former state prosecutor Paul Butler recently highlighted the scale of institutional injustice built into US policing in 2015 with this insight into the police perspective:

> If we prosecutors asked the officer too many questions about how he obtained evidence or if we questioned his credibility in any way, he would catch an attitude. 'Don't treat me like a suspect' communicated that officer's belief that he didn't have to follow the same rules as the citizens he serves and protects. The Law Enforcement Officers Bill of Rights makes that double standard the law in 14 states. (Butler 2015)

If due process becomes a cover for injustice then the law is turned upside down. A brutal process of untrammelled crime control, operated by the state's agents of social control, represents an abuse of citizens' right to justice—their civil rights—and therefore provides a justification for resistance to this process of violent social control.

Matza proposed an alternative approach:

> The growth of a sociological view of deviant phenomena involved … the replacement of a correctional stance by an appreciation of the deviant subject, the tacit purging of a conception of pathology by new stress on human

diversity, and the erosion of a simple distinction between deviant and conventional phenomena, resulting from a more intimate familiarity with the world as it is, which yielded a more sophisticated view stressing complexity. (Matza 1969, 10)

Sadly, this attitude was not on view from authority figures in Baltimore. The city's African American Democratic Party Mayor, Stephanie Rawlings-Blake, claimed the city should not be destroyed 'by thugs, who, in a very senseless way, are trying to tear down what so many have fought for. Tearing down business, tearing down and destroying property' (Reuters 2015). Most Americans, black or white, don't run businesses or own property. Is it reasonable to demand they respect the very things they lack? Their actions are not those of 'senseless thugs'. Rather, it is their empathy with the plight of Freddie Gray and their determination to prevent further police killing that has driven the actions denounced as a riot. Also, those holding political office have failed to appreciate the feelings of so many Americans who find themselves unable to vote because they have a criminal record resulting from the waves of mass incarceration in the USA over the last 40 years. Michelle Alexander, rightly, calls this 'the new Jim Crow'. Her book opens with a case study that lays bare the centuries of a racism that still endures:

> Jarvious Cotton cannot vote … Cotton's great-great-grandfather could not vote as a slave. His great-grandfather was beaten to death by the Ku Klux Klan for attempting to vote. His grandfather was prevented from voting by Klan intimidation. His father was barred from voting by poll taxes and literacy tests. Today, Jarvious Cotton cannot vote because he, like many black men in the US, has been labelled a felon and is currently on parole. (Alexander 2010, 1)

Words like appreciation and respect sum up the approach criminologists and others need to take if they are to explain this phenomenon. Matza explained: 'appreciation of deviant phenomenon requires a consideration of the subject's viewpoint. Though it hardly requires an acceptance of that viewpoint, it does assume sympathy with it' (Matza 1969, 18). Rawlings-Blake's denunciation is an example of an 'incapacity to separate standards of morality from actual description' (Matza 1969, 17). Describing the

West Side Studies research programme carried out in New York for the Russell Sage Foundation, he locates their failure in their detached corrective stance:

> It rarely transcends the limitations incumbent on the outsider. Although the observers toured the world of the West Side and sympathized with its residents, they developed little appreciation for its integrity and thus its workings. Being outsiders—and never transforming themselves—the observers were barely able to describe or comprehend the moral and social life of their subjects. Indeed, the virtual absence of moral life is taken as a cardinal feature of the West Side. (Matza 1969, 21)

Matza's approach is more involved, it embodies the notion of commitment:

> Appreciating a phenomenon is a fateful decision, for it eventually entails a commitment—to the phenomenon and to those exemplifying it—to render it with fidelity and without violating its integrity. (Matza 1969, 24)

He believed all research should adopt this approach: 'until appreciation is instituted as an ordinary element of disciplinary method, firsthand contact with a deviant world seems the surest way of avoiding the reduction of the phenomenon to that which it is not, thus violating its integrity'. This is the only way to avoid taking the outsider viewpoint: 'intimate knowledge of deviant worlds tends to subvert the correctional conception of pathology' (Matza 1969, 24, 25).

To move beyond seeing deviance as a pathology means acknowledging the agency of the subject, in other word recognising that people make their own history. This requires 'an understanding of the unusual ways in which a subject relates to the circumstances that allegedly move and shape [her or] him':

> An object, being merely reactive, is literally determined by circumstance. Life, being adaptive, responds to the circumstances making up the milieu … But mere reactivity or adaptation should not be confused with the distinctively human condition. They are better seen as an alienation or exhaustion of that condition. A subject actively addresses or encounters his circumstances;

accordingly, his distinctive capacity is to reshape, strive toward creating, and actually transcend circumstance. (Matza 1969, 92–93)

Matza's words here echo Gramsci, who Marable cites in attempting to stress the liberating potential of humanity when struggling collectively:

> It is essential to conceive of man [*sic*] as a series of active relationships (a process) in which individuality, while of the greatest importance, is not the sole element to be conceived ... man changes himself, modifies himself, to the same extent that he is a nexus. (Marable 2000, 214)

One of the leaders of the Congress of Racial Equality, James Farmer, provided a concrete example of the political power of activism, claiming: 'the picketing and the national demonstrations are the reason that the walls came down in the South, because people were in motion with their own bodies marching with picket signs, sitting in, boycotting, withholding their patronage' (Marable 2011, 214).

As an academic at the University of California, Berkeley from the 1960s onwards, Matza worked alongside the founder of symbolic interactionism, Herbert Blumer, 'culminating in the founding of the Institute for the Study of Social Change in 1976':

> The subversive implication of this stance is that the rationality of deviance could be understood and celebrated as a condition of oppression and the definitions and meanings imposed by those in power could become contested. (Lemelle 2010, 187, 188)

This approach was mirrored in the commitment to radical criminology amongst a number of Berkeley staff. As an editorial in the journal *Crime and Social Justice* noted:

> In 1970–71, the radical wing of the School provided a great deal of support to the campaign for community control of the police; in 1972, many people from the School helped to organize a huge prison action conference which mobilized and consolidated the growing prisoner support movement.

Others participated in a local anti-rape organization … All in all, it was a period of intensive political activity, generated by the broader social conditions of revolt and resistance, and nourished by specific experiences at Berkeley. (Editorial 1976, 2)

Angela Davis was also caught up in this maelstrom of resistance and repression. Arrested in 1971 for her 'role' in a hostage-taking incident in a California courtroom which was helpfully resolved by the police shooting and killing both kidnappers and court officials, her prison letter claimed 'the entire apparatus of the bourgeois democratic state, especially its judicial system and its prisons, is disintegrating'. They were 'instruments for unbridled repression, institutions which may be successfully resisted but which are more and more impervious to meaningful reform' (Davis 1998, 14). Back at Berkeley, alarmed by this degree of activism, the university management closed down the School of Criminology. One academic who lost his job, Herman Schwendinger, explained how students and staff were broadening their critique of society whilst riding this wave of radicalism:

Of course, radicals at the School contributed to this demystification of ruling institutions and ideology. Given their professional interests and outlooks, they naturally debunked the traditional rationales for class, gender and racially biased law enforcement policies. As political dissent intensified, their targets expanded. They began to include class control of government and America's political economy. (Schwendinger and Schwendinger 2014, 146)

These redefinitions of criminology have been taken further in subsequent decades with the development of the discourse of 'social harm'. They would not have happened without the wave of struggle—the explosion of 1968 and all that—which challenged the workings of capitalism in so many ways. Matza's *Becoming Deviant* was very much a product of that time and sought to explain how people's sense of what is possible can shift in the process of change itself: Matza details how consciousness can change when subjects are involved—are acting 'inside the phenomenon, actually doing the thing and possibly being with others who also do it, the subject becomes so situated as to sense the meaning of affinity':

> [She or] he builds its meaning … One way of summarizing that amplification is to say that the meaning of affinity becomes concrete or relevant. The subject may now reconsider, in light of the disclosed meaning built into the course of experience, whether his initial understanding of his own affinities—as he pictured them—was sound. (Matza 1969, 118)

So people aren't swept away—this is no subconscious or irrational process: their viewpoint may change on the basis of new perceptions generated by their active involvement. From the standpoint of those resisting injustice, the order of society and the necessity of actively challenging it, things look different. The need to remain a passive observer, accepting the status quo, is actively reconsidered in the light of a police action, for example. The protester reconsiders his or her stance, and chooses to take sides. Matza continues: 'that reconsideration is the project that links affinity to affiliation. The subject discovers himself in the process … In the context of experience, consciousness may shift itself so as to incorporate new terms of reference, new issues of relevance … the very tissue with which meaning is built and disposition discovered' (Matza 1969, 118–119).

Dario Melossi has recently reminded his readers 'it is in times when class division and conflicts are more pronounced that these critiques are more liberally advanced' and in todays more conservative atmosphere criminology has seen the marginalisation or even 'the removal of the sensibilities linked with the so-called *labelling* approach, the radical consequences of which had culminated in David Matza's *Becoming Deviant*' (1969), (Melossi 2015, x). Ironically, the growth of a radical activism at Berkeley in the 1960s and 1970s in the wake of the first US civil rights movement ended with the university authorities shutting down the school of criminology, and arguably the study of crime went on a steady retreat from overt political commitment over the next four decades. We still discuss political issues, to be sure, but often fail to draw out the radical and emancipatory conclusions. Melossi's book is about migration and crime and concludes: 'if we want to decrease the participation and involvement of migrants in criminal activities we have to do exactly the opposite of what we have been told for years, i.e. we have to welcome migrants in our midst' (Melossi 2015, 90). A similarly radical and political response to riot and protest would be for criminology to show more appreciation for the context and advocate the sort of policies which would really mean that black lives matter. However, the experience of Obama in office shows us that it is not enough simply to want these more progressive policies. Even if you are the president, the nature of state power and capitalist control over the political machine makes these dreams unlikely to be realised through winning an election. It can only be won through a struggle, another and final lesson for today from those earlier days. Melossi points out:

> The years between 1969 and 1971 marked the climax of the social and political conflict in the United States (and indeed not only there). It was within these conflicts that 'the State' resurfaced—'evoked', we might say, by the writings of intellectuals such as Matza—as the image of 'the enemy' of those various movements and of any project of democracy and freedom. (Melossi 2008, 176)

The principal purpose of this book is to provide evidence for the way that, as Marx and Engels described it in *The Communist Manifesto*, 'the class struggle is the motor of history'. So much that our society's rulers and the media label as anti-social, or riotous, or the actions of a mindless mob are in fact elements of that struggle seeking an avenue to make a change from the unbearable conditions of exploitation, violence or political tyranny that oppress most of the people most of the time. With the type of appreciation of these labelling processes that were pioneered by Tannenbaum (1938) and developed by the likes of Becker and Matza, we have more chance of setting crime in its context—and indeed identifying what really constitutes a crime and what is a justified reaction against the oppression, violence and exploitation sanctioned by the law and its agents of social control.

References

Akram, S. (2014). Recognising the 2011 United Kingdom riots as political protest: A theoretical framework based on agency, habitus and the preconscious. *British Journal of Criminology, 54*(3), 375–392.

Alexander, M. (2010). *The New Jim Crow: Mass incarceration in the age of coilor-blindness*. New York: The New Press.

Alexander, P., Lekgowa, T., Mmope, B., Sinwell, L., & Xezwi, B. (2013). *Marikana: A view from the mountain and a case to answer*. London: Bookmarks.

American Civil liberties Union (ACLU). (2014). War comes home: The excessive militarisation of American police. http://tinyurl.com/nneqyrk

Badiou, A. (2012). *The rebirth of history: Times of riots and uprisings*. London: Verso.

Baker, S. (2012). Policing the riots: New social media as recruitment, resistance and surveillance. In D. Briggs (Ed.), *The English riots of 2011: A summer of discontent*. Hampshire: Waterside Press.

BBC. (2012, August 13). Reading the riots: The rioters in their own words.

Bauman, Z. (2011). Interview: Zygmunt Bauman on the UK riots. *Social Europe Journal*. http://www.social-europe.eu/2011/08/interview-zygmunt-bauman-on-the-ukriots/. Accessed 15 Aug 2011.

Becker, H. (1963). *Outsiders: Studies in the sociology of deviance*. London: Macmillan.

Breitman, G. (Ed.). (1966). *Malcolm X speaks*. London: Secker and Warburg.

Briggs, D. (Ed.). (2012). *The English riots of 2011: A summer of discontent*. Hampshire: Waterside Press.

Butler, P. (2015, June 2). The police officers' bill of rights creates a double standard. *New York Times*.

Callinicos, A., & Jones, J. (2011, January). The student revolt and the crisis. *International Socialism, 129*, 3–21.

Campbell, J. (2013). *Crime and punishment in African American history*. Basingstoke: Palgrave Macmillan.

Carlyle, T. (1912) [1843]. *Past and present*. London: Dent.

Chomsky, N. (2012). *Occupy!* London: Penguin.

Clark, K. (1965). *Dark ghetto: Dilemmas of social power*. London: Gollancz.

Clement, M. (2012a). Rage against the market: Bristol's Tesco Riot'. *Race and Class, 53*(3), 81–90.

Clement, M. (2012b). The urban outcasts of the British city. In W. Atkinson, S. Roberts, & M. Savage (Eds.), *Class inequality in austerity Britain: Power, difference and suffering*. Basingstoke: Palgrave Macmillan.

Clement, M. (2013). Manufacturing austerity in the Eurozone. *Human Figurations, 2*(1). ISSN: 2166-6644. http://hdl.handle.net/2027/spo.11217607.0002.106

Davis, A. (1998). *The Angela Y. Davis reader*. Oxford: Blackwell.

Dorling, D. (2014). *All that i8s solid: The great housing disaster*. London: Allen Lane.

Editorial. (1976). Berkeley's school of criminology, 1950–1976. *Crime and Social Justice, 6,* 1–3.

Forbes, F. A. (2000). Point no. 7: We want an immediate end to police brutality and the murder of black people. In J. Nelson (Ed.), *Police brutality: An anthology.* New York: Norton.

Greenburg, I. (2013). Everyone is a terrorist now: Marginalizing protest in the U.S. *Radical Criminology, 2,* 131–143.

Guardian. (2014, August 20). Under fire in Ferguson.

Hall, S., & Winlow, S. (2014). The English riots of 2011: Misreading the signs on the road to the society of enemies. In D. Pritchard & F. Pakes (Eds.), *Riot, unrest and protest on the global stage.* Basingstoke: Palgrave Macmillan.

Hallsworth, S. (2015). Råd för framtiden 2015. When the rules went down: Rethinking riots as performative acts. https://www.youtube.com/watch?v=fYLfkFhvMy8

Harvey, D. (2013). *Rebel cities: From the right to the city to the urban revolution.* London: Verso.

Harvie, D., & Milburn, K. (2013). The moral economy of the English crowd in the twenty-first century. *The South Atlantic Quarterly, 112,* 3.

Hessel, S. (2011). *Indignez vous!* Montpelier: Indigène éditions.

Howard S. B. (Winter, 1967). Whose side are we on? *Social Problems, 14*(3), 239–247.

IRR (Institute of Race Relations). (2015, June 19). A round-up of the latest news on BAME deaths in custody. http://www.irr.org.uk/news/a-round-up-of-the-latest-news-on-bame-deaths-in-custody/downloaded

Killed by Police Website (US). http://killedbypolice.net/

Lea, J. (2013). Book review: Daniel Briggs (Ed.), The English riots of 2011: A summer of discontent. *Theoretical Criminology, 17,* 417–420.

Lemelle, A. (2010). David Matza. In K. Hayward, S. Maruna, & J. Mooney (Eds.), *Fifty key thinkers in criminology.* London: Routledge.

Macaulay, T. (1889). *History of England volume 1.* London: Longmans.

Marable, M. (2000) [1983]. *How capitalism underdeveloped Black America.* Boston: South End Press.

Marable, M. (2011). *Malcolm X: A life of reinvention.* London: Allen Lane.

Matza, D. (1964). *Delinquency and drift.* New York: Wiley.

Matza, D. (1969). *Becoming deviant.* New York: Prentice-Hall.

Melossi, D. (2008). *Controlling crime, controlling society.* Cambridge: Polity.

Melossi, D. (2015). *Crime, punishment and migration.* London: Sage.

Molyneux, J. (2011). *Will the revolution be televised?* London: Bookmarks.

Neate, R. (2015, May 22). McDonald's workers in mass protest to beef about low pay. *The Guardian (UK)*.

NPR (National Public Radio, US) (2015). http://www.npr.org/2015/06/29/418490411/arsonists-hit-6-black-churches

Olende, K. (2015, May 5). Baltimore cops are charged over Freddie Gray death. *Socialist Worker (UK)*.

Ovenden, K. (2015). *Syriza: Inside the labyrinth*. London: Pluto.

Platts-Fowler, D. (2013). "Beyond the loot": Social disorder and urban unrest. *Papers from the British Criminology Conference, 13*, 17–32.

Pritchard, D. (2014). Unrest and inequalities: Comparing welfare states. In D. Pritchard & F. Pakes (Eds.), *Riot, unrest and protest on the global stage*. Basingstoke: Palgrave Macmillan.

Reel News. (2011). Tottenham rebellion. http://reelnews.co.uk/issue-29-sept-2011/

Reuters News. (2015, April 28). www.reuters.com/article/2015/04/28-us-usa-policebaltimore

Schwendinger, H., & Schwendinger, J. (2014). *Who killed the Berkeley School? Struggles over radical criminology*. Brooklyn: Punctum.

Sky News. (2011, August 12). Looters.

Slater, T. (2015). The neoliberal state and the 2011 English riots: A class analysis. In H. Thörn, M. Mayer, O. Semhede, & C. Thörn (Eds.), *Understanding urban uprisings, protests and movements*. Basingstoke: Palgrave Macmillan.

Smith, N. (1984). *Uneven development: Nature, capital and the production of space*. Athens: University of Georgia.

Smith, N. (2011). Revolutionary ambition in an age of austerity. *Upping the Anti, 13*. http://uppingtheanti.org/journal/13/13-neil-smith/

Spence, M. (2015, May 1). Black suspect died after "rough ride" in Baltimore police van. *The Times*.

Squires, P., & Lea, J. (Eds.). (2012). *Criminalization and advanced marginality*. Bristol: Policy Press.

Sutterluty, F. (2014). The hidden morale of the 2005 French and the 2011 English riots. *Thesis Eleven, 121*, 38–56.

Tannenbaum, F. (1938). *Crime and the community*. Boston: Gunn.

Taylor, I., Walton, P., & Young, J. (1973). *The new criminology: For a social theory of deviance*. New York: Harper and Row.

Tilly, C., & Tarrow, S. (2015). *Contentious politics* (2nd ed.). Oxford: Oxford University Press.

Treadwell, J., Briggs, D., Winlow, S., & Hall, S. (2013). Shopocalypse now: Consumer culture and the English riots of 2011. *British Journal of Criminology, 53*(2), 1–17.

Trotsky, L. (1969). *The permanent revolution and results and prospects.* New York: Pathfinder Press.

Trudell, M. (2015). Racism and resistance in the US after Ferguson. *International Socialism, 146*, 76–95.

Wacquant, L. (2001). Deadly symbiosis: When ghetto and prison meet and mesh. *Punishment & Society, 3*(1), u95–u133.

Wacquant, L. (2008). *Urban Qutcasts: A comparative sociology of advanced marginality.* Cambridge: Polity Press.

Webb, J. (2014, September 16). Justin webb in the US. *The Times.*

Whitehead, P. (1985) The writing on the wall London: Michael Joseph.

Winlow, S., Hall, S., Treadwell, J., & Briggs, D. (2015). *Riots and political protest: Notes from the post-political present.* London: Routledge.

Younge, G. (2002, August 17). The politics of partying. *The Guardian.*

Younge, G. (2011, August 14). These riots were political: They were looting not shoplifting. *The Guardian.*

Žižek, S. (2011, August 19). Shoplifters of the world unite. In *London Review of Books.*

Žižek, S. (2012). *The year of dreaming dangerously.* London: Verso.

Index